THE EMPTINESS OF OUR HANDS

THE EMPTINESS OF OUR HANDS

47 DAYS ON THE STREETS

PHYLLIS COLE-DAI
JAMES MURRAY

Photography by
JAMES MURRAY

 Bell Sound Books

Bell Sound Books
An imprint of Back Porch Productions
46855 200th St.
Bruce SD 57220-5210
backporchproductionsllc@gmail.com

Ordering Information: For special discounts on quantity purchases contact the publisher.

This is a work of nonfiction. For protection of privacy all personal names have been changed, except for those of the authors' friends and relatives and those of public figures whose identities would be impossible to conceal.

Front cover image by James Murray.
Pinhole photography by James Murray.
Cover Design by www.e-booklaunch.com.

Printed in the United States of America

The Emptiness of Our Hands / Phyllis Cole-Dai and James Murray.—3rd ed.
ISBN 978-0-692-08085-6

To all of us,
that we might learn
through the tender and tough tutelage of spirit
to be more present to one another

We must love one another or die.
—W. H. Auden

CONTENTS

PART 1: INTO THE BETWEEN

PART 2: LIFE AS OVERFLOW

PART 3: ON THE RIVERBANK

PART 4: END TIMES

PREFACE TO THIS EDITION

From February 17 to April 4, 1999, James Murray and I lived by choice on the streets of Columbus, Ohio, the fifteenth-largest city in the United States. We went to the streets with a single intention: to be as present as possible to everyone we met, offering them our sustained and nonjudgmental attention. Such attention is the heart of compassion.

Those forty-seven days changed our lives forever.

We later chronicled our streets experiences in *The Emptiness of Our Hands*, a meditative narrative accompanied by James's pinhole photographs. This is the third edition of that book, lightly edited. It will thrust you out the door of your comfortable life, straight into the unknown. It will force you to confront what might happen to you, and who you might become, if suddenly you had no home.

Though the events recounted in these pages occurred in 1999, this book remains as relevant as ever. More than half a million Americans are without homes on any given night. Under the policies of the current presidential administration, that number is almost guaranteed to grow, as the income gap between the wealthiest and poorest Americans continues to widen. And the prevailing cultural climate, so polarized and full of spite, will only perpetuate the epidemic of violence against homeless individuals across the nation.

James and I intend to resist the ugly cultural forces now in ascendance however we can. That's why we've chosen to issue this new edition of *The Emptiness of Our Hands* and to distribute it in new formats. I'm also making available for the first time *Practicing Presence: Insights from the Streets,* based on a series of blog posts I published in 2009 to commemorate the tenth anniversary of our time on the streets of Columbus. A companion reader to this book, it contains forty-seven brief chapters, one for each day we were out. Each chapter fleshes out an excerpt from *The Emptiness of Our Hands* at a decade's remove from actual events. The book also includes photographs that have never appeared in print until now. Using it alongside this volume, you will further enhance your understanding of the streets and the practice of being present.

If you happen to be Christian, you might consider using one or both of these books as resources during Lent and Holy Week, which served as a backdrop for the period James and I lived on the streets. However, you don't need to be a Christian to take this stumbling journey into the practice of presence. Just allow these forty-seven days to be for you what they were for us: a deep embrace of core values that human beings around the world have held in common for millennia. These values might best be articulated as questions:

> How do we treat others as we would have them treat us?
> How do we love our neighbors, including those who seem
>   "alien" and "other?"
> How do we extend hospitality to strangers, allowing them an
>   honored place among us?

These age-old questions have no simple answers. They must be answered with our lives.

James and I hope that your reading of this book will heighten your awareness of people who experience homelessness and strengthen your compassion for them. More broadly, we hope it will inspire you to intentionally practice presence on a daily basis in the various settings of your life. Practicing presence isn't easy, but it's powerful. It can change lives, including your own. It can even change the world.

THE EMPTINESS OF OUR HANDS

47 DAYS ON THE STREETS

ACKNOWLEDGMENTS

We're immensely grateful to all of you who offered us unconditional and generous support during those forty-seven days in 1999. There isn't space enough to identify all the particular forms your assistance took, but in reading your name below, please be assured that we remember.

For special thanks we wish to single out a few people on whose dependable and skillful help we constantly relied while on the streets: Mary Sartain, who collected, organized and stored our little scraps and bundles of notes; Ellen Puckett and Sarah Reeder, who quickly developed James's negatives so that he could gauge the progress of his pinhole photography; Gwyn Stetler, who helped inspire this journey and was for us a witness, and a rock, throughout; our families, who, walking with us in spirit, were always there to listen when we phoned; and most of all, Phoebe Walker and Jihong Cole-Dai, who loved us enough to let us go.

Blessings to you, and then, to all of these sweet souls: Maggie Atkinson, Nancy and Spence Badet, Alice Barbera, Rick Bauman, Atlee and Winnie Beechy, Phyllis Berman, Gordon and Lucy Bixel, Mary Brennan-Hoffman, Marcia Broucek, Patti Carrigan, Elliot Charrow, Barry Cole, Carol and Lynn Cole, Dave Cole, Dortha Cole, Father George Deas, Bob and Joan Deaton, Tim Durham, Jody Dzuranin, Patsy Ernsberger, Dan Everly, Melanie Ewing, James Ford, Bob Gillespie, Peter Gold, Nick Gumprecht, Ann and Jack Harris, the Hellraisers, Bill Hill, Sharon Johnson, Bernie Khunsman, Judy and Rob Limekiller, Donna Link, Beth Lonn, Diane and Ron Mattox, Michelle Mau, Dorotha Mengert, Pat and Paul Miller, Theda Oberholtzer, Ami Peacock, Betty Persons, Sandra Ritchie, Susan Ritchie, Barbara Ryan, Christie Sabol,

Deya Murray, Eileen Murray, Jerry Murray, Sandy Murray, Scot Murray, Jack Schwarz, Ron and Doris Seward, Peg and Fletcher Shafer, Jamie Smith, Warren Smith, Madelyn Snyder, Ryan Snyder, Max and Marjorie Stacy, Jerry Strine, Tyler Studds, Chuck Thomas, Cheryl Throwe, Marela Trejozacari, Ethel Umble, Linda and Norman Walker, Ruth Wood, the photography department of Kenyon College, the Dublin Unitarian Universalist Church, the Columbus and Marion spirituality groups, and the Westerville Senior Citizens Center writing group.

Our thanks to all who shared in our noontime meditations, whether you actually came downtown to the Statue of Peace or joined us in spirit from a distance, as (we later learned) did various individuals and communities of faith in Ohio, Indiana, Illinois, Michigan, Kentucky, North Carolina, New York, Connecticut, Maine, New Mexico and California. However you became aware of our undertaking, you helped sustain us, and more so the homeless people in and beyond Columbus with your prayers, good will and collective intention.

We're also indebted to the many strangers in Columbus who, without knowing who we were, gifted us in uncountable ways while we were on the streets. Among them we especially lift up our homeless neighbors along the Scioto River; staff members of the Agora, the Five Loaves Bakery, and the Interfaith Hospitality Center; the Take It to the Streets organization; the cooks and volunteers in the food lines at Central Presbyterian Church and the Holy Family Soup Kitchen; the workers at JOIN and The Place to Be; the lenient librarians at Main Library and the tolerant employees of McDonald's and White Castle; the congregation and staff of St. Joseph Cathedral; and various staff members in city shelters.

We deeply appreciate the counsel that was so graciously provided by Maura Casey, Jay Erickson, Susan Ritchie, Jack Schwarz, Gwyn Stetler, Amanda Stewart and Tyler Studds, all of whom served as critical readers for our manuscript-in-progress. You helped bring this book to life.

Finally, we wish to acknowledge Bernie Glassman Roshi. In the stream of inspiring events eventually leading us to the streets, your book *Bearing Witness: A Zen Master's Lessons in Making Peace* was the last and most compelling. With our hands at gassho, we offer you, in humblest gratitude, the words of Bashō, the Zen poet of seventeenth-century Japan:

> *The temple bell stop*
> *But I still hear the sound*
> *Coming out of the flowers.*

This list of acknowledgments is long, and could be endless; nothing was insignificant. We apologize to anyone whose name we've failed to include. Sometimes bounty overflows the baskets.

We offer to all of you, and to every reader, the Hebrew blessing of a Jewish friend who graciously sent us off on our journey: *Yashir koach.* "*May you grow in strength.*" May your souls forever bear witness to that unnameable Mystery in which all life has its being.

INTRODUCTION

I will take with me the emptiness of my hands
What you do not have you find everywhere
—W. S. Merwin

From February 17 through April 4, 1999, James Murray and I lived voluntarily on the streets of Columbus, Ohio. This period of forty-seven days, beginning on Ash Wednesday and ending on Easter Sunday, coincided with the Christian observance of Lent and Holy Week.

We didn't go out on the streets to satisfy idle curiosity or to experience a strange new world. We didn't go out to find answers to questions or to search out solutions to problems. We didn't go out to save anyone or to hand out donations of food and blankets. We went out for one primary reason: to be as present as possible to everyone we met—homeless person, volunteer, university president, cop. In other words, we set out, in our own way, to love our neighbor as ourselves, with eyes open, minds open, hearts open, hands open as wide as they could be, not ignoring potential risks but not looking for trouble either. Doing so, we were reminded just how difficult the practice of compassion can be, not only because of external obstacles and distractions, or physical hardships, but even more because of our own judgments, assumptions, fears and desires, all of which harden our regard for and behavior toward other people.

James and I have been told, more than once, that spending those forty-seven days on the streets of Columbus was a crazy thing to do. But then worthwhile things do often seem a little out of the ordinary, and they change you in ways you could never have imagined. Still, let us be clear: James and I are not thrill-seekers. No thirst for adventure drove us to do this. It's more like Annie Dillard says in her poem "I Am Trying to Get at Something Utterly Heartbroken":

> *This is not a thing that I have sought,*
> *but it has come across my path and I have seized it.*

(from *Mornings like This*, p. 12)

An apt description. The Thing comes—the calling, if you will—and you realize, deep down, it's come for you, and you can't turn your back, or toy with it. The Thing demands you take it up with single-minded passion, even though you never asked for it, or even want it. The Thing's here, and it's yours. You don't ask why it has come, for who would know the answer, and besides, the why doesn't matter. You trust the Thing totally, and that's enough. Finally, you don't ask how you'll survive it, if the Thing is hard and will break your heart. Now is not the time for asking that, but for telling your husband that this is what you've been given to do. And because he understands you, and loves you, and is a remarkable man, he says, "If this is what you have to do, what can I do to help?"

The Thing came across my path on a hot day in August, 1998. At the time, I'd been living and writing in Columbus, Ohio, for thirteen years. James, a dear friend and gifted photographer with whom I'd collaborated the previous year, was just finishing his studies in religion and art at Kenyon College, an hour north of the city. By chance, he and I had a meeting scheduled the afternoon of that August day. When during our meeting I announced my intention to go to the streets, explaining my reasons as best I could, he seized the Thing, too.

"Can I go?"

As he later confessed, the words escaped his mouth before he realized, but he didn't want to take them back, even though (at the time) going to the streets seemed less his calling than mine. Over the previous year, he'd watched the issue of homelessness tapping me on the shoulder again and again, taking on faces, names, stories. Deeply affected, I'd been waiting to see where it all would lead. Now, suddenly, the Thing had appeared to me in full and was pulling me toward the unknown heart of the city.

The unknown is the crucible of the human spirit. If we give ourselves to it with faith, inevitably we undergo a change, and little by little the world changes with us. This is why James wanted to go with me. He didn't know what it would mean to be truly present on the streets, with every security stripped away, and he didn't know what would happen if he tried, but try he would.

James and I share Christian roots (his Roman Catholic, mine Methodist) as well as a deep appreciation for eastern philosophy and meditation. We also share an intuitive sensibility, and an abiding interest in spirituality and art. Other than that, and our both being Anglo, we're not much alike.

Thirteen years younger than I am, James is a sturdy six-foot-four inches tall, with shoulder-length curls; I'm a slender five-foot-six, with straight hair bobbed short. He grew up in a New York City penthouse near Central Park, attending private schools and spending weekends on Long Island; I was raised on a hog farm in northwest Ohio. He's a bold extrovert; I'm more inward and cautious by nature. He loves looking at life through a lens; I avoid cameras, and make love to the world through language. All these differences, however, meant little that hot day in August, and still do. In general, we're both more concerned with what people hold in common than what sets them apart. So when he offered to accompany me to the streets, I gladly accepted.

Now, on the other end, I know I wouldn't have lasted, in body or spirit, had he not gone along.

Borrowing from our Christian roots, we decided that we would leave home the following February on the first day of Lent, a traditional season of self-examination and fasting. If all went as planned, we would return home on Easter, the springtime festival of resurrection and cosmic renewal. This liturgical backdrop would provide a rich spiritual context for what would probably be the most raw experience of our sheltered lives. We had no doubt those forty-seven days between February 17 and April 4, 1999, would be incredibly tough. Just how tough we rarely speculated, not wanting to shadow-box with what-ifs and could-happens.

In the ensuing months we made certain promises to each other. While on the streets we would, first of all, try to avoid staying in homeless shelters, since we didn't want to take up beds. Second, we wouldn't tell anyone exactly why we were out, since the truth would color every interaction. If questioned, we would be vague or evasive; we would directly lie only if it was necessary to prevent harm. Third, we would each do whatever we could to support and protect the other. Lastly, either of us could quit at any time. If one of us left the streets, the other would be free to follow, or not.

We naturally considered chronicling our time on the streets through his photography and my writing. Our artwork could be a companion on the streets as it was elsewhere in our lives, challenging us to greater awareness. Someday the work might shape-shift into a book that other people could grapple with, wring some blessing from, but we didn't dwell on that possibility. The last thing we wanted to take to the streets was a confused mix of motives. Come February, we would go to the streets prepared to pick up the pencil, to shoot the picture, but we would actually do so only if it helped us be present. Only if it proved another way to love our neighbor.

Our biggest artistic question was how James would manage his camera work without being conspicuous. The answer was soon clear: pinhole photography—a method so basic that even grade schoolers can learn. If he carried certain supplies onto the streets, he'd be able to build crude cameras from boxes or cans scavenged from dumpsters. We both liked the symbolism of recycling trash into cameras, plus the pragmatism was unbeatable: whenever he took a picture, he'd appear to any casual observer just to be holding a container of some sort.

Though basic in its method, pinhole photography isn't easy. It's imprecise, frustrating, time-consuming guesswork, much more complicated than the ethical code James would follow in his shoots. That code consisted of two fundamental rules: No taking photographs of people, since he couldn't ask their permission; for the same reason, no taking photographs of shanties or other makeshift homes.

His exposures would be picked up periodically by one of his photographer-friends, taken to a darkroom and developed into negatives, to await his return home. Then he would transform the best of those negatives into black and white prints.

As you'll see in this pages, the images he shot over those forty-seven days turned out as bleary and rough as our experience of the streets themselves.

Our first night on the streets was—to be frank—hell. It so traumatized us that we were tempted to quit and go home. Paradoxically, however, it also convinced us that we were exactly where we had to be, doing what we had to do. And part of what we would have to do, if we somehow managed to remain, was produce the book that until then had been merely a shadowy prospect. We would have to speak up. Of this, we were now certain. If only in a limited way, we had to portray how being without a real home can devastate the human spirit. After a single night, we already had some sense of this. Then, too, perhaps the book could inspire its readers to reflect on their own ability to be more present, more compassionate, in their small corners of the world.

I asked James if he would help me write such a book, and he graciously agreed. Photographer turned storyteller.

It wasn't easy after we came off the streets to make sense of our fragmented notes, scribbled whenever and wherever we'd had the energy and the paper. Nor was it easy, in fleshing out our notes, to relive the hardship all over again. Thanks, James, for the gift of your perspective. Thanks, too, for entrusting me with the editing of your words.

An ordeal doesn't mean much until it begins to lighten a little. Until then, you're just in shock, or in pain, dragging beneath its weight. Though James and I came off the streets in early April, 1999, we couldn't muster the heart to write about them until the very end of October. By then, he'd moved from Ohio to Connecticut. States apart, the two of us were alone for the first time with the fullness of the Thing, grappling with it even as we were still struggling to get our energy back, still suffering panic attacks, still trying to readjust to the pace and perks of "ordinary life."

Now the book is done. We've tried to be as loyal as possible to what we remember. But however true it might be, this story is also a fiction; less a recital of objective facts than a montage of perceived events, snatches of conversation, dream remnants, scraps of ideas, fleeting impressions. The fragments are more organized, their language more polished, than they should rightfully be. That's for your sake. If we didn't make the Thing intelligible, you might give up reading. This is your advantage over James and me. On the streets we had no narrator to help make things sensible, or sane.

Perhaps you know Columbus. Perhaps you know the artsy Short North, trendy German Village, the impoverished Bottoms, blue-collar Whitehall, affluent Bexley, the downtown around Broad and High Streets, Capitol Square with its Statue of Peace. Perhaps you know how the golden crown of the LaVeque Tower lights up the skyline at night, or how the Olentangy and Scioto Rivers unite at the heart of the city like long-lost lovers. Perhaps you know how gloomy and gusty Columbus winters can be, wind chills often dropping well below zero, and how in some years spring is here barely a week before the hot humidity of summer swallows it whole.

When James and I hit the streets, Columbus was the nation's fifteenth-largest city, with 1.5 million residents in the metropolitan area. With a booming white-collar sector, it had rock-bottom unemployment, yet the poverty rate was rising. Many people in the working class struggled to rent, let alone own, a home. A minimum-wage worker had to put in at least eighty-three hours a week to afford even a modest two-bedroom apartment.

Whether such an apartment would be available was another matter. The number of affordable housing units had dwindled as the city had grown—an estimated 22,000 additional units were needed. This lack of affordable housing, together with deepening poverty, had been largely responsible for the dramatic increase in the city's homeless population (as across the United States) over the previous two decades.[1]

The number of people sleeping in Columbus shelters had doubled just in the 1990s. Often the shelters were filled to overflowing. Additionally, there was a substantial street population, though its size was understandably difficult to judge. (Estimates ranged from 150 to 1000 per night.) And an unknown number of people was living temporarily with friends or in other unstable housing arrangements, a very common occurrence.[2]

No one can say with any certainty how many people in Columbus were living without homes during 1999. Let's say simply that there were too many. Even one person would have been too many, but to quote the director of the Community Shelter Board, Columbus had practically "a small city" of homeless people.[3] If all the "small cities" of people experiencing homelessness in this country around that time had been consolidated, we'd have had a virtual metropolis: an estimated two million in 1998,[4] about the same number of people as were living within the city limits of Philadelphia and Boston combined.[5] All the more tragically, one in every four of these persons was a child.[6]

Then as now, homeless persons in Columbus tended to be individuals who had suffered a temporary setback, such as loss of employment, relationship problems or eviction. Contrary to popular belief, while many of these persons suffered from mental illness or chemical dependency, they did so only at around the same rate as the general population.[7] However, use of alcohol and drugs did seem to be the strongest single predictor of whether a person who was temporarily without housing would become chronically homeless.[8] James and I ended up spending most of our days and nights among chronically homeless persons, especially those residing on the riverbanks of the Scioto River.

Columbus was more tolerant of its homeless population than were some other cities in this nation, where efforts to criminalize homelessness often violated basic human rights.[9] Of the fifty largest U.S. cities, 38% had recently initiated crackdowns on homeless people—for example: having the police dump them at the city limits; forcibly bussing them out of town; arresting them if they refused to be transported to a public shelter; passing ordinances against begging or sleeping (or even "covering oneself with a blanket") in a public place, sitting on the sidewalk, and so on. More than half of the fifty cities studied had conducted police sweeps simply to remove homeless people from public view.

According to a source in the city sheltering coalition, Columbus also had an unspoken policy of trying to keep homeless people out of sight. This unspoken policy had made its way into several anti-homeless ordinances, including one against sleeping in public parks. Nevertheless, the city was also seeking constructive ways of addressing the perceived needs of the homeless population. Its "Rebuilding Lives" plan, meant to move chronically homeless men out of shelters into permanent housing linked with job training and support services, has been hailed as a national model. But whether real change, and compassionate change, is happening in Columbus, only time will tell.

All of this is background to the pages that follow. It's part of the sidewalks you'll be walking with James and me, part of the food you'll be scavenging from dumpsters. It will be there in your shivers, your insomnia, your sweat, your stink, your longings, your limp. Let it sink in. Let it settle into the marrow of your bones, like a disease, and hope for recovery.

If you do this, you'll be ahead. When James and I hit the streets on February 17, 1999, we weren't aware of any homeless statistics or policies. We were scarcely aware of any services (shelters, soup kitchens, clinics) available to homeless persons. We had done little research at all, wanting to go out as thousands do each year in this city who suddenly have no place to call home and must stumble their way through the not-knowing.

About the only serious inquiries we made beforehand were into ourselves. As earnestly as we could, we dragged up into the light of day all the things we'd ever heard, or believed, about homeless people; all the stereotypes and prejudices and assumptions, not even sure how they'd become part of us —*Homeless people are dumb, lazy, on the streets because they want to be, mentally ill, violent, lucky not to have any responsibilities, inarticulate, dirty, rude, mostly male, mostly black, mostly drunks and addicts, many of them Vietnam vets....*

These were the things we "knew" best—not that a homeless woman could be so lonely, she would ride up and down in a shopping mall elevator, just to be close to other human beings. Not that a young man, unable to cope with the tragic deaths of his wife and infant daughter, would abandon his home for the streets, intent on destroying himself.

Before you read further, James and I invite you to reflect on what you think you know about homeless people. Ask yourself what you believe it's like to live without a real home. Be honest.

Now, lay all that aside, if you can. The Thing's about to cross your path. Empty your hands, and seize it. Let it lead you out the open door, away from the comforts of your sheltered life, from your usual sense of what's necessary, and real, and meaningful, and good. Go with it where you might never have gone alone, not that you might be entertained there, or even find wise answers to hard questions, but because there are people—*lives*—at stake. Dare to exist in the in-between, that place where nothing is secure, and everything is significant, if you'll allow it to be; a place where you can see most anything and, in good faith, do almost nothing except feel a shattering, and sometimes a mend; a place where you think and think and think and still, in the end, know precious little but for the fact that you've been where you've been, and anguished there, and were scarred—and now, on the other side, if you've been lucky enough to return home, you have no regrets at all, just much work to do.

LIST OF ILLUSTRATIONS

PART 1: INTO THE BETWEEN

DAY 1

WEDNESDAY, FEBRUARY 17

DOORS

I've walked through thousands of doors in my life; left some of them standing wide open, closed others, locked my share. But I've never walked through a door quite like this one—my own front door, a plain slab, not very thick or heavy but looking sturdy as steel on this brisk, gray morning. And I've never pulled a locked door securely shut behind me, as I'm about to do now, without a key resting in my pocket or under the doormat so I can easily go back inside. Today there'll be no easy way back in, no easy changing of the mind. Only the leaving....

Ash Wednesday: what T.S. Eliot called "the time of tension between dying and birth." I pause just over the doorsill, James behind me on the porch, my gloved hand clinging to the knob. It's a little after 8 AM. Jihong has already left for work, as if this were just a usual day in our marriage; Phoebe, James's girl-friend, has started for her home in Connecticut, as if this were just the end of another too-brief visit. They couldn't bear to stay here at the house and watch us go, and we couldn't bear to leave them behind, so they'd been the first out the door, just after the four of us made our parting, borrowing the strength of ceremony.

In a small bowl we'd combined wood ash from the fireplace with the finer, sweeter ash of incense collected from the meditation room. Then we'd marked each other, as Cain is said to have been marked by God before setting out into the unknown, better to learn the keeping of his brother. The faint dust marks, so tenderly imposed on the skin of our foreheads, were our sign of belonging—to each other, to this set-apart time, and to a world that covers us with the dust of sufferings and miracles alike.

Now I look over my shoulder at James, hand still full of knob.

"Are we ready, Irishman?"

His body visibly braces: he's feeling the edge. Who empties his bags, rather than packs, before a long, hard journey? He breathes deeply, bright tears staining his cheeks. His eyes lock mine. "Okay. Ready."

I step down, tug the door home, test the lock. Ready or not, the thing's done.

MILES

Between the front door of my suburban home and the heart of Columbus, where most of the city's homeless population is found, stretch fourteen miles of pavement. A long march into godknowswhat.

It's all James and I can do, the first block, to put one foot in front of the other. Reality is setting in. For the next forty-seven days, we won't have any material comforts of home—no thermostat to turn up, no refrigerator to raid, no lights to switch on, no bed to sleep in, no toilet just across the hall, no morning shower, no clean clothes in the closet, no locked doors. We won't have the intangibles of home, either—especially the sense of belonging. What we *will* have, for sure, is fear. Uncertainty. Struggle.

Still, as our stride picks up and hits a rhythm, an inexplicable lightness of spirit sets in. Perhaps it's the gift of deep conviction, or maybe, after months of anticipation and sometimes dread, it's just relief that we're finally under-way. We laugh, even, at James's scruffy first beard, sprouted just for the occasion.

At a traffic light we stand waiting. People stare at us from stopped cars. We smile back. The eyes glower, glance away. Ten minutes from home, already we're perceived as different, it seems. Is it because of our clothes?

We're dressed for winter. I wear two old pair of long underwear, worn blue jeans, knitted leg warmers, thermal jacket, pullover sweatshirt, Jihong's ski sweater, heavy overalls, and a down coat blessed with many pockets, which a friend had intended for the Salvation Army. Two pair of gloves for my hands, three pair of wool-blend boot socks and insulated boots on my feet, and finally, for my head, two knit hats and a neck warmer. Only the boots are new.

In my pockets I carry little: a baggie of vitamin C tablets; my driver's license for identification; a card with emergency contact information; a love note from Jihong ("This is me," it begins, "when you are out and about"); a photograph, given me by a friend for good luck, of a Native American mask he'd carved from wood. On a cord around my neck, two amulets from other friends, along with my wedding ring. These lie over my heart.

Over his long underwear (a Christmas present from Phoebe, so she could be close to him every day on the streets) James wears wool pants, thin turquoise trousers, turtleneck, wool army sweater, hooded sweatshirt, and hooded coat, beige with furry brown lining, a style from the seventies. Old boots, two pair of socks. Hat and mittens.

His pockets hold a toothbrush, emergency information, ID and vitamin C. Around his neck, two amulets from friends and a ring identical to one Phoebe wears. Over his shoulder, a medium blue duffel that contains, along with an extra pair of gloves and socks, the supplies he'll need for pinhole photography: flat black spray paint, electrical tape, masking tape, 5"x7" photo papers, lightproof film-changing bag, black storage bags for exposures, and a pocket tool kit, about the size of a credit card. This tool kit, a gift from his father, he prizes mainly for its two-inch knife and three-inch rule, which he'll use to build cameras.

The temperature is in the low thirties. Snow begins to fall, light flakes like so much ash, drifting, never reaching the ground.

Within a half hour we both start to chill as sweat saturates the clothing next to our skin. I scrounge in a trash bin for a large plastic bag, peel off some outer layers of clothes and stuff them in. Then I search the ground for a stout stick. As a child I'd listened spellbound to my grandparents telling stories about depression-era hobos. Now, bag propped on the stick over my shoulder, I'm the proverbial spitting image of one.

A couple miles east along the busy commercial strip of Route 161, then we turn south along High Street. This is the yellow brick road leading to the heart of the city. We've entered Worthington, an affluent historic suburb with a colonial New England feel. Its brick sidewalks are clean and even, its houses distinguished, its grounds carefully landscaped.

As we pass through the village green on the main square, city workers are trimming tender young trees with long-handled pruning shears. We identify with the trees.

TEETH

A sign outside a dentist's office reminds me that I need to acquire a toothbrush and paste. No time like the present. Leaving James on the sidewalk, I go inside the building, heart pounding. I don't know what it is to be a beggar. I've never been someone to readily ask for help. Now I'm offended by my pride.

I remove my hat. The receptionist scowls. Clearly she'd rather not deal with me.

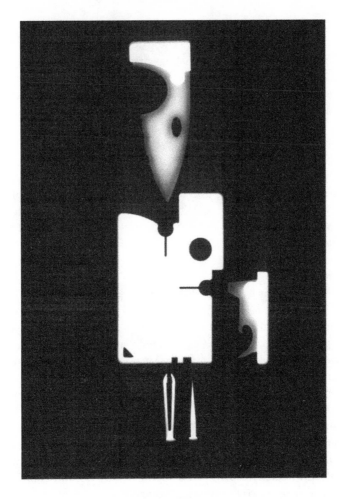

James's tool kit, in pieces

Smiling, I request her kind assistance. The scowl deepens. "I'll have to check." Red-faced, she abruptly leaves her desk. Muffled voices confer behind a door.

I no longer care what happens. It's been enough, just to try.

Waiting for me outside, James has ventured around back of the dentist's office, where he finds several dumpsters. Trash receptacles like these will be our cupboards and closets for the next one-and-a-half months. Neither of us is a stranger to scavenging for hidden treasures at flea markets and thrift stores. But out here we'll be rummaging in trash, by necessity. For food, especially. As soon as this morning's pancakes have worn off, we'll be scrounging for discarded leftovers. Expired goods. Spoilage. Anything for a meal.

Curiosity lifts the lid on the underside of a dentist's world: empty supply boxes, used rubber gloves, crinkled plastic wrappers and warning labels, wadded tissues. James's first taste of dumpster diving is about as appealing as getting his teeth cleaned.

Back inside the dentist's office, the receptionist finally returns. Somehow now she's smiling. Beaming, almost. She hands me a brand-new Oral-B toothbrush and two thin sample packets of Crest, then wishes me well. Rejoining James outside, I wonder at the change in her demeanor.

On the sidewalk, a half-eaten Granny Smith apple. James and I each relish a bite before tossing away the core.

SESAME STREET

Cookie Monster, wedged in a chainlink fence. Strange place for a toy, far from Sesame Street.

A row of dumpsters is barely visible behind a pharmacy across High Street. They're a hundred yards out of our way, but on a hunch we cross four lanes of traffic to check them out.

The largest bin is full. At first glance it seems empty to our needs. Then I burrow down.

"Cookies!" James exclaims, at the sight of a plastic package, still half full.

Our hands unearth twenty more packages, still sealed in their wrappers, twenty-four chocolate-chip cookies in each. Laughing, we dance an awkward jig in our heavy boots, shouting, "We have food!"

Munching down, we stuff all the packages into one large trash-bag. James heaves the load over his shoulder, and we're off. From here on, we mark our trail down High Street with cookies, dropping packages at bus stops, on benches, on tenement steps. The giving is energizing.

"C is for cookie," Cookie Monster sang, "that's good enough for me!"

DIAMONDS

Around noontime we take a break at Whetstone Park, behind a neighborhood branch of the Columbus Metropolitan Library. With Worthington, the Graceland Mall area and residential Beechwold behind us, we've entered popular Clintonville, with its Roaring Twenties housing. Not far ahead lies the Ohio

State campus scene. Then there'll be a stretch of tumbledown row houses, storefronts and abandoned buildings, the artsy Short North, and finally, downtown.

Backs of my legs burning, I collapse on a park bench beside a baseball diamond. Field one, out of four.

James, chewing on cookies, gravitates toward home plate. Suddenly he takes off running the bases. With the recent light snow and cold rain, the base path is muck. As he rounds first, his left foot slip-slides under his right. He catches himself, barely, from a full-body sprawl. As I cheer him on, he kicks up mud on a full-tilt slog to second base. Third. At last, home again.

"*Safe!*" we yell, in our best umpire voices.

EYEBROWS

We meditate in the library's garden, desolate in winter. Seated on a bench, cold settling into our bones, we shiver but aren't in a hurry. It's essential, in these moments, to remember why we're on the streets: to be as present as possible to our surroundings and everybody we meet; to offer the gift of attention, without judgment, without pity.

Silently I renew these intentions. Then, focusing on my breath, I gradually let go of thought—my questions, my worries, my plans, my fears.... At last there's only the breath, moving in, moving out.

In, out.

In. Out.

This is life. So simple. Just this.

After a while I feel more rested; strangely fortified, too, as though by a company of unseen helpers, wise ones who know what it means to live with a heart as open as a clear blue sky, as passionate as the summer sun, as patient as rain on rock.

A Zen saying burrows into my quiet, becomes a prayer: "May I walk hand in hand with the ancestors, the hair of my eyebrows entangled with theirs."

The empty garden is full.

BORN-AGAIN

Mid-afternoon, maybe four miles from downtown, we get our first hazy view of the city skyline. We think of having to nest somewhere tonight amidst steel and concrete. Emotions surge. We crawl forward.

Soiled royal-blue pants hang over the rim of a trash can—34" long, James's size, with permanent creases. In the last mile or so, with the air temperature noticeably dropping, James had wondered aloud whether he might need a fourth layer for his legs after the sun goes down. Gratefully now he stuffs the blue pants into his duffel, just as we're approached by a middle-aged white man walking a dog.

The man introduces himself as Pete, a born-again. "Need any food?" he asks.

"Yeah," we say, famished.

He leads us to a storefront mission a block away and unlocks the door. "A Better Way," the place is called. He directs us to sit down on folding chairs, then disappears into the back. When he returns, he's carrying a grocery bag. Canned goods bulge against white plastic.

"How long you been out?" he asks, then says, "Not long, I guess." He looks pointedly at me. "You born again?"

"Yeah," I say, meaning something quite different from what he does. His concern for my soul is touching, but I'm not interested in debating religion. I'm interested in the contents of that grocery bag.

"How about you?" he says to James.

"I'm a spiritual person."

"In other words, you're *not*." He looks both of us up and down. Finally he announces that he suspects James is on the lam, and I'm a person in deep pain, needing to be healed. Jesus is the answer. It's not too late. A Better Way has the power to help us change, if we'll only come back for Bible study and worship. They'll even feed us dinner, Pete says.

James and I stand to go. Pete hugs us both, sniffing James, presumably for liquor. Then he hands me the grocery bag. We thank him, sincerely, and hurry out the door.

Sidewalk inventory: one can government-issued peanut butter, one can boiled potatoes, two cans tuna, one can chicken and noodle soup, two cans pork and beans. We're rich—and very lucky that James has a tiny can opener in his tool kit.

NESTING

4 PM. Seated in the plaza outside the forty-story headquarters of Nationwide Mutual Insurance, we celebrate our arrival in the downtown, feasting on cold beans and dumpster cookies dipped in government peanut butter. Businesspeople walk briskly past, paying us no mind. We remove our boots and prop up our sore stockinged feet, trying not to think about our blisters.

Rest is short, though. We need to find a place to spend the night, homeless shelters being an absolute last resort. Instinct soon draws us west toward the Scioto River, where we scout possible sleeping sites.

Low spreading evergreen bushes surround a large office building between Front Street and Civic Center Drive. Exploring them, we spot a number of human nests, some abandoned, others seemingly still occupied, given the backpacks and other possessions lying around. This area feels right. We choose a deserted nest, then begin to scavenge the nearby streets for plastic, cardboard, foam, whatever we can put between the cold, hard ground and our hope for sleep.

Once our beds are ready, we have leisure time. To get warm we hike over to Main Library, where in the past I've sometimes noticed (apparently) homeless people reading newspapers, browsing the stacks, using the computers.

James drowses at a table. Across from him I write on the back of a poster-size print pulled from a dumpster earlier in the day: *Signing of the Treaty of Greene Ville, August 3, 1795.* A famous painting, by Howard Chandler Christy. Chief Little Turtle is surrendering to General Mad Anthony Wayne, concluding another war conducted by the U.S. government against the native inhabitants of this territory. White pioneers had been hungry to settle the land, so the government drew a map, charted a line, and forced the Miami, Chippewa and Potawatomi, among other tribal nations, to move to the other side.

Today, in Columbus, it's not farmland our leaders are hungry for. They want a brand-new professional hockey arena, a relocated Center of Science and Industry, an expanded Veterans Memorial Building, revitalized business in the old Franklinton neighborhood … on goes the list. All this development is taking place just across the river from downtown, in an area where several homeless shelters are situated. The shelters might be closed down or re-established elsewhere in the city. The picture's not yet clear. Lines are still being drawn. Homeless people, whom one civic leader has called "bums, winos and druggies," don't fit into the developers' plans.

QUARTERS

Leaving Main Library, we stop by Grant Hospital to see if it hosts any Twelve-Step meetings. James, who's in recovery, would like to find one soon. He assures me that he isn't afraid for his sobriety. He just wants to be with people who won't stare at him and judge. "Besides," he grins, "there'll probably be donuts and coffee."

The woman behind the hospital's reception desk is aloof. "No meetings here," she says, when James asks.

"Do you maybe have a phone book so I could look up the number for Central Office? Maybe they could tell me where to go."

In a huff the woman pulls out the White Pages. James looks up the number and scribbles it on a slip of paper. "Could I please use your phone?"

She frowns, gesturing over her shoulder. "There's pay phones over there."

James stares at me helplessly. Neither of us has change for a phone call. "Thanks anyway for your help," he tells the woman. We turn to go.

"Wait—" She reaches down for her purse, retrieves two quarters. Somehow she's smiling, now.

PICNIC

James and I lounge atop a hot-air vent behind a warehouse, eating a dinner of cold canned tuna and soup, with more cookies and peanut butter for dessert. Closing his eyes, James jokes that he almost feels like he's at the beach. Tropical. But instead of salt air, the faint smell of laundry exhaust.

INTOXICATION

Our little nest in the bushes, we notice now, is on the grounds of the Ohio Departments Building (ODB), one of many state government buildings in the downtown. We lean against its gray western wall as the sun sets over the Scioto River. Engraved on the building's frieze high above us:

THEIR SACRIFICE GUARANTEE OF POSTERITY

FREEDOM

OPPORTUNITY

Streetlights shimmer gold on the river. The calm is intoxicating. We almost forget our weary bodies.

We jot notes. We speak of high things: how we might get to know the street people living among the bushes, and share with them our little store of food, and all of us watch out for one another.

We bed down in the bushes around 9 PM, as best we can tell without watches. "What do you want to do in the morning?" James asks, as we're settling in under low, prickly branches.

"Morning seems far away. Let's wait and see. Yashir koach, Irishman." *May you grow in strength.* The Hebrew blessing of a Jewish friend, received in the mail before we left home.

"Yashir koach."[1]

THE STATE

No sleep for me. I feel trapped. Under the low evergreens I've scarcely room to move, even to lift my head. I bear it as long as I can, then instinct takes over. My body erupts into frantic struggle. I blunder up and out of the bushes, escape into air, stand panting under an indifferent moon.

I bed down again thirty or so feet from James, in a gap between the bushes and a wall of the ODB. Here I'm more comfortable and able to move freely, but since I'm more exposed, I'm also much colder, even wearing my many layers of clothes. With legs drawn up to my chest, I tuck in my head and exhale long and hard into my coat, time and again, as if blowing up a balloon.

It's no use. There's no getting warm.

Hours go by. I toss and turn in shivering exhaustion.

Suddenly I hear footsteps—

Quiet—quiet—

More steps on the pavement—coming my way—

Don't make a sound—

A mag light shines down, blinding me. I shield my eyes.

"Come out of there right now!" A male voice.

Slowly my eyes adjust. The voice belongs to a state trooper, middle-aged, black. He demands a form of identification, then radios a dispatcher, checking for outstanding warrants. As we await the report, I ask the trooper for the time.

"Around midnight," he says, kindly enough. "Why aren't you in a shelter?"

"I prefer not to be, thanks."

"If you hadn't been rustling around, I wouldn't have known you was here."

James wakens to shivers and voices. He listens closely as the trooper questions me. Occasionally the beam of the trooper's mag light falls on the bushes where he lies, motionless. He wonders if he's been spotted; if he should just crawl out, give himself up.

He decides to wait.

My warrant check is clear. I feel a strange relief, as if it could have been otherwise.

"This property belongs to the state," the trooper says, crisply. "You got to move on. If you stick around, I'll have to arrest you for loitering."

Who's the state if not the people? I want to say, but choke back the words. *Let it go. The man's just doing his job. Move now, and quick, or James'll get rousted, too.*

The streets of downtown are empty, and dimly yellow. Completely spent, very much alone, I'm filled with foreboding. *Don't go where there isn't light.*

James is still hidden in the evergreens, hoping he won't be made. But once I've left the premises, the trooper's mag light sweeps directly to his face.

"Come out of there! Let me see your hands. You have any weapons?"

"No, sir."

"Base," the trooper radios, "I have a male Caucasian, approximately six-foot-two, under some bushes, close to where the woman was…. You have any identification?"

James scrounges for his driver's license.

"If you don't have any outstanding warrants, I'll let you go with a warning. This is state property. You can't sleep here."

"Yes, sir."

"Why aren't you in a shelter?"

James shrugs.

"Yeah, that's pretty much the same answer *she* gave," the trooper says, pointing in the direction I'd gone.

James gathers his duffel and the food bag. "Could you please tell me what time it is?"

"Almost twelve-thirty."

James moves out, shivering and in a daze.

I'm nowhere to be seen.

PARKING

On the very top level of the parking garage attached to the Riffe Center for Government and the Arts, I hide between stacks of construction materials and try for sleep. It doesn't come. I'm just too cold, starting to shake uncontrollably.

My body needs warmth, my body needs rest. The flesh-and-blood part of me realizes this and begins to feel an urgency, even desperation. Yet the part of me that is mind is strangely detached from what's happening, as if convinced this is just an episode in a bad dream, and soon there will be a waking up.

James trudges the streets of downtown. He's fairly new to the city. What a way, what a time, to orient himself. He crosses through a major intersection at the slowest pace he's ever walked. No traffic. No pedestrians. Only him. Unsettling.

His eyes search constantly for any sign of me. Misery, wishing for company.

A ramp to a parking garage looks inviting. He takes a couple steps up the incline before two security guards turn the corner and wag their heads at him.

MAN OF GOD

I decide to risk sneaking from the parking garage into the Riffe Center. Once inside, I might be able to catch some sleep in a janitor's closet or backstage in one of the theaters. Anyplace warm. Anyplace out of the way. I shuffle toward the door.

"Stop right where you are!"

A uniformed guard, out of nowhere. Another black man; in his twenties, maybe. He radios in to the security detail, reporting my trespass. Then he says with seeming reluctance that he'll have to escort me down to street level.

On our way down the man tells me his name is David. He draws out his wallet, hands me three dollar bills. "This is all I got. If I had more, I'd give it to you."

"I don't need money," I say, trying not to sound ungrateful. "I just need a place to sleep."

"When a man of God tries to give you something," he declares, *"you don't say no."*

SANCTUARY

Where to go now?

Mind is numb. Legs are lead.

Where to go—

A church. All I can think of. The closest I can remember is on Capitol Square, due east of the Ohio Statehouse, right in the heart of downtown.

"Trinity Episcopal," the church sign reads. I circle the building on the corner of Broad and Third, trying the doors. Every one is locked. I circle again, this time inspecting the building for a bit of shelter. Finally, on its south side, I locate a nook between two jutting walls, just wide enough, with my knees slightly bent, to sit in sideways. The stone church is cold against my back, the ground frozen beneath me, but I feel relatively safe. It's refuge enough.

I draw my line. If somebody tries to roust me from this spot, I'll refuse to go. "This is a sanctuary of God," I'll tell them, "and I will not be moved."

Unknown to me, James has arrived on the grounds of the Ohio Statehouse, just across the street from the church. A pine tree on the east side of the capitol offers the promise of shelter, but he hesitates. At least one state trooper is probably patrolling the square. If he's caught again on state property, he'll likely be off to jail. Two strikes, you're out.

His eyes take in a scrolling bank sign: *1:23 AM ... 24º ....*

The tree tempts. It has thick cover. Its lowest branches droop, skirting the ground like a full gown.

He crawls under. The thick, dead grass around the tree trunk is matted down; he won't be the first person to have lain here. Fatigue covers him like a blanket. Pillowing his head on pine needles, he fades off.

TEASERS

Mustn't sleep, I tell myself, battling hypothermia. Every few minutes I stand up, stamp my feet like a child, run in place, do squats and jumping jacks, fire-breathe from my belly till I begin to feel warmer.

I sit down again and try to meditate. Sing in whispers. Talk to Jihong. Watch for any lightening of the eastern sky. Cloud cover reflects the city lights, painting the sky a pale orange-rose, like dawn. A cruel tease. *Mustn't sleep.*

Under his tree at the Statehouse, James shivers awake, needing to relieve himself. No time for modesty, no thought for propriety. He does his business between the tree and a concrete wall, then hurries down the hill to the side-walk. "Got to move," he says to his sore, tired body. "Got to get warm."

2:47 AM, according to the bank. He doesn't wait for the temperature to scroll by. He knows it's dropped. He doesn't want to know how much.

Eventually he returns to the hot-air vent where he and I ate dinner. Small comfort, now. The blasts of heat make the night around him feel even colder.

ICE

French bakery next door to the church—Au Bon Pain—means "good bread," probably, but looks like "good pain"—

Nonstop shivers—ribs ache like I've cried for days—

Blow into gloves—no fast way through the night—each minute is ice—*just endure—no way around but through—*

James—still asleep in our nest? Other people in the bushes—rousted?

SANTA MARIA

James walks aimlessly. In his exhaustion, he's not afraid anymore. Numb. His legs, his joints are wood, don't want to move. Marionette limbs without a puppeteer.

Lights ripple on the Scioto River. Beneath a bridge, a homeless person lies wrapped in blankets, suitcase wired to one leg. Not far away, a replica of the Santa Maria, flagship of Christopher Columbus, half frozen in ice at its moor-ing. The original never made it home.

BREAD

I stand outside the night-forsaken bakery—exhaust vent above me—luke-warm air swirls down—smells yeasty sweet—I salivate—

James, wandering through a grid of alleys behind the State Supreme Court, discovers some bread in a dumpster. Whole wheat and white. The wheat's soggy, so he tosses it back. He stares hungrily at the white in his gloved hand, but finally he throws that back, too, doesn't know why.

A wider alley, now. Halfway down, a stray cat lunges. James jumps back, terrified, suddenly aware. This is no place to sleepwalk. He heads back to his tree near the capitol.

SYMPATHIES

Bakery light switches on—

Maybe get inside now—use bathroom—beg hot water—somewhere to nap—please —just till they open—

In kitchen, man in white—back turned—fussing with oven—clock—red digits—*5:25 maybe—can't see—*

I rap on window—man glances around—shuffles over—peers through windowpane—

I raise my arms—open them wide—*harmless—*

I gesture for drink—*please—*

Man's face fills with disgust—arms wag me hard away—he turns on heel—back to kitchen—

I pace by window—fifteen minutes—half hour—back and forth—*ignore me again—*I tell him—*decide—not to help me—again—*

SOMEWHERE ELSE

James huddles against his tree trunk. Almost dawn, he's hoping, the sky dull orange between sagging branches. But no, the bank clock says hours to go. There's no way to speed the night—

He stands up—shakes legs, rolls head, swings arms—*where's Phyl?*

Morning—coming—

Oh, to wake up—somewhere else—

GLORY

Bank across alley from bakery—no guard at lobby desk—*maybe*—*please*—

I hobble on numb feet—shove through the revolving door—slam into a wall of heat—head swims—knees buckle—I sink to marble floor—

Across the lobby, a plate glass wall—*glory*—I see from my knees—McDonald's across Broad Street—lights on—*open!*—6 AM, must be—*night*—*finally* —*over*—

DAY 2

THURSDAY, FEBRUARY 18

SURVIVORS

In McDonald's I beg a free cup of hot water at the counter, then collapse at a corner table in the back of the restaurant, head in hands. All around me, voices. At first, to my dull senses, they're no more than ghosts of sound, but finally I'm warm enough to hear them, and I gather myself enough to look up, amazed that I'm not alone. Maybe a dozen people, men mostly, all apparently homeless. Teenage to elderly; white, black, Latino; some scruffy like me, others neatly groomed or in the process of cleaning up, slipping in and out of the restrooms to wash, shave, comb their hair.

A white guy asks me for 25¢. I slip him one of David's dollar bills, money from the man of God. The rest I'll save for James. I don't know what shape he'll be in when I find him. *Whenever* I find him.

Another Anglo, fiftyish, immaculately dressed, his belongings piled on the seat beside him, tosses me a copy of yesterday's *Ohio State Lantern*.

A young Latino asks if he might join me. Over his coffee cup he tells me his problems, trying to reassure himself that he can make it.

"The sun's coming up," I tell him. "Try to take one day at a time." Out here, no cliché.

"That's exactly the attitude, miss," says a graybeard across the aisle.

"We got to have faith," the Latino agrees. "I'm innocent, you're innocent, and a loving God wouldn't *do* this to us. When we're the most cold and tired, God's right here with us. That's what I believe."

He tells me how difficult it is to have patience, to hang in day after day after day, without enough sleep. "Some nights," he sighs, "it's just too *cold* to sleep." Sometimes, when he's desperate for a little rest, he's tempted to make up a crisis in order to get admitted to a mental hospital. "But then they might decide I'm nuts and keep me."

Once the sun's up, I leave McDonald's to search for James, hoping against the odds that he'll still be where we camped, outside the ODB. Stepping into a stream of work-bound pedestrians, I'm swept down the sidewalk along Broad, across High, and past the Riffe Center. There I'm startled to pass by David the security guard, man of God, so near I might have touched him before we're carried away in opposite directions. His face, still so kind.

No, I hadn't dreamt him. *Angel.* I float.

ARMS

Two hours later, I'm limping up State Street toward Main Library. James wasn't in the bushes at the ODB. He wasn't at the hot air vent. He wasn't along Front Street. He wasn't anywhere. The library, about to open, is my last hope, for now. I don't have it in me to walk much more, the street keeps sliding sideways—

But, oh, there he is—two long, skinny arms, waving wearily outside the front entrance—

Even from here I can see his grin. I thrust my arms into the air, pumping my fists in triumph. Irishman made it through the night.

WICHITA

Periodicals section, third floor of Main Library. I'm not writing because I want to. I'm frantic to sleep, but it won't come. James, seated across from me, has his head down on the table like a schoolboy. He might have slept a total of four hours last night, he told me. I envy him those four hours. I envy him, sleeping now.

Just behind me, a homeless man is slumped over in his chair, snoring into a magazine.

When James and I compared nights, we realized that we'd been separated by less than a hundred yards, pine tree to church. Tonight, having learned our lesson the hard way, we'll stay in city shelters. We won't try to sleep outside again till we find some blankets and a more tolerable place to bed down.

My eyes skim a rack of newspapers and catch the lead headline from Wichita, Kansas: "How Secure Will You Be?"

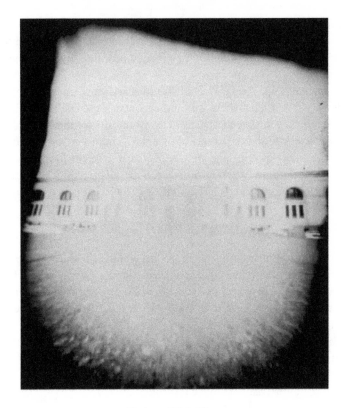

The front of Main Library

BLANKETS

Around 10:30 AM James and I part ways to either track down some blankets or beg money with which to pay for some.

At a homeless shelter James offers to buy one for $2, the remaining money from the man of God. The staffer sees COLD stamped on James's forehead and says, with a touch of regret, "Sorry, our blankets aren't for sale."

Meanwhile, mid-morning business is slow at The Place to Be. This café is housed in the basement of Trinity Episcopal Church, only steps from where I'd drawn my line during the night hours. I ask several employees behind the counter for money, assuring them I'll spend it on blankets.

"Sorry, we can't help you," they say, "but shouldn't you be staying in a shelter? It's too *cold* to be sleeping out there!"

I drag myself back up the steps to street level. Icy snow is falling. A bank clock reminds me that it's nearly time to meditate at the Statue of Peace, on the Broad Street side of the Statehouse. In the weeks before leaving home, James and I had decided to meditate there for a half hour each day at noon. We told friends and relatives they'd be welcome to join us at a distance.

I start shuffling slow as pain toward the capitol grounds, only to be stopped by shouts. One of the café employees, a young Anglo sporting a base-ball cap and full white apron, trots up behind me, thumbing through his wallet. "Here—" breathless, he hands me a $10 bill— "maybe you can get a blanket at a thrift store. Maybe get yourself something to eat, too."

Tears.[2]

INITIATION

Wings outstretched, cape billowing, gown flowing, the angel strides, her face determined and strong. Her right hand, raised overhead, holds a leafy olive branch. Her left hand steadies a shield, tip resting on the ground.

At least twelve feet tall, cast in bronze and installed on a granite base, the statue had been unveiled on June 26, 1923. She was meant as a tribute to the Ohio men who'd fought during the Civil War with the Grand Army of the Republic, as well as the women who'd labored in support of them. The inscription: "Let Us Have Peace."

In the shadow of the angel wait a number of our friends. In their presence James and I break down, weep, cling. This close mingling might attract atten-tion (Statehouse visitors and street people don't often hug), but we don't care. Today, at least, we need the comfort of touch. There's no meditation; only tears, and the effort to speak, to somehow assign words to a night unlike any we've ever experienced. Initiation, we begin to call it.

I ache for Jihong, but he's teaching his chemistry class at Ohio State. Maybe it's best that he isn't here to witness what's already become of me.

BUDGET

Our exhaustion plain, our friend Gwyn urges us to go to the Agora and try to get some sleep. Located across the Scioto River, a fifteen or twenty-minute hike west of the Statehouse, the Agora houses a socially concerned Mennonite congregation as well as a day-center for homeless families.

The day-center is operated by the Interfaith Hospitality Network, which Gwyn directs. Homeless families can stay all day at the center, receiving assistance from social workers; then, in late afternoon, they're bussed for the night to makeshift living quarters in synagogues and churches around the city.

On our way to the Agora, James and I stop at a Volunteers of America thrift shop. Earlier he'd scouted its racks for any blankets, afghans or

Looking up at the Statue of Peace

comforters. Now he points out a wool blanket. Heavy. Full-sized. $2.99. This morning, it was beyond our budget.

That was then. This is now.

I lay the café employee's $10 bill on the counter.

THE AGORA

We arrive at the Agora footsore and ready to drop. Two staffers whom Gwyn has apparently told about our undertaking hurry to set up cots in a small meeting room. "Thank you, thank you, thank you," we say.

James falls headlong onto the nearer cot. His big feet hang well off the end. Two deep exhalations, and he's out cold.

The staffers cover us both with blankets, pull the blinds, turn off the lights, and close the door against the din from the day-center: crying babies, ringing phones, the shrieks and laughter of children, adult voices chatting in the hallway, the click and clatter of a typewriter, a TV's drone....

THE BOTTOMS

In thirty hours I haven't slept more than one, but I can't relax. Maybe I'm high on adrenaline, or wired on the sugar from the cookies I've devoured. A vegetarian at home, I usually don't eat many sweets.

After much fitful, frustrated tossing, I give up. I leave my cot and wander out front to Five Loaves, the Agora's bakery/café. Its profits support the church's many outreach ministries.

Rebecca, a youth minister, is behind the counter, taking her turn serving pastries and sandwiches. During a lull in business, she tells me that she feels called by God to work with the teenagers in this neighborhood. "The Bottoms, that's what they call it. Thirteenth-poorest white ghetto in the country. Most of the kids here don't know it's a good thing to eat three meals a day, or get lots of sleep, or wear clean clothes, or go to school, or even have parents who love them. They've never had it, never seen it, never been taught, so how would they know?"

She shakes her head. "The kids don't have any dreams. They think it'd be a great life, growing up to work at McDonald's."

A customer appears at the register. I retire to a small table to write. Yesterday in Main Library, drafting on the back of the *Treaty of Greene Ville*, I'd composed. Ink flowed. Themes were sustained, sentence structure was varied, word choices were deliberate. My handwriting, though inelegant, was quick, slashing, confident.

Today I scribble, with a pencil found yesterday at the baseball field. *Was that only yesterday?* Like a young child I grip too tightly. I bear down so hard that my fist smears lead. My marks on the paper are crude. My thoughts clot in simple sentences, abrupt phrases, single words. I struggle to spell, familiar words not looking right. I abandon punctuation. *Just get it down.* Style belongs to somebody else. *Whatever will help you remember.* Concern for diction, obsolete. *Or forget.* The page glares up at me. *Don't tell me to stay between the lines.*

Sitting at the next table is Peggy, a social worker on coffee break. Over the space between us she tells me the story of Isaac, a homeless child, five years old. Last summer she'd been trying to arrange permanent housing for his family and employment for his parents. Then, in September, a car struck and killed him near the Methodist church that was sheltering his family for the night. Soon after, his family disappeared. They haven't been heard from since. She still grieves.

Before she returns to work, Peggy kindly buys me a huge deli sandwich, a bowl of vegetable soup, and a bag of potato chips. I'm hungry as a dog, but the feast will have to wait till James wakes up.

NUMBERS

3 PM, standing at an Agora payphone. In my hand are the phone numbers of two homeless shelters, one for men, one for women. Before James and I hit the streets, a contact on the staff of a city shelter had recommended we call these numbers if we ever needed a place to spend the night. We'd be taken care of, few questions asked.

We'd hoped never to use these numbers, not wanting to take up the beds. Still, our contact had told us not to worry, there would always be enough space for those in need. No matter how crowded the city shelters, nobody would be turned away, especially in inclement weather.

I drop my quarter and dial. On the fourth ring, somebody at the women's shelter picks up. "Call back around six," a husky female voice says. "We'll know then if we have room for you."

If we have room.

James calls the men's shelter when he wakes up, around 4:30. The guy on the phone tells him that he'd better come right away if he wants a bed for the night.

Right away. If he wants a bed.

The men's shelter is located way back across the river, but James can walk the distance. I, on the other hand, will have to catch a bus to the women's shelter —*if* I'm told I can come. Should I be turned away, my options will be severely limited. To my knowledge, most city shelters serve either single men, families, or individuals battling addiction. Where to go if you're female, childless and sober?

I accompany James as far as High Street. There, as we say goodbye, I smile a little. "My bus fare to the shelter will be a dollar-ten," I say, forcing myself to sound optimistic. "You're getting off easy."

"I don't like leaving without knowing for sure you're in."

"I know."

He waits for words. Finally he says, "My instincts tell me you'll be okay."

"We'll both be okay."

"Why don't we meet at McDonald's on Broad, first thing in the morning?"

"I'll be there." I give him a tight hug. "Yashir koach, Irishman."

SHELTER

Outside the men's shelter James sidles through a loose crowd of cliques and loners, guys loitering, smoking and shooting the bull. He walks past the security guard stationed at the front door and gets in line at the reception desk. Straight ahead is a room painted baby blue, a scripture passage barely legible on the wall. Rows of hardwood pews face a battered podium and a big-screen TV playing a third-rate movie. Some men are watching. Others are milling about, restless.

Instantly James is nervous.

A new guy, he's told to register. He fills out an information form and signs a contract, agreeing among other things not to have alcohol, drugs or weapons on the premises. To complete the paperwork, the intake staffer asks him basic questions, all of which he answers vaguely.

"Why you here?" the staffer wants to know.

"Separated from my girlfriend," he says. It's as true an answer as he can think of, since by now Phoebe's back in Connecticut. The staffer marks the "Relationship Problems" box under *Cause*.

After the interview he's searched by a security guard. When asked to surrender any weapons or sharp objects on his person, he takes out his tool kit and hands over its miniature can opener. Somehow he doesn't think to mention itsknife.

He'll be told where to sleep at 9 PM. Hours to go. In the blue room he claims a spot in the very back pew and chucks his duffel underneath.

Now time presses in, turning thick, quicksand pulling him down. Whenever he makes eye contact, he nods a "What's up," trying to appear more relaxed than he feels. Some men creep around the room as if in pain. Others dart like water bugs. Many, like him, are just lounging in the pews, each keeping close watch on his own suitcase, satchel, backpack, pile of plastic bags.

Back on High Street I drop another quarter on the women's shelter. I'm calling an hour earlier than I'm supposed to, but I can't endure the wait. I hold my breath as the phone rings.

The same voice answers. "We've got room," the woman says. "Come on over." She tells me which bus to take, which stop to get off at. "Our location is confidential. Many of our residents have been battered by husbands and boyfriends. So don't you tell anybody—I mean *anybody*—exactly where you're going. Got it?"

During the half-hour bus ride I meet Sweetness, a smiling, middle-aged black woman who's been staying at the shelter. She's just made arrangements to rent an apartment. "Soon I'll be in my own place. Girl, I can't wait!"

"How's it been, living at the shelter?"

"You'll want to watch your *ps* and *qs*, girl. Some of them women is tough customers. Had to be, to survive."

AD-LIBBING

Name, most recent address, age, Social Security number, marital status—so many questions.... After two strenuous days without sleep, I can scarcely digest the intake staffer's words. Now and then her voice is drowned out by bantering and laughter, weeping, petty accusations and arguments, a TV turned up loud. Women crowd the cluttered desk where we're seated, noisy with complaints, requests, demands.

The staffer studies my driver's license. "Why aren't you living anymore at this address?" She's almost shouting to be heard.

I don't know what to say. "So sorry. So tired. Can't think."

She tries to help me by reading down a standard list of reasons women become homeless: financial problems, eviction, unemployment, domestic violence, divorce, separation—

"*That's* it." I cringe inwardly at the doublespeak, but at least it isn't an outright lie. "My husband and I are separated."

"Why's that?"

"It's sort of hard to talk about."

The staffer escorts me up a flight of wooden steps. Unlocking a door, she leads me into a suite of three rooms and a bathroom. Situated in one corner of the large main room is somebody's ad-libbed home: a set of bunk beds, cracked wall mirror, busy dresser, and shabby chair tossed with clothes. The rest of the room is empty except for a small sofa that's well past its prime and a few twin-sized mattresses scattered on the floor. They're for temporary "overflow girls" like me. The two far rooms, quite cramped, are for longer-term residents who are making a gradual transition to more permanent housing. Apparently the shelter is a hive of suites like this one.

The bathroom shower, I learn, is for resident use only. What I wouldn't give to laze under the shower head, water steaming hot! But as an "O-girl," I'm at the bottom of the pecking order. I can't risk breaking the rules. Not on my first night, anyway. Grateful for a bit of soap lying on the sink, I take a spit bath and wash my hair, toweling off with my sweaty long johns. Then I scrub out my underwear and socks and lay them out to dry.

I spread the rest of my clothes over one of the mattresses on the floor and lie down on top ("the best way to keep somebody from stealing them," Sweetness had said). I cover myself with the wool blanket bought at Volunteers of America. At last, for the first time in days, I drift toward sleep—

Angry shouts—feet running up and down the stairs—women rushing in and out the door—a rowdy fight downstairs—glass breaking—

I yank the blanket over my head.

EL DIABLO

A dirty, potbellied Latino, barely five feet tall, lightly touches James's shoulder as if they're old friends. Through a heavy accent he invites him outside the shelter for a cigarette. James doesn't smoke but somehow can't say so. He rises to follow. The Latino points to James's duffel, indicating he should bring it along.

The two are watched intently as they go, though the stares are furtive. Most of the men, James noticed earlier, won't acknowledge the Latino's presence. The Latino disapproves of them—his eyes tell it—and his disdain, if nothing else, seems to have made him an outsider. Now the men are probably wondering who James is, what his alliances are.

He steps from the shelter into night.

"Your first time here?" the Latino says, and James nods, amazed it was so obvious. He reaches out his hand, introducing himself. The man returns a firm grip. "Manuel," he says, laying his free hand over his heart.

A wrinkled brow, a round unshaven face, lackluster eyes, Manuel has the look of somebody grown used to despair. Forcing a cigarette into James's hand, lighting it before his own, he begins to unburden himself. He complains in a mumble about the other men in the shelter, switching rapidly between English and Spanish. James struggles to understand, to respond.

Their conversation deepens. Soon Manuel is confiding problems with his marriage, his finances; an entire life in turmoil. Finally James says, "Manuel, what keeps you going? Do you believe in God, or—?"

The man swells with emotion. "I believe in God," he replies, "but...." —a long pause— "El Diablo es El Diablo." *The Devil is the Devil.* This much, James understands.

Manuel draws on his cigarette, shaking his head. Then he looks up at James. His eyes fill with tears. "I can *cry!*" he exclaims. The tears spill over, slide all the way down to his jawbone before he wipes them away.

FIRST-TIMING

James reclaims his old spot in the back pew. He asks guys sitting around him where to get food, where to do laundry. One-word replies mostly.

A few pews up, a black man wearing a Kelly green cap and matching down jacket turns around and says, "This your first time here?"

James nods.

"Don't worry about it," the man says.

Manuel paces.

A blond Anglo, built like an offensive lineman, plops down nearby. He appears to be around James's age—a rare thing; at twenty-three James might be the youngest man here. After some chitchat, the blond guy leans in, asks James if he has any weed.

"Naw, man."

"Want to smoke some with me?"

James shakes his head.

"You going to stay here?"

"Yeah, if they let me."

"Well, I'm just here to get a bus pass. Been living in the basement of a building out east—some guy lets people stay there. You leave there by bus first thing in the morning, and if you want to, you can go back there at night."

James doesn't know what to make of this information. It sounds sketchy. Homeless people living in somebody's basement? After getting bus passes from a city shelter? It doesn't make much sense, but out here nothing much does, so far.

OVERFLOW

After four hours of waiting and a food-line meal, James is told the shelter is full. He and nine other men, including the offensive lineman, will be transported to an "overflow shelter" in Bexley, on the city's east side. Since no buses run to that part of town this late at night, a staffer orders two taxis.

At 10:30 PM the cabs drop the men at a rec hall in a city park. The entire building is dark except for the dim red light radiating from two EXIT signs. Once inside the doors, the men proceed down a flight of stairs, then through a steel door, and finally down three more steps into the basement. This, James figures, must be the place the big blond had been talking about.

After signing more papers in a small staff room, he pulls a flimsy collapsible cot from a depleted stack and paws through a pile of ratty blankets till he finds one his nose can tolerate. Then, on to the sleeping room, the largest room in the basement. It's wall-to-wall men, maybe seventy in all; little space left for latecomers. Three rows of cots, set side by side, run the entire length of the room, separated by narrow aisles. The men's cots are only inches apart.

"What's up," he says to his neighbor, unfolding his cot in tight rank. He stows his boots and duffel underneath. The vinyl sheeting of the cot droops so low, the duffel bulges against it.

His neighbor introduces himself as Bob. He seems in a daze. An ugly red gash extends from his hairline down the left side of his nose to his upper lip. "Car crash," he says, when James asks. "Been in a coma the last three days. Just came out of it today. I'm from out of town. Totaled my car. Nowhere else to go."

Bob sounds bewildered, almost like he'd rather be back in the coma than staying here. Looking at him, James wonders how many other men with physical ailments might be sleeping tonight in this shelter. Chances are, some of them have serious infectious diseases, like tuberculosis or hepatitis.

"This place is worse than the state pen," gripes the new guy settling in on his right.

James digs down in his duffel, takes out a copy of *The Big Book*, borrowed for the night from the downtown shelter.

"What you got there?" Bob asks, his voice weak.

"I've had a problem with alcohol. This book's about recovery. It's helped me out a lot."

Bob nods, as if he can relate.

James flips to a page, tries to focus. He reads the same paragraph three times. The sour stench of blankets and bodies is turning his stomach. Finally he sets his book aside and tries to relax, his body tense as a Wall Street nerve.

The lights go out.

PART 2: LIFE AS OVERFLOW

DAY 3

FRIDAY, FEBRUARY 19

WAKE-UP CALLS

"Five-thirty! You're out of here!"

Fluorescent lights flicker on. The air fills with shouted commands and the grumblings of exhausted men. James lifts his head, eyes screwed in a squint, trying to get his bearings. One whiff reminds him not to inhale through his nose. He forces his body up, instructs it to dress, fold cot, toss blanket on the pile.

As a staffer distributes bus passes for their trip back into the downtown, the men are herded outside. Together they slouch toward a bus stop some distance away. No loitering. Bexley is a wealthy suburb. The residents want all the homeless men transported from the rec center before sunrise. At least, that's the scuttlebutt. Last night, after the lights went out, one of the guys had piped up, said, "Shit, since we're sleeping in Bexley, maybe tomorrow we'll *all* get rich!" Everybody had laughed, a little.

Waiting for the bus, men still half asleep lean down to the pavement, pick up old cigarette butts, relight them for a single drag. Morning extroverts curse the cold, shifting their weight from one foot to the other, trying to keep the blood flowing. Homeless calisthenics.

James hunches his shoulders, stamps his feet, breathes clouds. Lights flicker on in nearby mansions. Crows caw. The sky begins to brighten.

"Got to get up! It's six o'clock!"

I peer at a backlit figure in the doorway. "Yeah, okay, thanks." I roll over, covering my head with my blanket.

"You got to leave in *one hour*. You and the rest of the O-girls."

The door bangs shut. I stay on my mattress. Not much primping to do.

At 6:30 I'm rousted again, this time by a staffer who whispers my name and shakes my toes gently through the blanket. I feel like a child being wakened for school, early on a dark winter morning.

"You're a mother," I murmur.

The staffer moves on with a sigh.

MORNING COMMUTE

James isn't actually homeless, but from the disgusted looks he's getting as he moves up the aisle, the passengers on this bus believe he is. He hurries to find a seat. *No special section for our kind,* he thinks to himself. *We're scattered all over the bus.*

Up front a homeless man gives up his seat for an elderly woman. He stands, she smiles. James feels a little warmer.

The bus running the route near the women's shelter is early. My new friend Sweetness, walking with me and the other women on the snow-dusted sidewalk, sees it coming and grabs my arm. Together we run slipping and sliding for the stop. Once on board, I fumble for fare: another $1.10 into the downtown. The money in my pocket, courtesy of the café worker, is dwindling fast.

I ask Sweetness how she manages the round-trip fare every day. Rather than answer me directly, she lets me know that free one-day bus passes are available at a place called JOIN.

"Men," she complains, "*they* get bus passes at *their* shelters, no problem. Not us. They think long's we got *cootchy coo,* we can always get the money we need. That's what they think. It's not right."

Downtown, at the bustling intersection of Broad and High, Sweetness and I get off the bus, exchange quick goodbyes in the flurrying cold.

"Just be positive, child," she says (when we first met I was "girl," but now I'm under her wing). She gives my arm a squeeze. "If you *want* help, you'll *find* it. God bless."

STAYING

McDonald's on Broad Street. James's appearance after his first night in the men's shelter is shocking: heavy dark circles under his eyes, face sallow and swollen from tiredness, head and shoulders sagging. Through exhausted tears he tells me the story of his stay. Then, at the end, a burst of hysterical laughter.

"What are we doing, Phyl? This is nuts."

"Do you want to end it?"

He grows quiet. Shakes his head. Not a "no," exactly. Bewilderment. "I'm broken, Phyl."

"I know." *How to tell him you're sorry, you never expected, never wanted, the streets to hurt him like this?*

His hands gesture helplessly. "I feel like I've lost big pieces of me, and it hurts like hell."

"What do you feel like you've lost?"

"I don't know … trust, maybe. Trust that I'll survive. Trust that I won't lose my mind. I don't know. Maybe I just want to believe that my life matters more than it seems to, out here."

For a while we don't speak. Then he wipes the tears from his eyes. "What about you? How was your night?"

I tell him about Sweetness, the shelter, the noise, the fighting. Apparently an O-girl was thrown out for assaulting a staffer. She won't be allowed to return.

"My biggest worry is the bus fare," I say then. "It'll cost more than two dollars a day, getting out there and back."

"Last night I heard there's a women's shelter, here in the downtown, where if you tell them you're battered, you can stay, no matter what."

"I'm not going to lie, James."

"Figured you'd say that, but had to tell you anyway. Any cuts on your face, you're in."

"What do you want, an excuse to beat me up?"

We laugh. It feels good to laugh, even at a joke in bad taste.

"So you're doing okay?" he says.

"Much better than yesterday. Getting some sleep helped."

"Want to keep going?"

I nod. "But if *you* need to quit, that's okay. I understand."

"Just be sure to quit for the right reason—that's what we said, coming out."

"Yeah. Right now, I've got to stay. I'm where I've got to be."

He smiles weakly. "Count me in."

ILLUSIONS

An uncanny connection seems to exist among street people. You might not know each other, but you easily recognize each other. Maybe it's the scruffy clothes that give you away, or the hollow pain in your eyes. More likely it's the

Alley view of downtown

way you walk, down and heavy, like a constant ache. The backs of the legs complain. You don't hurry unless you have to. You fill your steps.

So much walking. So much walking in straight lines. Sidewalks: right—left —up—down. Streets: this way—that. Doors: in—out. Suddenly the world's a grid; life, unswerving conformity. Spirit in a straitjacket.

Already I feel light-years from home, and lost, even from Jihong. I see him everywhere—turning the corner, entering a building, getting on a bus. Always he disappears. My mind puts him there, real enough. The next instant, it erases him without a trace.

I so want to speak to him face to face, to touch his cheek, to hold him close and be held by him, yet I doubt I could, even if I had the chance. That where he is and where I am could be the same world seems impossible. What word, what caress, would suffice to close the distance between us?

I try to reassure myself that the two of us aren't as distant as we seem. Separation is, at the heart of it, an illusion; nothing, nobody, in the world stands essentially apart from the rest. Still, the illusion of separation is convincing, sad, and sometimes almost unbearable. It's love that helps me withstand the strain of it. Headline from the *Employment News*, a curbside weekly: "Why Can't We All Just Get Along?"

RITUAL

James, off on his own, is hitching along toward the Broad Street bridge, feeling downright elderly, when some dead plants next to the sidewalk catch his eye. Milkweed, waist-high. Fluffs of seed rise from open pods, migrate on the breeze. Inspired, he pockets a couple of pods, then hurries off to find me.

The sidewalk gods have smiled on me: a small tube of Crest, not quite empty, and a clean rag to use as a washcloth. I throw away a sheet of plastic I've been toting around for protection in case of rain. *Don't accumulate stuff that's not essential. It fast becomes a burden.*

James is rushing toward me with obvious purpose. His face is much brighter than its early morning gray.

"What's happened?" I ask.

"Follow me. I have a surprise."

My imagination prospects for gold as he leads me west on Broad: a stash of blankets, maybe, or some out-of-the-way place he's stumbled upon, secure and warm enough to spend the night.

Halfway across the Broad Street bridge, he stops suddenly and leans against the rail. For a few minutes the two of us watch the river swirling muddy brown below. Then he yanks off a glove and reaches into his coat pocket.

"Hold out your hand."

He lays a milkweed pod in my palm. Dead-brown, brittle, barely open. I look at him, puzzled. He has another pod in his hand.

"I thought we could release the seeds over the river. Kind of a ritual: for each clump of seeds, we can name something we've got to let go of, in order to keep going out here."

"Wonderful," I exclaim, knowing exactly what he means. There are so many things he and I wish we had out here; things we're used to having; things we might never have during these forty-seven days. (How intensely we humans crave a perfect life, in which we have everything we want and nothing we don't. How bitterly we resent the inevitable disappointment.)

We dare not cling to our desires. They're too heavy, too burdensome to carry. They get too much in the way. *Empty your hands.*

I tug off my gloves, better to grasp the tufted seeds.

"You first," James says.

"I let go of my need for a good night's sleep," I say, casting a cottony fluff.

"I let go of my need for three meals a day."

"My need to be warm."

"To feel safe."

"To have more money."

"To be clean."

"To know what's coming next."

More and more white wisps of milkweed down float gently over the churning water, like tiny parachutes. A few of them will make it to land. Maybe one of them will survive to become a milkweed plant. And maybe one day a monarch butterfly will lay her eggs on the underside of its leaves.

"I let go of my need to feel loved."

The necessity of the lowly milkweed: a monarch butterfly will lay her eggs nowhere else.

"I let go of my need to be me."

JOIN

"Joint Operation for Inner-city Needs," the sign reads—a relief agency run by the Catholic Diocese of Columbus. It's open for a couple hours each weekday morning and afternoon. Waiting in a slow line behind a dozen people, I finally make it to the receptionist's window. She takes my name, checks my ID and asks what I want.

"A bus pass, please."

"You'll have to wait. *Next!*"

Off to one side, clothing racks and cardboard boxes full of hand-me-downs. I'm pawing through, looking for anything that might serve as a blanket, when my name's called. I'm led at once through a locked door into a small cubicle, where sits Ethel, a smartly dressed seventy-something volunteer.

"So," she says flatly from behind her neat desk. "You want a bus pass."

"Yes, ma'am, it'd be a big help."

She's not convinced I need a bus pass, and says so. She starts shooting questions at me. I feel pinned down. Who am I—why am I on the streets—don't I have any family to help—where am I currently living—

She scowls at my last reply. "How could you possibly be staying *there?*" she says accusingly. "That shelter is only for long-term residents."

"I'm what they call an overflow girl," I say. To prove I'm telling her the truth, I describe the shelter and the entrance interview. I even identify the shelter's confidential location. She still doesn't believe me. Beginning to feel irritated, I take a deep breath and calmly suggest that she call the shelter staff and confirm I stayed the night. She refuses.

Baffled, I don't know what else to say. What makes this woman so skeptical, so unyielding? Maybe she's been too often lied to, or too much taken for granted, or too long exposed to people in trouble. Maybe she's frazzled from working so hard to help while nothing ever seems to change.

She leans back in her chair, stares me down. "What made you decide to do this? Or did you just say to yourself, 'This is what I'm going to do,' and then you just did it?"

I'm stunned. *It's as if she knows.*

When I don't respond, she says, "Well, this will be *quite* an experience. Maybe you can write a book about it someday." She laughs suddenly, loudly, and quickly administers a bus pass. "Good for one day. By rule, that's the only pass you're allowed this month."

TABLE TALK

Lunchtime in the men's shelter, downtown. The older man sitting beside James goes by the name of Colonel. Rumor has it that he has plenty of money but prefers to live here in the shelter. "A lifer," the men call him, as if doing hard time behind bars.

All around James and the Colonel the crowded lunch tables are buzzing with the news of Wilford Berry's execution by lethal injection, the first execution in Ohio since 1963. Nicknamed the Volunteer, Berry had objected to all appeals on his behalf, preferring death to spending his life in prison for murdering a baker.

"It's just not right," a guy across from James says. "He should've repented."

"He had some balls, I tell you," says another.

"God have mercy on him and his family."

"Didn't say a single word to his own relatives before he died—how *could* he?"

"Ah, he was a bastard."

BUFFET

A whole loaf of white bread, dumped on the ground under a bush; stale, stiff to my touch, probably meant for squirrels.

A generous serving of spaghetti and meatballs, spilled from a styrofoam container onto the sidewalk. I bend over and sniff.

Hot sausage sandwiches, greasy, topped with sautéed onions, red and green peppers. "Honey mustard," the street peddler cries to the air. "Special sauce, if you want it!"

EYES

Near where I sit, waiting for James at the Statue of Peace, busloads of elementary schoolchildren are arriving for a tour of the capitol complex. My tired eyes luxuriate in the children's bright red boots, pink hats, turquoise mittens, yellow coats. Somebody has loved these little ones enough to bundle them up.

Their energy's a delight, even as their teachers scold and cajole them into straight lines. They don't look at me, though. Not till they think I'm not looking at them—then they study me like a brand-new picture book. Already they're learning well the art of avoidance.

Rarely am I able to make eye contact with men and women I pass on the streets. Pedestrians almost always lower their eyes when we meet, or stare deliberately ahead, or turn sharply to glance back over their shoulder, as if somebody behind them has just called their name.

It's been said that an infant first gains some sense of her existence, and some sense that she's loved, from the gaze of her parents. But what happens when a grown woman loses her way—when she no longer perceives (if she ever did) that her life has substance, and matters? In whose eyes might she still see reflected her fundamental worth?

HIS FIRST

In early afternoon James attends a Twelve-Step meeting in the Bottoms. The smoke-filled room, the stale donuts and bad coffee, the round-robin discussion—all these are a comfort. He's dirty and disheveled but not judged. Not that he's aware, anyway.

Scattered around the room are large coffee cans serving as ash trays. The nearest holds a couple hundred cigarette butts. When the meeting ends, he picks it up and asks the chairperson if he can have it. "Yeah, sure," the man says, giving him a strange look.

His first pinhole camera, maybe.

He meets me at Deaf School Park, behind Main Library, anxious to work. Before hitting the streets, he'd made several pinholes, poking needles of various widths through thin pieces of brass, one-inch square. Now, to make a camera, he has to mount one of these brass pinholes over a hole in his coffee can to serve as a lens. First, he drives a nail through the can, using a light metal mallet we found yesterday. After removing the nail, he light-proofs the can, spraying the inside with black paint and masking its plastic lid with black electrical tape.

Once the paint is completely dry, he'll select a brass pinhole and securely tape it over the larger nail hole. Finally, he'll cover the pinhole with a piece of electrical tape, which will act as the camera's shutter. To shoot a photograph, he'll simply peel back the tape, allowing light to pass through the pinhole lens and expose a 5"x7" sheet of photo paper positioned inside the can.

After every photo he shoots, he'll have to conceal the camera in his light-proof film-changing bag, then blindly transfer the exposed photo paper to a black storage bag. Every few days one of his darkroom assistants will pick up a package of exposures and take them home to develop into negatives. He'll want to see those negatives as soon as possible in order to judge the camera's performance. Pinhole photography is mostly trial and error. He can't easily judge exposure time, appropriate distance from the subject, or lens angle. Some shots, if he doesn't get them right the first time, he'll simply miss. Others he'll be able to shoot over and over, trying to get images that satisfy.

WEED

A major snowstorm is headed toward Columbus. Many homeless people who ordinarily sleep on the streets will take refuge tonight in city shelters. The rec center in Bexley, responsible for the overflow of men from those facilities, is likely to be overcrowded. Latecomers might not get a bed. James signs in early, wanting not to sleep on concrete.

"Want to go outside, smoke some weed with me?" asks the guy lying in the next cot. Last night: the same man, the same question, and a simple "no" had sufficed. Now, to discourage the overtures, James says that he's allergic.

"Really?"

"Yeah."

"Do you get a rash?"

James nods, another lie to put the man off. The fellow leans toward him, his expression serious. "Oh—you know, I think *I* get a rash, too." Standing up to go, he laughs. "I smoke it anyway."

James tries to imagine being high, all five senses hyped to the max, in this place, so crowded and noisy and rank and tense. The thought sickens him. *But hey,* he says to himself, *if getting high would help a guy laugh in this hole, maybe it would help him survive.*

PACK

Boarding the bus in early evening to return to the women's shelter, I ask the driver to please tell me when we're approaching the stop nearest my street. He frowns, stares straight ahead. "Don't want to," he says.

I don't want to ask him again and possibly provoke a scene. Uneasily I take a seat. How will I ever get off the bus at the right stop? Last night, on my way to the shelter for the first time, I was too exhausted to read street signs. But Sweetness had been there, guiding me like a mother hen.

Tonight, though, I'm alone, and anxious. I have to get off at the right stop. Wandering these streets after dark wouldn't be wise. It's a tough part of town.

Staring out my window, I see an elderly man hobbling down the sidewalk through a stinging snow, wrapped in a thin blanket. I shiver, deep and hard.

An older black lady sitting beside me leans into my shoulder, says in a low voice, "You going to the shelter?"

I nod.

"Me too," she says, relieved.

No longer alone.

In all, five of us women get off the bus. We hurry in a pack the few blocks to the shelter, as fast as we can go.

LAUNDRY

Tonight's intake worker, contradicting last night's, says that yes, even though I'm an O-girl, I may take a shower. She even rummages in a messy closet and brings out a clean bath towel and a variety of toiletries, as well as a sheet and a tattered orange afghan to use on my mattress. I'm overwhelmed.

Upstairs, at the bathroom door, I'm intercepted by Cindy, a long-term resident in the suite. She hands me a red sweater and white bib overalls, two pair of socks, and a brown nightshirt to sleep in. All of them her own clothes, freshly laundered. "Take these," she says over my protests, "and give me your dirty ones. I'll do them up for you."

"Why're you helping me like this?" I ask her, close to tears.

"Why not?" she says, voice matter-of-fact. "People helped *me* when *I* was down."

I stand under the shower, water steaming hot, till my skin is smarting red.

CONSPIRACY

I'm startled awake in the night by a resident's screams—she's hysterical, just across the room—the door into our suite won't open, from either side—won't even budge—she's claustrophobic, totally panicked—two other women are trying to console her—a third's furious, late for a date—staffers outside the door can't agree on what to do next—loudly they curse the repairman who supposedly just fixed the knob—"Maybe he wasn't really no handy-man!"—"Maybe he planned the whole thing! You know, like, *sabotage!*"—"Yeah, he probably hates women"—

DAY 4

SATURDAY, FEBRUARY 20

BOTTOM LINE

Approaching noon in the downtown. I'm feeling woozy. Barely a bite since yesterday's lunch of tuna and beans, the last of our canned goods from born-again Pete. Energy's spent. So cold. So much walking.

James says he's holding up, having eaten breakfast at a men's shelter. "Why don't you buy a cheeseburger at McDonald's?" he suggests.

According to the restaurant's menu board, a cheeseburger will cost me 89¢. Nearly a dollar. My belly wants to spend the money. My mind wants to save it for bus fare.

I withdraw from the counter without placing an order.

Out the window, a homeless man is moving a mountain of aluminum cans, his shopping cart piled high with bulging black trash-bags. Every bump and crack in the sidewalk threatens his load. Pennies, they'll pay him. He vanishes behind a curbside bus.

Suddenly I remember: Last night at the women's shelter, one of my suite-mates had finagled a rare bus pass from a staffer and slipped it to me on the sly. She's already saved me $2.20.

I return to the counter and order my burger. It's barely warm, but I savor every bite, $1.31 to the good.

JUST SAM

We're digging in a dumpster across the rear parking lot of St. Joseph Cathedral. I toss James a Reese's Peanut Butter Cup, still in the wrapper. "Yum," he grins.

A plain wooden angel, country craft style, lies buried under a heap of garbage bags. James sets it on top of the bin as decoration just as a man in black walks up. A priest, maybe. He asks what we're doing.

"Just looking around."

"Are you hungry?"

"Yeah!"

"Come with me," he says, with a friendly motion of his hand.

Without hesitation we follow the stranger across the lot to the rectory's back door. Leaving us on the stoop, he goes inside. Soon he returns with a bologna sandwich, an apple and two cookies for each of us. "You can come here for food any day of the week. Nine o'clock in the morning, four in the afternoon. Got that?"

We thank him.

"What's going on with you guys? Why are you on the street?"

"Just got to sort some things out," we say.

His eyes brighten with tears. "Well," he says, collecting himself, "you take care, okay?"

We ask his name.

"Oh," he says, "I'm just Sam."

LANDSCAPE

A sacred landscape has begun to emerge over our first few days on the streets: McDonald's on Broad, where we meet first thing each morning to debrief after our nights in the city shelters; the Statue of Peace, where we meditate each noon, and where dear friends often bless us with precious eye contact from a discreet distance; the third floor of Main Library, where we relax and read out of the elements; Deaf School Park, where we write and construct pinhole cameras, or simply laze, when the sun's warm enough; and now the rear door of St. Joseph rectory, where we can beg sandwiches. In these places we feel safe. Sometimes we even feel a sense of belonging, or at least of having the right to be on the premises, if only for a while.

But nothing's absolute. As we've discovered today, some of these places restrict their hours on the quiet downtown weekends. We adapt, but with sadness, a melancholy out of all proportion.

How quickly a place can become a haven. How little is required.

James and Phyllis walking the streets, photographed by Jihong Cole-Dai from his car

CHICKEN

Late afternoon. The back door of the Salesian Boys and Girls Club opens. A man tosses a couple of large foil roasting pans into the trash. James elbows me in the ribs.

The lukewarm remains of chicken casserole. We draw fast-food forks from our coat pockets, and the banquet begins. Shriveling orange halves round out our meal. We nip the clean, fleshy parts like vultures picking at a carcass.

After a few minutes, we notice a cop car just down the block. Hastily we pocket our forks, jump a chainlink fence and slip down the nearest alley.

VISIBILITY

End of our day. We take leave of each other at a High Street bus stop, headed for our respective shelters. James hesitates, looks at me oddly.

"What is it?" I say.

"You're all eyes."

"All eyes?"

He nods. "That's mostly what I see of you, all day long. You're always bundled up against the cold, face-warmer pulled up over your nose, hat pulled down to your eyebrows. Your eyes are the only part of you that's visible. But they're all I need to see to know how you're doing."

"How am I doing now?" I ask him, my eyes full of tears.

KINDERGARTEN

As the men in the shelter wait for dinner, an Anglo preaches about Jesus. In the very back pew James drifts off, exhausted, till one of the preacher's friends starts playing a guitar, leading a hymn. James rouses himself to join in. The lyrics leave him unmoved, but he feels a power in the unison male voices.

Once the singing ends, the guys in the first two pews queue up to enter the cafeteria. Each man signs his name on a tablet before going in to eat. The line trickles through the door.

Just as the next two rows are called, a staffer starts yelling at a guy named Marvin, accusing him of butting into line. "I was up here the whole time!" Marvin protests, and the men around him confirm he's telling the truth, but he doesn't stand a chance. The staffer strides across the room and gets in Marvin's face. "Go sit down in the back of the room! You'll eat last, after everybody else!"

This place is like kindergarten, James observes from his pew. *Once you've been labeled a troublemaker, you can't do anything right.*

Marvin's too angry to sit. He paces back and forth behind James's pew like a hungry lion in a cage stupidly left unlocked. One brush of the big cat's body and the door will swing open.

At long last, pew #17 is called. James hurries to get in line. Marvin, still fuming, curses him. "Get the fuck out of my way!" Glaring at the staffer seated at the desk, he screams, "What gives, man? What gives?"

SECONDS

The residents in the women's shelter feasted tonight. Their leftover fried chicken, mashed potatoes and gravy, succotash and chocolate cake are still on the table, getting cold, but if you're an O-girl, you can't touch. I learned that lesson last night: residents eat dinner, O-girls eat snacks.

I hover near the food, feeling desperate. Pat, the staffer in charge tonight, finally relents under my hungry gaze. "Look," she says, "eat whatever you want. I'll get in dutch for it—somebody'll tell for sure—but I think it's a stupid rule that the overflow can't eat and everybody else can."

I dish up a plate, in heaven for her trouble.

Over by the intake desk is a new woman. She's been beaten up by her man. As Pat tends to the woman's pulpy face, one of the residents keeps interrupting, like a child jealous of her mother's affection. "I want a soda, I want a towel, I want to use the phone...." With each interruption the new woman's eyes seem a little more dead. Tears slide down her cheeks, mixing with blood, trickling into the corners of her swollen mouth.

I spoon up seconds.

When Pat finishes her first-aid, the new woman takes up a position just inside the door of the main room, leaning wearily against the jamb. Residents and O-girls brush past her, saying nothing, eyes averted. Sometimes the woman murmurs hello as they pass, then gestures weakly toward her bandaged face, mewling like a kitten.

For godsake, do something. Uncertainly, I set down my plate, my fork. *Anything.* The crowded room seems full of obstacles. *Just get up (what to do?), try—*

Suddenly Sweetness is there. She wraps an arm around the new woman's shoulders, walks her over to a sofa, shoos away a couple of residents, settles in with the woman, holds her hand, lets her cry....

Helping can be so simple, if you'll let it.

SPECIAL DELIVERY

Two black women set up ironing boards to press their jeans for work. I've never ironed a pair of jeans in my life, let alone starched a crease down the legs, but Toots and Billie could do it in their sleep. Over hot irons the two of them jive about their jobs, their men, their looks, their cooking. Other women gather around, egging them on. Toots is the crowd favorite. She taunts, brags, razzes, rhymes, mocks. Sometimes her voice is music, sometimes sass, sometimes prophecy or preaching. Sometimes it's just plain meanness.

"Ain't I free?" somebody shouts.

Toots laughs, says, "Honey, if you know you is, you *is*. Since you don't know you is, you *ain't*."

An hour or so later, the ironing done and jiving past, there's a sharp rapping at the front door. All around me women shriek and yell. They rush as one body into the back room and huddle in a tight hush of fear, their eyes fixed on a staffer as she calmly, warily, goes to answer the door. Maybe it's somebody's abusive lover, or a husband drunk with rage—

"Special delivery," the man says. "Sign here."

SNAKE EYES

"Get the fuck away from my shit, man!"

James jerks awake. Not far from his cot, some guy's yelling in the dark. Instinctively James gropes, checks his gear.

Seeing what you see when you're awake is hard enough. But like a snake you've got to sleep with your eyes open, too.

DAY 5

SUNDAY, FEBRUARY 21

INDULGENCE

8 AM mass at St. Joseph Cathedral. We've come here because we have nowhere else to go. This being Sunday morning, public buildings in the downtown are generally closed, at least till noon, and the weather's too nasty to remain outside.

We've come here too because this elegant cathedral, the seat of the Columbus diocese, is filling with people—people wishing not only to worship, but also to *be together*, acknowledging the higher, the truer, the loving, the just. Like them, James and I want to commune. We want not to be alone.

We can also indulge our senses here. There'll be gold metalwork gleaming with light, and candles glimmering in hidden drafts of air. There'll be colorful liturgical cloths and garments appropriate to the season. There'll be music— pipe organ and choir, hymns and chants soaring to the vaulted ceiling, then drifting as echoes into silence. Quite possibly, there'll be incense burning; if not that, then the mingling of perfumes and colognes. There'll be prayers as we kneel on soft cushions, and the barest taste of bread and wine.

At the Passing of the Peace, congregants stand to greet those sitting around them, blessing them, wishing them well. The older white man directly in front of me, wearing an expensive suit, casually turns around to shake hands. When he sees me, shock registers on his face. I smile and grip his hand hard.

James and I would both like to be more presentable, this first Sunday of

Lent. Back when we were kids, the dress code for church services was strict: for James, a collared shirt and dress pants; for me, my best dress and shoes. Proper attire was a way of showing respect, though to whom, God or neighbor, was never clear. It was simply a necessary part of the ritual: good clothes, like good music, made for good worship. Those memories of religion in childhood remain strong, even after all these years.

Today our clothes are dumpy, dirty, sweaty, infested with fuzz balls. Both of us, upon arriving, had peeled off a few layers, hoping for a less nappy look, but with each garment we removed, our body odor intensified. Fuzz and dirt, we decided, was better.

The priest's homily is based on Jesus's testing by Satan in the wilderness. He describes Lent as a time when we must face and overcome our temptations, especially through the practice of fasting. In his view, fasting is a temporary sacrifice of excess. For a period of forty days, we give up something we possess too much of, or do too often. What happens after the forty days are up, well, the priest doesn't say.

This interpretation of fasting, depending as it does on excess, strikes me as privileged. It tends to exclude those who have little while easing the conscience of those who have much. What if fasting, instead of being a temporary modification of lifestyle for the relatively well to do, were a deliberate change of heart undertaken by us all? What if it were less about giving up red meat or cigarettes or clothes-shopping for a few weeks, and more about giving up, bit by bit, our rigid expectations of what the future should hold, our fixed assumptions about how the world should operate, our categorical judgments of how people should act and who they should be? Considered this way, fasting isn't a privileged practice—all of us can do it. Nor is it restricted to certain season of the year, but instead is a daily challenge.

The point in fasting isn't for us to become perfect, beyond reproach, but simply to exercise faith, opening our minds and hearts as best we're able and learning from our mistakes. Over a lifetime of practice, something might rise up in place of the fear or greed or ignorance we've fasted away—something we've helped bring about but can't take credit for. Maybe our joy is fuller, our compassion wiser, our kindness quicker, our patience longer, our suffering more humble, our determination to respond to the suffering of others deeper and more enduring,

James goes forward for bread and wine, welcome as a Catholic to partake. When he returns, he opens his hand to reveal a communion wafer. Breaking it in two, he passes half to me, and together we consume the host. A sense of belonging, born from a simple gesture.

The man who had earlier passed me the peace returns from the front of the nave still chewing his wafer. Spurning his original seat, he takes another, several pews further up the aisle.

GOSPEL

James and I arrive at Central Presbyterian Church just as they're closing the breakfast line, run every Sunday morning for poor and homeless people. On today's menu: sausage gravy over biscuits, sliced peaches, cold milk, Little Debbies. Though famished, I save the sweets for later. Who knows if there'll be supper.

Nine of us stragglers remain at the tables in Fellowship Hall, trying to eat while the minister and a pianist lead us in worship. It's hard to sing hymns with your mouth full, hard to concentrate on a sermon when your mind's set on the hope of a second helping of biscuits. I wrestle my attention back to the minister, preaching now about how we poor folks will only find God in two places, the Bible and the church. "That's where God is. His *only* address. Folks like you ought to know—if you don't have the right address, you'll never find who you're looking for."

Those of us who stay through worship are rewarded afterward with sack lunches. Too bad that God, so confined within sacred pages and hallowed walls, won't be with us on the streets when we eat them.

A PLACE OF OUR OWN

In gentle flurries outside the church, we chat with Jeff and Maddy, an Anglo couple we just met over breakfast. They tell us that they've been camping in a woods, south of downtown, though they're careful not to say where, exactly. With a tent, tarps, sleeping bags and blankets, they're managing to stay warm enough, and dry. The weather is wretched, but they'd rather camp than sleep in city shelters, which don't allow unmarried couples or the use of alcohol.

Jeff pokes fun at Maddy. "She's been a bad girl. Got herself kicked out of two shelters for drinking. Can't never go back. Don't matter, though. They treat you like shit in them places."

Taken by the idea of camping, James and I ply Jeff and Maddy with questions. James, especially, can scarcely contain himself. He's excited just thinking about a place of our own. He'd do almost anything to live in a place where he could get some decent sleep at night, nobody rolling over in sleep and slapping him, nobody moaning, nobody picking a fight, nobody looking to steal his stuff—

A place where he could breathe deeply and not wish he hadn't; where he could take his clothes off and not feel the dirtier for it; where he could relax and not be assaulted by the hungry, angry, lonely, tired energies roiling in the room—

A place where at the end of the day he wouldn't have to see any more brittle and broken men, or listen to their stories, or witness how shabbily they can be treated, and how shabbily treat each other; where he could just close his eyes and not be bothered, and could be quiet if he wanted to, or talk, or cry when he needed to, instead of holding back—

A place where he could just—*be*....

He'd do almost anything.

END OF A ROLL

Downtown slows to a crawl on weekends, nearly empty of pedestrians, traffic flow light. After only a few days, weekday life on the streets has a familiar feel, a rhythm almost, and this carries a comfort, but now this weekend strangeness, and James and I are a little lost, like boats adrift.

Sweets, though, from the sidewalks: a Baby Butterfinger, a small bag of Reese's Pieces, two Certs from the end of a roll. Sharing the Certs, we improvise a TV commercial for breath fresheners—two mangy, stinky street people sucking on cool, clean peppermint. We're laughing hysterically when suddenly there's a furious flapping of wings up from the sidewalk near our feet.

A mourning dove. She settles onto an overhanging branch. Dangling from her perch in the tree is a string of gold beads. They're *Mardi Gras* beads. Mardi Gras, or "Fat Tuesday," is traditionally the last day of merrymaking and indulgence before the fasting of Lent.

The dove stares down.

PIECES

Cindy, the shelter resident whose clothes I wear, is putting together a 1,500-piece puzzle, for the second time.

She tells me she misses Texas, where she grew up. She's been living at the shelter for two months, trying to put her life back together so she can go south again. "It's okay, being here, but I don't like mingling with the others. Especially, you know, the *niggers*."

Her use of the word stuns me. I walk away.

Before settling down to sleep, I read from *Cry, the Beloved Country*, the South African novel by Alan Paton. I borrowed it the other day from a bookshelf at the Agora. Stephen Kumalo, a Zulu minister, despairs of saving his son Absalom, arrested for murdering a white man. Each page cries out with the pain of apartheid, the crimes made possible by racial prejudice, poverty and fear.

"The tragedy is not that the world is broken," Paton writes. "The tragedy is that it's not being mended."

RENT

Lying on his cot in the Bexley overflow shelter, James glances around at his fellows. *We don't pay any money to sleep here, but staying isn't free. We pay psychological rent. Every face shows it. Nobody brightens, entering this room. Might as well be a sign hanging out front:* CHECK JOY AT DOOR.

He smiles to a new friend across the room. The man smiles back.

If only, James says to himself, *nobody had to be here....*

DAY 6

MONDAY, FEBRUARY 22

PRAYERS

Now and then, especially when we're outside, James and I offer spontaneous prayers of gratitude to inanimate objects: *Thank you, Bench. Thank you, Boots. Thank you, Ground. Thank you, Sun.* Everything is so immediate, and so graciously there, blessing it seems the natural thing to do.

Some scholars of religion say that primitive worship arose from overwhelming fear. I wonder if it sprang from thanksgiving instead. But then, perhaps profound fear and deep gratitude aren't so easily separated.

BEGGARY

Brilliant sun this morning, the kind that makes you think it cares, but I'm running low on money, and sunshine won't pay tonight's bus fare back to the women's shelter.

Outside a thirty-story building along High Street, James is begging on my behalf, soliciting passersby for money as if he's done it all his life. "Sir—ma'am —can you spare some change for the bus?" Nobody responds. Most won't even look at him.

Meanwhile, I stand on a street corner near St. Joseph Cathedral, eyes homed in on a smartly dressed businessman just down the block. As he comes my way, I rehearse my line, drawing a deep breath at the last—

I let him pass. I don't say a word. The scent of his cologne lingers before a breeze snatches it away.

I'd like to be more like James, but I'm loath to panhandle from strangers on the street. My needing the money simply isn't enough. Desperate as I am, I've got to earn it. *Deserve* it. I don't want to feel this way, but I do. It's in the marrow of my grown-up-Protestant bones: money's the measure of your industriousness, and therefore also of your virtue. The more you work, the more money you have, the better person you are, the better life you lead.

This is a myth without mercy, reducing the value of your life to your ability to make and spend (or save) a buck. It's a myth I've tried not to live by, but here on this corner it's my Mr. Hyde, and I feel powerless as Jekyll.

I go to the back door of St. Joseph Cathedral and beg for an hour's work, without success. Then, on to The Place to Be, the café at Trinity Episcopal. Baseball Cap isn't around, fortunately. He's done enough, having chased me down with a $10 bill a few days back.

"Do you have some odd job I could do for pay?" I ask the balding man behind the register. "I need a dollar-ten in bus fare to get to a shelter tonight, and another dollar-ten to come back downtown tomorrow."

The man surprises me by opening the register. He counts out $2.25, then exchanges the quarter for two dimes and a nickel. He smiles. "Dimes are better for bus fare, aren't they?"

Back on High Street, James closes his eyes in the flurrying snow, centers his thoughts and briefly prays a blessing on all the pedestrians on the block. When he opens his eyes again, he notices a tall, strapping businessman sporting a blond ponytail. As the man passes, James gives his spiel.

The man burrows into his pockets. "I'll see what I have."

James hears the jingle of change. His heart lifts.

"There you go." The man lays some coins in James's hand, the exact amount needed for fare.

"Thank you, sir. *Bless* you."

James bounds across four lanes of traffic, off to find me. He's as excited as a little kid who just sold his first glass of lemonade.

My grandparents and other members of their generation have told me stories about the Great Depression, when begging was common and, as they put it, you practically had an obligation to respond. Whether that's truly how it was or just how they remember it, I don't know, but they tell me they'd give the beggar whatever they could—a dime, a meal, a drink of water, a place to sleep. "We didn't think twice about helping. It was just what you did back then, because everybody was in the same boat. But things are different now."

Exactly how things are different now seems difficult for them to say, but beggary's no longer acceptable. Perhaps there was always some degree of shame in the asking, but now there's more resentment in the being asked. Those who beg must have some weakness in character that has reduced them to the indignity. Whether the beggars are unfortunates or miscreants, most of us "upstanding folks" think we're nothing like them. A distance has opened, with blame as the wedge. Now we don't have to look the poor in the eye. We don't have to listen to their stories. We don't have to give them a dime, a meal, a drink, a place to sleep. If we're careful, we might not even have to acknowledge their existence, despite the fact they're everywhere.

Even as street beggary has fallen into disrepute, institutionalized beggary has become commonplace, and tax-deductible charitable giving has emerged as a middle-class virtue. Beggar, if you want our money, don't stand on the sidewalk and try to panhandle our pocket change. Hold a fundraiser. Solicit us through the mail. Call us during a phon-a-thon. Deduct a designated contribution from our pay....

Charity in large measure has become depersonalized, reduced more or less to a financial transaction. Certainly there are reasons, however good or bad, for the change, but I wonder: has it helped to spawn the shadow side of street beggary which today so intimidates and offends us? To the degree that we regard those who beg from us as less than ourselves, we regard them, and often treat them, as less than human. Then we're surprised when some of them respond in kind, hassling us, lying to us, and worse. The shadow form of beggary has no honor and no heart, but I suspect it has taken all of us to create it.

Begging is increasingly restricted and now illegal in some cities. By law in Columbus I can't approach a car stopped at a traffic light to ask for help. I can't panhandle near an ATM or near the entrance to certain business establishments. I can't block the path of a pedestrian in order to beg—

As if I would. I couldn't even get up the nerve to ask a businessman for a quarter.

TRIFLES

Any color, in whatever form, to relieve sidewalk gray: Plastic red poinsettias. Yellow school buses. A building by the river, painted olive green. A purple mail box. A sapphire blue convertible. Tonight's copper sunset, dancing on skyscraper glass and metal....

Small courtesies: A stranger taking the time to search his pockets for loose change instead of rushing past you, pretending not to hear your pleas. A man giving you dimes instead of quarters for bus fare. A motorist waving you across a pedestrian crosswalk instead of making you wait. A woman bumping into you, then saying "I'm sorry" instead of "Get out of my way."

Nothing's inconsequential.

SLAVES

Mid-morning, waiting in line for JOIN to open, James and I hear a middle-aged black man describe Columbus as a "come-up city."

"You can get a leg up here, if you hang tough," he says to the queue. "The jobs don't pay much and the bosses treat you like slaves, but you can make it here. Maybe."

GRUBB

Aptly located on a street named Grubb, operating out of what was once a Catholic parochial school, is Holy Family Soup Kitchen. "The best soup kitchen in the city," in the opinion of our new friends Jeff and Maddy.

On a cinderblock wall flanking the soup kitchen's parking lot is the fading artwork of children long since grown: painted trees, stick-figures, hand prints, and in the middle of it all, a single question, brushed on in red, surrounded by empty gray space—

Why?

Inside the building, James and I become #116 and #117, according to our index cards, and are instructed by a hallway monitor to join the food line when our numbers are called.

After entering the basement cafeteria, we sink onto folding chairs. The place is a mayhem of clattering trays and cups, shouts and table talk, scraping chairs, laughter, mad rushes up to the food line, banging pots and pans. It's swarming with people of every age, from stooped white-beards and wizened women to skittish preschoolers. Some of the adults are dressed as impeccably as executives, others are casual; most look rough, like we do. Eyes: glazed, sharp, bleary, crazed, darting, twinkling, soft.

Stacked to our left are boxes of grapefruit, apparently free for the taking. Straight ahead are four rows of tables, set end to end the entire length of the room. The main serving line runs across the very front, beneath da Vinci's painting of *The Last Supper*. Beverages, bread and desserts are being distributed at tables here in the back.

Waiting for our numbers to come up, I read an article about the soup kitchen in a stray copy of the *Franklinton News*, the thin newspaper of the

Question on the schoolyard wall outside Holy Family Soup Kitchen

Bottoms. Established nearly twenty years ago by the Holy Family Parish and its revered monsignor, Francis Schweitzer (his portrait hangs on the wall), the place now serves 300-500 people a day, Monday through Friday, with only one paid staffer. The rest of the labor is supplied by volunteers. Much of its food comes from Second Servings, a program that redistributes surplus food from restaurants, hospitals and other facilities.

"111 to 120, 111 to 120!" a voice booms through a megaphone. James and I leap to queue up. Before us, a cornucopia of food: fried chicken, mashed potatoes, spaghetti, mixed vegetables, baked beans, chicken noodle soup, tossed salad…. Our mouths hang open in disbelief, and gratitude. The servers ask James, ahead of me in line, what he wants and how much. Soon every inch of his tray is covered.

My turn now, but I'm speechless. So much to choose from!

A memory rises up of Jihong's mother, visiting us from China, on her first trip to an American supermarket. In the produce section she wanders wide-eyed among enormous piles of green peppers and onions, potatoes and cabbage, fresh ginger root. She has cooked with these ingredients her entire life, but now, stunned by the sheer abundance of food, she's incapable of choosing, seems almost afraid to touch anything, till finally she reaches out and closes tentative fingers around a single head of garlic.

Today, Mama, I understand.

"Yes, please," I say, to a chicken breast. My first selection made, the rest is easy.

Once everybody in the cafeteria has been served, many people return to the food line for seconds, or to fill small containers with leftovers. James and I rummage in our pockets, come up with two small baggies. We stuff them with spaghetti for our supper.

This place being open for lunch five days a week is the best news we've had. From now on, hunger won't be so much of a problem.

WIDE ANGLE

Lying in sunshine on the frozen ground of Deaf School Park, mid-afternoon. Suddenly I sit bolt upright, look over at James. "We never had lunch today!"

He bursts out laughing.

"What's so funny?"

"You *are* joking, right?"

I stare at him blankly.

"A few hours ago we gorged down a huge meal at the soup kitchen. Don't you remember?"

Dismayed, I sink back to the ground. *How could you have forgotten?*

James examines a gift box he found this morning in a garbage can, preparing to transform it into a pinhole camera. He measures it with the rule from his tool kit, 5"x6"x3". "The perfect dimensions!" he says.

"Why's that?"

"Pinhole cameras of different sizes and shapes create different photographic effects. The coffee can's images will be curved. Pictures from this box, wide-angle."

Across the way a majestic white dog is on a romp. I can't take my eyes off him. "Here, boy!" I yell after some minutes of watching, and I'm overjoyed when he doesn't hesitate to come. *You don't care what I look like.* He lets me rub him down, whimpering and licking my face as though we've been too long apart. My body thrills at the affection. *Go ahead, touch me all over. You don't care who I am.*

His companions, a young white couple, keep their distance from me, but they don't order the dog back. "What's his name?" I call to them, laughing.

"Gord."

"Thank you, Gord," I whisper in his ear, and instantly he bounds away, a mighty lord of a dog.

ROUTINE

In a courtesy kiosk outside the Ohio Statehouse I drop change in a payphone and dial the women's shelter. Every night, around 6 PM, the same routine: make the call, ask if they're taking overflow, and hold my breath. Tonight I'm told that I'm lucky, I'll be getting the last bed. My heart leaps, then sinks.

The last bed. What about the next woman who calls?

A trooper materializes on the High Street side of the kiosk, presumably intent on chasing me off. It's happened before. With security cameras all over the capitol grounds, state troopers are quick to roust anybody who looks suspicious. I slam down the phone and flee through the Broad Street door.

SLIPPERY

I'm in a different suite in the women's shelter tonight. This one's occupied, among others, by a chic but mentally ill woman I call the Lazarus Lady. Nobody seems to know her name.

A couple nights ago, she and I had gotten off the bus together at the poorly lit shelter stop. Chicly dressed, carrying a large Lazarus shopping bag, she hurried up the dark street. My clodhopper boots couldn't keep up with the quick click of her stiletto heels.

"How's it going?" I called over her shoulder, hoping she'd slow down. We'd both be safer, walking together.

"They don't know what they're talking about."

"Excuse me?"

"Can't cross that street, you know. Like, business is bad. Everything's rumbling. I can't wait to go. And then there's tomorrow. Believe it. Maybe I can work it out, if the century goes on. The store's still open. *So slippery.* Dim those lights!"

Lazarus Lady's mad monologue had continued all the way to the shelter. Anything I said merely dropped into the breaths between her disjointed thoughts and was swallowed whole.

Now, anxious to take a shower, I strip off my many layers of clothes in the tiny bathroom. I'm down to my undies when suddenly the Lazarus Lady throws open the door. Unleashing a hysterical tirade, she gestures wildly for me to get out. Her words are totally unintelligible, but one thing is clear: This is her territory, and she wants me gone. No negotiations. Hastily I gather up my clothes. There'll be no hot shower for me tonight.

· · ·

James has spent five nights in the Bexley overflow shelter, but up till now, rank and dirty as he was, he just didn't have the energy to shower. Tonight, finally, his desire to be clean is greater than his need to rest.

The showers, cordoned off by three moldy curtains, are located in the small staff room. At the moment, nobody's in line. He grabs a thin towel from a pile, slings it over the shower rod, then peels off his umpteen layers of clothes.

The concrete beneath his bare feet is slippery with suds and slime. He stoops his tall frame under one of the two shower heads, turns on the tap, and picks up a sorry cake of soap.

TIGHT

A guy's griping about having to sleep only inches from the men on either side of him. He wants to move his cot. A staffer tells him, sternly, to leave it where it is. "Look," the staffer says, "our numbers are high due to the weather. We need to accommodate as many guys as possible. Space is going to be tight."

Both men have a point, and neither is about to back down. They square off with strong language. Tension mounts till finally another staffer, a brawny black man with a calm voice and presence, steps in and manages to resolve the dispute.

James appreciates this staffer's manner. He treats the men like human beings. Just this morning, when the lights had blinked on at 5:30, the staffer wandered the room, gently nudging him and the other lazies who had automatically rolled over in bed and covered their heads. "Hey guys, come on now, you got to get up," he'd coaxed, rather than hollering obscenities and kicking the men's cots like other staffers did.

Many members of the staff act like roosters strutting and crowing in a barnyard. They're always telling the men exactly what to do and how to do it "or else." One guy scolds incessantly. Earlier this evening, when a toilet had gotten clogged, he construed it as a sign of disrespect. He gave a stern lecture on toilet etiquette. Once he cleaned up the mess, he marched all the men into the bathroom. "I want you to see what a fine job I done."

The lights go out. Exhausted men toss and turn on their flimsy cots, settling in, trying to get comfortable. The room begins to fill with an odd music of coughs, wheezes, belches and moans. Snores too, finally, though nobody sleeps soundly for long.

The men are constantly rousted. Night shift workers need to be woken at various hours. Time after time, staffers flip on all the fluorescent lights, bellowing for this man or that to "haul his ass out of bed." Every time the entire room stirs with a tired growl. James, coming to, can never remember at first where he is. When suddenly he does, there's a rush of fear (*maybe some-*

*body's stolen your boots, maybe somebody's searched your duffel, found your supplies,
is wondering who the devil you are...).* Gradually the panic subsides, till he's calm
enough to feel the itch from the wool blanket, to smell again the hundreds of
men who've used it since it was last washed. He starts willing himself back to
sleep. He's only inches away when the lights flicker on again and somebody
shouts, "So and so, move your sorry ass—"

DAY 7

TUESDAY, FEBRUARY 23

HUMAN ENOUGH

Horn blast—James and I yank each other back to the curb—

Crossing the streets of downtown has become hazardous. Strangely unaware of traffic, both of us regularly step into the path of oncoming cars and trucks. We're not real enough to be struck down: this isn't what we think but how we act. The body comports itself according to what it senses, and after only a week on the streets, our bodies have gotten the message, loud and clear: we're not here enough, not substantial enough, not human enough, to matter.

Blessings on that driver for laying on his horn.

SQUATTING

Inspired by Jeff and Maddy, we've decided to establish a camp, possibly in the woods along the Scioto River. Staying in the city shelters, James is getting precious little sleep, and I'm struggling every day to conjure up bus fare. Then, of course, there's our old ambivalence about taking up the beds. Though camping will pose its own difficulties, we believe it's the better long-term option. Quieter, cheaper and in some ways safer than the city shelters, it'll also provide the solace of something our own. We hope to be camping by Saturday night.

This afternoon, having hiked south out of the downtown, we've been scouting the east bank of the Scioto for signs of human habitation. We'd prefer to pitch camp near some neighbors, possibly even Jeff and Maddy. But hours have trudged by, not a soul in sight.

Bone-tired and hungry, we're about to end the day's search when suddenly we spot a tent in the trees; then, an old refrigerator tipped on its side, with a pair of shoes neatly signaling its occupation; next, a couple of shanties, and a truck camper without the truck. So many camps, all apparently deserted for the moment.

Full of energy now, we explore the area for a suitable campsite of our own. Soon we find one in a strip of dead and immature trees between some railroad tracks and a water treatment plant. The site is well above the river, flat and somewhat concealed. We choose the precise spot to build a shelter, then clear away stones, sticks, bricks, bottles and broken glass, leaving duff to cushion the ground.

It's a start.

Done for the day, we set off again for the downtown, following the railroad tracks. As a southbound train approaches, we wave our arms gleefully at the engineer. He responds with an earsplitting blast on his horn. It feels like a friendly acknowledgment, welcoming us to the neighborhood.

My face breaks into a grin. "*He* doesn't care!" I holler at James, in a punch-happy burst over the screech and rumble of the railroad cars.

He whoops, gives me a spirited high-five.

Nobody will roust us out here.

PROSPECTS

Aching for rest, ornery burrs stuck to our clothes, we slog along the potholed city streets. Whiffs of country-fried chicken, greasy kung pao and fresh donuts coax growls from our empty bellies. A hard hour after leaving our campsite, we finally collapse on a bench outside Main Library and jerk off our boots. They sit, steaming, on the sidewalk. Our feet sweat perfect footprints onto the pavement through three thick pair of socks. If we can, we'll have to replace our heavy boots; otherwise our feet will take a beating, hiking the roughly two miles between camp and the downtown twice each day.

We're inspired to have prospects. To have an idea that holds promise. To have something tangible to work on, to make with our hands, even from junk and rubbish. My notes are fragments. James's cameras are trash. Now our home will be fashioned from household refuse and workplace scraps.

We have no idea what kind of shelter we'll build, but this morning, before our hike to the riverbank, we'd stashed our first supplies: a large plastic banner, plus a length of purple burlap, bigger than a blanket, scavenged from a museum dumpster. This is the opposite of what people usually do when constructing their home: first they brainstorm a design, then they create a blueprint, then they order the materials. Out here, the materials have to come first. Once we find them, they'll tell us what to do. We trust the process. It's a lesson we've learned from dumpster diving: you don't know what you need till you find it; once you find it, you know precisely how to use it.

Whatever form it takes, this new home of ours won't mean an easy life, if only because of the frigid weather. All this week the nighttime temperatures have been in the low twenties, even the middle teens, before the chill factor. At least the city shelters were heated; no such luxury in camp. I try not to dwell on this. Somehow we'll manage. Somehow we'll build a shelter that can keep us warm and dry, that can withstand wind, sleet, snow, rain. Once we've moved in, it'll probably take a blizzard to make us leave.

MIRACLE

Fed up with his uncomfortable boots, James stops in the Salvation Army thrift store. When he tries on a pair of used white sneakers, he moans a little in relief. "Like heaven," he says to me.

They're priced at a whopping $6. He offers the clerk 75¢, all the money he has. By some miracle, her manager approves the deal.

CHANCES OF WINNING

In the crowded TV room at the women's shelter, the women talk over the top of a romance turned up loud: The pros and cons of letting a man give you money. The dangers of letting him dominate you. How to get your kids back in court. Today's lottery numbers and the chances of winning. Classic TV shows. Sickness and body ailments. Sex. Weed. Folks you'd love to see again. The shelter staff. Caseworkers. Bosses. Horoscopes....

In the Bexley men's shelter a pudgy black guy is talking smack to Winfield, a tall, dignified black man, fortyish, powerfully built, mentally ill. Something the pudgy guy says prompts Winfield to cock his sturdy cane, as if to strike him.

"Yeah, come on, old man!" The troublemaker raises his fists, punching air. "*I'll* take you!"

James, no more than ten feet away, watches anxiously from his cot. The tip of Winfield's cane waggles like a baseball bat in the hands of a dangerous hitter.

A staffer rushes over to stop the fight before it escalates. After hot dispute, the cane is confiscated. Peace is made. Tentative, uneasy peace.

DAY 8

WEDNESDAY, FEBRUARY 24

THE WAY

So many men stayed at the overflow shelter last night, there aren't enough bus passes this morning to go around. James misses out. He's facing a two-mile hike into the center city on an ailing foot.

Wet snow falls. Every step splashes slush.

His new Salvation Army sneakers are torture. The way they feel, their last owner must have been extremely flat-footed. They cramp his arches, dig into his ankles, lock up his knees. He tries walking bull-legged. It doesn't help. He cuts slits in the leather with his knife, hoping for a little give. That doesn't help either, and now the shoes leak. He can't switch back to his old boots. They're miles away, wrapped in plastic, stashed under a bush near St. Joseph Cathedral, too heavy to lug around. All he can do is accept the inevitable: today his feet will be cold, soggy and sore.

A vanity plate on a hotrod parked on the street: UR WHAT UR.

He stops at a small park to rest in a gazebo. A large metallic sculpture on the grounds catches his attention. It's somehow familiar. Eventually he realizes that its creator was one of his old art professors. The strength and grace of its abstract lines touch him deeply. While this morning he feels neither strong nor gracious, just to be reminded of his prof—the man's lighthearted encouragement, and the way he would accept almost anything from his students except lack of effort—is an inspiration.

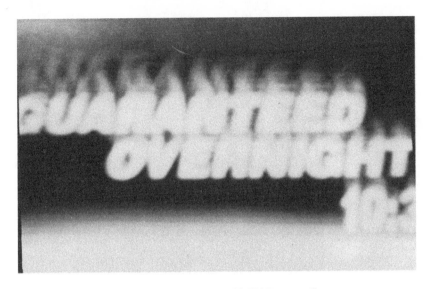

"GUARANTEED OVERNIGHT": UPS Express mailbox

RED

At Grant Hospital James consults with a nurse about his right heel, festering and ugly from all the walking.

"Do you have any money?" she asks.

"No, ma'am."

"Here, take this." She hands him a dollar bill from her pocket. "Go buy yourself some hydrogen peroxide. That's what we'd treat you with here, along with lots of red tape."

On the street corner near the hospital, a UPS Express mailbox. All packages, it reads, are "GUARANTEED OVERNIGHT."

I wish I were, James says to himself. *I wish we all were.*

REVOLUTION

He needs somehow to secure a bus pass for tonight, otherwise, come sundown, he might be limping all the way back to the Bexley shelter. After noon meditation he hobbles to a men's shelter in the Bottoms to beg a pass.

A bearded, long-haired staffer who might have been a hippy in the seventies invites him to sit next to his desk. "Hey," he says, after introducing himself, "what's going on?"

James tells the staffer his situation.

"You on the streets over a girl or what?"

"Separated from my girlfriend."

"Well, let's see what we can do." The man starts asking the usual questions, filling out the usual forms.

After a minute the staffer leans back in his chair. "Where's the spark in your generation? There's wars going on all over the world, and nobody protests. I'm worried about you guys."

This staffer seems interested in more than just giving a handout. It's rare, out here, when somebody seems sincerely to care about how you're feeling, what you're thinking. James looks at him squarely and says, "Well, I'm not that worried about us. I see an inner revolution going on in my generation. Its focus is on spirituality."

"I hope so," the staffer says skeptically, "but I don't see much of it." He reaches into his wallet for a bus pass. "Here you go. Take care of yourself. If you ever need a shower or a meal, you can come here."

DISTANCE

"Excuse me, do you work here?"

I'm standing on the third floor of Main Library, where James and I have come to get out of a driving snow. I'm smelly, dirty, clomping around in clumsy boots and too many layers of bulky clothes, the top half of my coveralls actually hanging down loose around my waist—is this woman *seeing* me? Can she truly believe I work for one of the top-ranked public libraries in the entire country?

"No, ma'am," I say, "I don't work here, but I'd be glad to help you—"

Suddenly her eyes widen, and she backs away, as if afraid I might hurt her. "No—no—that's okay," she stammers, and hurries off.

Meanwhile, a white boy, maybe ten years old, just walked past James at our library table. James smiled and tried to make eye contact, but the boy lifted his chin and snubbed him. Earlier, he'd noticed the same boy observing him curiously from the stacks.

He understands the youngster's ambivalence. As a boy growing up in Manhattan, he, too, had learned to studiously ignore "the bums" who fascinated him. One homeless guy had routinely perched outside a church on uptown Madison Avenue. Instead of asking passersby for spare change, he'd say, "Can anybody spare a couple hundred dollars?" His humor (or gall) amused people, and enticed some to give who normally wouldn't. As a friend of James liked to say, "If you can get them to laugh, you can get them to cry."

As a boy James had seen this same beggar several times. The man aroused his interest, even got him to drop some change once. But James had mostly exercised his curiosity about homeless people from a distance. Perhaps like the boy who had just snubbed him, he'd been too scared of their unpredictability to let them know he cared.

LONG DISTANCE

James dials Phoebe's number in Connecticut, then leans back against the wall and slides wearily down to the thinly carpeted floor. Other library patrons are in and out of the modest courtesy room, making phone calls, photocopies, change for dollar bills.

Finally, on the line, a far-away "Hello?" At her voice, he sighs, full-body.

As he and Phoebe take turns telling the goings-on of their lives, he wishes for privacy. He wishes for right words. Everything he says is flat, cool, thin, though just beneath that surface ice is a river, currents so powerful they'd sweep him away in an instant if he ever broke through.

At the end, "I love you." What he means to say is "Help me," but she, so distant, has no way to hear.

LONGHOUSE

Pitching camp on the riverbank, after the morning's snow. In a weed patch adjacent to the woods, we discover a half dozen rusty lengths of steel reinforcement mesh, the kind used when pouring a concrete floor to increase its strength. Three of the sections are bent into crude crescents. Instantly we know what to do.

We drag the mesh to our campsite and arrange the crescents side by side. Lashing them together with wire and pieces of extension cord, we rig the framework of a miniature longhouse. We anchor it to the ground with rocks and bricks, then step back to examine our work.

The structure is maybe 5'x9'—a little cramped, but the smaller, the warmer. It's wide enough that when we're sacked out side by side, each of us will be able to roll over once. It's long enough to accommodate James's length plus supply some storage space. The ceiling's quite low, sloping from four feet at the front door to three or less at the back. The entrance will face south, away from fierce north and westerly winds.

We're actually ahead of schedule. Another good day's work, and we should be able to move in. The energy we have for our homemaking is remarkable.

SOLACE

Settling onto his cot in the Bexley overflow shelter (last row, in the corner), James leans against the wall. Peeling paint flakes off onto his clothes. He doesn't bother to brush it off. The shelter seems mellower tonight—or maybe

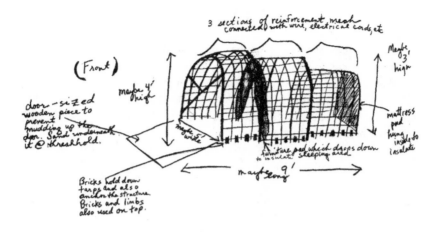

Rough sketch of the shelter built on the riverbank

the change is in him, now that he knows he'll soon be giving up his cot for a campsite.

John, the white guy on the next cot, volunteers to get him a job on his paint crew.

"Maybe," James says. "Thanks for the offer. I've got some things to work out first."

The man nods.

"Hey John, if you don't mind my asking, why are you here?"

"My girlfriend was too clingy. Needed some space, you know. I let her have the old apartment. I'm just here till I can scrape some money together for my own place."

He seems the reflective sort. James asks if he has a faith of any kind.

"Was raised Pentecostal, down in Tennessee, but I don't go to church very often anymore."

"You doing anything for Lent?"

He laughs. "Well, I gave up my dog and my house. That's enough. I don't feel compelled spiritually to give up anything else. I mean, *look* at us." He gazes thoughtfully around the room. "We've all got our cross to bear."

So many men. Aging Vietnam vets. Panhandlers who work the same spots every day on the streets. Men who day and night hide their eyes behind shades. Loners who stare at the ceiling. Pacers, wearing out the floor. Partiers, who every night ask James, "What did you get into today?" "Not much," he says, "how about you?" "Got blasted," they say, and sometimes brag their tales.

The same proportion of men ask him, with genuine interest, "Did you find work?"

Near James's cot stands a young Anglo, head shaved smooth as a melon. He's swilling coffee, going for a buzz, showboating all the way. Time and again, he refills his two styrofoam cups from the brewer in the staff room, chugs the coffee down with firecracker eyes, then goes back for more. "Aaah, this stuff is hot," he exclaims now, shaking out his tongue to attract attention. The other men ignore him.

All at once, the guy sets his coffee down. Removing a wad of paper from his pocket, he unravels it and says to James under his breath, "Pssst! Take a look—"

A single white pill. "Morphine," the guy says, and pops it down with his ninth cup of java in fifteen minutes.

James has had enough. The shelter hasn't changed much after all. The air is still crazy. Desperate for quiet, he sneaks out of the crowded sleeping room through a fire door, into a restroom that's off-limits. Sometimes, for sanity's sake, he ignores the rules and retreats here. He hand-washes his filthy socks at the sink. He always feels a peace in doing this; the only real solace he's ever felt in this place.

How ironic, he thinks. *I used to believe that "solace" was implicit in the meaning of the word "shelter." Not anymore.*

WEST BANK

"Are you college-educated?" a resident at the women's shelter asks me. Her name is Linda.

"Yeah. Why?"

"The way you talk. The way you carry yourself."

"Yeah," says Faye, the woman sitting beside her. "Almost like, what are you doing here?"

I smile faintly. "We all have our reasons."

"I went to college, too," Linda says. "Got a great job, but I messed up. Too much booze. I'm on my way back, though. I'm working the Steps, getting back on my feet."

Linda and Faye tell me briefly of their struggles. Lost jobs, lost kids, lost loves, lost dreams, lost, lost, lost. They don't indulge in self-pity, though; self-blame either. "We made our share of mistakes," they say, "but the tide is changing now."

"You know," Linda says after a silence, "there's not enough housing for homeless women."

"Why's that, do you think?" I ask.

"Not enough funding. The people with money—they don't want to believe women get beat up. They don't want to believe we can be alcoholics and junkies, or that we're lazy, some of us. They don't want to believe *any* of it, so they just make like we're not here."

The conversation sags. I smile a little, tell the women I wish them well. "This is probably the last time I'll be seeing you."

"How come?"

"My friend James and I, we're going to camp."

"God, girl, you're going to *freeze!* Where you going to camp?"

"By the river."

"The *river!* You be careful—there's some rough people over there. Bad scene."

"Yeah, I'd take me an *uzi,*" Linda says.

The women are right: the riverbanks do have a reputation. The west bank, in particular. To ease their minds, I tell them that it's quieter on the east, where we're pitching camp.

Cindy, who's been listening without comment from a nearby chair, abruptly leaves the room. She returns with some of my clothes that she has laundered and neatly folded, plus two more pair of heavy socks. "You'll be needing these."

Deep in the night—hot argument downstairs—many voices—
A plumbing break—the main floor floods—
Little sleep for anybody—
Soon you'll be out of here—
You're lucky to have the choice—

PART 3: ON THE RIVERBANK

DAY 9

THURSDAY, FEBRUARY 25

IRIS

While debriefing here in McDonald's on Broad Street, these early mornings after our shelter nights, James and I have become acquainted with a worker named Iris. She seems to have started her job wiping tables and restocking condiments about the same time we hit the streets. Developmentally impaired, her vision poor, she has eyes for more than appearances, and a heart that knows no impediment. Whenever she spots James or me, she breaks into a huge smile and hurries over to give us a hug. We've come to expect her pep talks. "Don't worry, things'll turn around! Have you found a job yet? You want to apply here? I'm sure they'd hire you! Have you thought about going back to school? Isn't it a beautiful day?"

Now I ask Iris if she might be able to spare any trash-bags. "We could really use them to move supplies to our new camp."

"How many do you need, honey?"

"As many as won't get you into trouble."

She returns with a fistful, and kisses.

STOOP

Needing more bedding for camp, James begs a staffer at the front desk of a men's shelter for a blanket. Old, stinky, thin, holey—any blanket will do. The staffer refers him to the shelter director, just descending the stairs from the second floor.

"Can you spare a blanket?" James asks.

"Why don't you stay here instead of on the streets?" the director says.

"I'd rather be out."

"Well, I won't give you a blanket. I'm not going to support you being out."

"*Please,* it's so cold out there—"

"No! You're not getting a blanket from me!" The director exits the building.

James pleads his case to several other staffers, without success. Finally, a security guard across the room winks at him. "Hey man," the young Latino says in a low voice, I'll get you a blanket." He escorts James to the door. "Go around back in two minutes. I'll leave a blanket on the stoop."

Sometimes the folks who show us the most generosity seem to have few resources and little status of their own—folks like this security guard; Iris at McDonald's; David, the man of God who emptied his wallet....

GAME

I'm on Broad Street, staring absently at the sidewalk, waiting for a traffic light to change, when an insistent tap-tap-tapping interrupts: the metal tip of an umbrella on cement. I glance up at the umbrella's owner, amused at the show of energy, or impatience. I recognize the man's face from the news. He's William Kirwan, president of The Ohio State University (one of my alma maters). He's a long way from campus.

I lean in, almost touch his shoulder. "What about that game last night?"

Kirwan, startled, looks down at me. The expression on his face is priceless —an initial boyish enthusiasm almost instantly overtaken by total bewilderment. For a swallow, he's speechless, perhaps stunned by the mere sight (or smell) of me, or by my having presumed to speak to him, or by the thought that a street person could possibly know that last night his beloved Buckeyes had upset the Wisconsin Badgers.

He's quick to collect himself. His eyes find their focus, and he breaks a wide grin that seems thoroughly ingenuous. Together we swap a few hoop dreams till the light changes and he disappears in a crush of pedestrians, umbrella tapping mid-stride.

MOVING DAY

Shoulders ache. Legs burn. Every step's an effort. James and I are loaded down with almost more bags and bundles than we can carry, some of them even lashed to our bodies.

This morning, after successfully begging two brand-new polyester blankets at JOIN, we'd gone our separate ways to scavenge provisions for camp.

James hit pay dirt: huge amounts of discarded packaging plastic and piles of insulation, four inches thick, perfect for weatherproofing the shelter. Carrying it all now in early afternoon, we count our blessings, but camp seems a county away.

SOMETHING LIKE HOME

Around 3 PM we finally reach the woods. We wilt, dropping our bundles with groans.

No time to rest, though. Our shelter must be habitable by nightfall. Only a few hours of daylight remain. We work quickly to cover the shelter frame with plastic, then with insulation and finally with tarps, securely tying each layer to the reinforcement mesh.

In late afternoon, I reluctantly take leave of James to rendezvous with a homeless woman I've promised to drive to Illinois.

James continues our homebuilding, concentrating now on the shelter's interior. He creates a floor by layering plastic and thick cardboard over the frozen ground. Then he fashions a nest from the few blankets and extra winter coats we've managed to gather. Lying on his back atop this bed, he carefully inspects the ceiling and walls, reaching his fingers through the reinforcement mesh to probe the plastic lining. If he's lucky, there won't be many leaks.

Just before dark he covers the open ends of the shelter with a meager hodgepodge of packaging plastic and trash-bags. It's the best he can do for now. He's out of supplies, and out of time. Tomorrow he'll make improvements.

He breathes a prayer of thanks to Jeff and Maddy for inspiring us to camp. This time yesterday he was on the bus to Bexley, dreading another tough night. What a relief, now, to be here.

Our shelter isn't exactly tidy, its skin of plastic and tarps held together by wire, electrical tape, bricks, rocks, and dead tree limbs. It isn't well-proportioned either, fat with insulation in some places, thin where we ran out. Still, it looks sturdy enough, and somewhat snug. Soon, maybe, it'll feel something like home.

He walks to the edge of the woods and surveys our new neighborhood. Bridges to the north and south. To the east, a high bluff, on top of which looms the last row of houses this side of the river. From the rear, illuminated by security lights, the old two- and three-story houses appear rundown. Dogs are barking in the backyards. Maybe they've spotted him.

At the bottom of the steep bluff are maybe a half dozen sets of railroad tracks, then the weedy field sloping gently to his feet. Not far beyond camp, there's the water treatment plant, and finally the river, with the Bottoms picking up on the opposite bank.

What do you think goes on around here, he asks himself, *after the sun's gone down?*

COMMUNITY

In early evening James meets two middle-aged Anglos by the railroad tracks. They're headed "up top" to a convenience store for beer. Residents of the riverbank, they tell him they know we've pitched camp.

The more slightly built of the two men sizes James up. "I don't want to know your story, and I don't want you to know mine."

James holds up his hands as if looking down the barrel of a gun. "Hey man, no problem."

The stouter guy is circling like a caged cat, blowing into his hands for warmth. "I'm Rooster," he says, in a not unfriendly tone. "This here's Jake."

James introduces himself. The three men shake hands all around.

"Who's your woman?" Jake says.

"Her name's Phyllis." James is amazed at how much the men already know. His mind flashes to me, tooling up the highway to Illinois. Were he in my place, gone from the streets, he doubts he'd have the strength to come back.

"Hey," he says to the guys, "we going to be alright down here? The cops going to bother us?"

"Naw," Jake says, suddenly all smiles, "don't worry about the cops. But we got to look after each other. We're all in this together. We got a little community here. There's Benny, who sleeps under the bridge—he's a security guard, works nights—and there's old man Calvin, next to you. Then there's me and my buddy Sarge. There's Rooster here, and Enid, his old lady—hell, there's people all up and down this river."

The men light up smokes and offer one to James as they watch a slow train coming down the tracks. Only three cars. As it rolls to a stop, Rooster says, "If you need anything, these railroad guys'll help you." He and Jake step up closer to the train. A crewman reaches down and hands each of them a courtesy kit, standard issue to railroad workers: toilet paper, bottled water, first aid supplies, earplugs. Both guys give their kits to James, along with a half dozen signal flares—"Good," they say, "for starting campfires."

"Hey," Jake says, "we might get a visit from Harold and Ada later. They bring food and stuff down here to help us out—"

"Ah, fuck them," Rooster says. "They should keep to themselves—"

"Excuse me, Rooster, but I'm *tryin'* to talk to our new neighbor here." Rooster scowls. Jake grins. "Anyway, James, as I was saying, Harold and Ada can help you out. And you can let *me* know, too, if you need anything. Alright?"

"Yeah, thanks, guys." James starts to walk away. "Have a good night."

"Hey man, you need another tarp for your camp?" Rooster calls after him. "Yeah."

"Well, there's an old green one under the bridge, *there*. It's all yours. Yeah, and there's a carpet factory up on the corner, *there*. You might want to look in their dumpster, see if you can get some remnants to lay over the ground. That ground gets *cold*."

SHELTERED

Outside our makeshift shelter James brushes his teeth, then yanks off his boots and crawls in. Lighting our only candle, a gift from the streets, he wedges it into the hole of an empty soda can, then sets the can in a boot to keep it steady. *Can't be too careful,* he warns himself. *This place is a firetrap.*

He pulls out some scratch paper, starts jotting down notes about the day. Now and then he raises his eyes to scan the ceiling and walls, still praying they're watertight. The plastic sparkles with candlelight.

He's uneasy. Despite himself, his thoughts keep returning to our first night on the streets, bedded down under the bushes outside the ODB. *Will tonight be any less an initiation?*

The shelter sits on a slight slope, he notices now. He struggles to get comfortable, adjusting the layers of cardboard and plastic beneath him on the floor, but nothing helps. Finally he blows out the candle, buries himself under the blankets, pulls them over his head. In the darkness he imagines Phoebe's hand playing with a strand of his hair, nestling in the small of his back....

Totally spent, he free-falls into sleep.

BIG MAMA

"James! Hey, James! Harold and Ada's here. Want to meet them?"

Jake's voice, just outside the shelter. James rouses himself and groggily pulls on his boots, still half in a dream.

Headlights dissect the night woods. He follows Jake up to the field, where stand a dozen or so people, mostly teenagers—Carl, Jane, Brian, Tim, Brenda, Louis ... nobody named Harold or Ada.

"Now," Jake says to the group, in a parental tone, "I should have checked with James before I called him out. He might have wanted some privacy. It's not proper etiquette to impose—"

"It's quite alright, Jake," James reassures him, but Jake's wearing a big grin, watching all these people so eager to help the new guy on the block. The group presents James with candles, a flashlight, a blanket and a meal in a styrofoam box. Overwhelmed, he's speechless.

The kids ask him if he needs anything else. "I could really use a sleeping bag," he says, dreaming big, and immediately an adult chaperone retrieves one from a truck. He can't believe the kindness. His first night on the riverbank feels like a poor man's Christmas.

The kids direct his attention to a black Blazer parked nearby. They urge him to go say hello to Ada Martin, the woman they affectionately call Big Mama. She organized this volunteer effort, they tell him, along with her husband Harold, who was unable to come tonight.

Ada rolls down her window as James walks up. Chronically ill, she can't be out in the cold. She's big-boned, black, with a pretty, round face and gorgeous eyes. She asks him for a hug. He leans in as far as he can, and she gives him a tight squeeze. "We love you, baby. We'll see you again soon."

DAY 10

FRIDAY, FEBRUARY 26

NEXT DOOR

Just after dawn James meets our closest neighbor for the first time. He lives almost directly beneath our shelter—a roly-poly groundhog. He always looks both ways before making a move. Rarely does he stare straight ahead.

CARPETBAGGER

Behind a carpet factory James tugs and wrestles large remnants out of the trash bin, enough to thickly cover our shelter's cardboard-plastic floor. He's stuffing them into two long, durable plastic bags when a cream-colored Acura pulls up. A white man steps out, glaring.

"Can I have these scraps?" James asks.

The man considers for a moment. "Yeah, okay, but if my boss comes out, I said nothing of the kind."

James hurries.

Behind the dumpster is a steep sixty-foot slope dotted with briar bushes and strewn with trash. He flips his two clumsy bags end over end down the hill, dislodging them from sticky briars with swift kicks, dodging broken-legged chairs, upended shopping carts and soggy mattresses.

At the bottom of the hill, he heaves the first bag over his shoulder like a wounded comrade-in-arms and lumbers off toward camp, maybe a half mile away. By the time he drops it in front of our shelter, his shoulders and back are stiff and sore, but he's excited, and returns at once for the second bag.

VISITATION

The slamming of car doors. The chatter and static of walkie-talkies.

Resting in the shelter after his carpetbagging, James peers out the door, heart racing. Two squad cars are up in the field. His gut turns.

Please don't roust me out, he thinks—*please—*

He watches as the cops head into the woods further downriver. A tense twenty minutes or so pass before they reappear. They're soon on their way again. *Who or what brought them down?*

BUMS

After meditating at noon near the Statue of Peace, James walks into the capitol to use the restroom. Noticing a neat stack of toilet paper rolls, he grabs one for camp. Somehow it seems fitting, not at all stealing, to let the State of Ohio care for our bums.

BED-IN-A-SACK

In a dumpster on the Franklin University campus, giant bags of shredded paper. James grabs two of them and sets out on the long hike back to camp, knowing just what to do. This morning he'd scavenged two garment bags from the boxes at JOIN. Once he stuffs them with shredded paper, they'll serve as mattresses.

On Front Street he walks past an Ivy Leaguer putting a squash racket into the trunk of a forest-green Infinity buffed to a high shine. A few hours ago, he'd encountered this same man just as he was climbing out from behind the wheel, his teeth clenched on a fat cigar, a Harvard v-neck sweater under his suit-coat. The man had thrown him a sneer before turning up the sidewalk toward a law office.

James chuckles. The man has changed into a jock's clothes. Pale, hairy legs show under his tan trench coat: the very image of a mad flasher. The eyes of the two men meet. No sneer this time. The ivy leaguer seems embarrassed to have been seen in public wearing duds other than suit and tie.

CORPSE

James meets up with Jake and Rooster along the railroad tracks. Rooster tells him how the cops had crashed his camp this morning after receiving a report of somebody carrying a dead body into the woods. "Them cops, they come right into my tent, pulled me out of bed! Grilled me good!"

Good god, James says to himself, *did somebody spot me lugging one of those bags of carpet and think it was a corpse?*

DAY 11

SATURDAY, FEBRUARY 27

URGES

With the subtlety of a drill sergeant, James's bowels roust him out of bed before dawn. Every inch of his body is sore and reluctant to move, but he's got to hurry. The nearest bathroom, at White Castle, is a brisk ten-minute walk from camp: south along the railroad tracks; then, at the bridge, up a steep embankment to street level, where traffic's already picking up. Early birds are on their way to work, night owls are on their way home. Headlights blitz his swollen morning eyes.

PLEASE SEAT YOURSELF

In the dumpster behind Einstein Bros. Bagels, James thrills to discover a clear garbage bag, tightly tied, full of bagels still soft to the touch. He chooses two garlic and onion bagels for himself and pockets two wheat bagels for me, hoping I'll be back today from Illinois.

After strolling around to the front door of the deli, he walks right in. Customers ogle as he casually seats himself at a small table. The shop is warm, yeasty.

Thumbing through a *Columbus Dispatch*, he chews his bagels, savoring the crusty flavors. He totally belongs.

IN THE PRESENCE OF GRACE

At McDonald's on Broad Street, James waves at me from behind the rain-beaded window. Serendipitous reunion. He's grinning but looks a fright. When I join him inside, he tells me his nights in camp have been tough—thankfully dry, but terribly cold, and deafening with trains.

"Looks like you haven't slept much yourself," he says then.

I sigh.

"Tell me everything," he says. "Start with Grace. Who was she, exactly?"

I smile a little. *Yes, who were you, Grace, exactly?* "She was an O-girl at the shelter," I say wearily, "but I didn't really know her." An understatement.

You and I had never spoken at the shelter, Grace—you seemed wary of everybody, and proud—but twice we'd met. One night, overhearing a staffer deny your request for a toothbrush, I'd given you a brand-new Oral-B, still in the box, found just that day on the sidewalk. Another night you arrived at the shelter after all the bedding had been taken, and I gave you my tattered orange afghan. You never said a word during these exchanges, never made eye contact. Your back was ramrod straight, your bearing dignified, your eyes cast down. Sensing your humiliation, I'd wondered who you were.

Early Thursday morning, as I was leaving the women's shelter for the last time, I'd seen you again. I was cutting through an empty lot to the bus stop, and there you were, an attractive young black woman in a tailored red coat, clutched against the cold behind a donut shop. Though I didn't know your name and would presumably never see you again, moving as I was to the riverbank, something compelled me to shout into the icy wind and wish you a good day. You didn't respond. Maybe you hadn't heard.

"Later that same morning," I tell James, "I bumped into her at JOIN. I didn't recognize her at first. Not till I noticed her red coat, and the way she avoided my gaze, even as she greeted me and drew me aside."

"May I speak with you?" you said, very politely.

Precise diction, and an accent. African, I thought.

"You are the one who gave me the toothbrush?" you asked, finally meeting my eyes.

I nodded.

"You have a driver's license?"

"Yes."

"You are a good driver?"

"Yes."

"You have insurance?"

At this I hesitated (which world was I living in?), then told you I wasn't sure.

Your name, you said, was Grace.

"She wanted to move to Rockford, Illinois," I explain to James, "northwest of Chicago. She wanted to make a fresh start." My voice is thin and raspy from exhaustion. I swallow hard, summoning more energy for words. "Problem was, her belongings, which were in storage, needed to be trucked out, and she didn't know how to drive. She asked me if I'd do it."

"Just like that?" James's eyebrows shoot up.

Your boldness startled me. "There's nobody else to take you? A friend? A relative?"

"No. I have asked everyone I know. Please." You obviously felt disgraced by the begging. "I am desperate."

I believed you. "When are you wanting to leave?"

"Late this afternoon—maybe five o'clock."

"That soon...." I thought of James and our shelter on the riverbank, not yet complete. So much to do, so little time, the cold dark only hours away. "Do you already have a truck?"

"Yes, I have rented a truck."

"Standard or automatic?"

"When she said it was an automatic," I say to James, "that pretty much cinched it. I couldn't have driven a stick. I asked her how I'd get back to Columbus, and she promised to buy me a bus ticket."

"Risky."

I shift uncomfortably in my seat. It offers no give. "Yeah, well ... anyway, after I left you at camp, I met up with her, and she got us on a bus out to the east side of Columbus. We wound up at a U-Haul rental. She had a storage unit there full of boxes. We needed to get them loaded into a ten-foot truck. But most were too big for us to move."

You insisted that we pick up some guys off the street to do the labor. So, despite serious misgivings, I cruised the neighborhood, daylight fading fast. Beside me in the cab you prayed fervently for a few good, strong men. To no avail. After half an hour I managed to convince you that we should return to U-Haul and offer a tip to one of

the employees for his help. I knew you could afford it. At the bus stop I'd noticed the
thick roll of cash in your purse.

"It was seven o'clock before Grace and I finally drove away from U-Haul. But I have to tell you, once we got going on the highway, it felt great, having my hands on the wheel of that truck. Moving at more than pedestrian speed. Watching the lights of the city fading in my rearview mirror. I was feeling pretty good, till all at once I remembered you. It was your first night in camp, and I had no idea what you were going through. After that, there was no leaving the streets behind, no matter how many miles I drove."

You wanted me to drive the estimated 350 miles to Rockford straight through. I told you I'd try. You'd brought a few snacks. I was terribly hungry, having eaten nothing since late morning, but I carefully rationed the chips and crackers you offered. My next meal could be a long way off.

You told me a little about what you were leaving behind, what you hoped lay ahead. As I listened, the details of your story impressed me less than the ice in your voice. With each mile I grew more uneasy. My anxiety only deepened when you claimed that God had willed every action you'd ever taken in your life. You could do no wrong, you said, so long as you called upon the Lord—

For some reason your voice cut through me like a shard of glass.

My fingers tear mindlessly at one of the wheat bagels James has brought, reducing it to pieces. "A couple hours up the highway," I tell him, "Grace and I stopped for a fill-up, and our truck died, right there at the pump. Not even a click when I turned the key. I called U-Haul, and they said a certified mechanic would have to check it out. There we were, parked at a service station, and we had to wait for U-Haul to dispatch a tow truck from forty-five minutes away!"

At long last, around 10:30 PM, a jump. Back on the road, you dozed in fits. I pressed hard on the intractable gas pedal, trying to ignore the throbbing ache in my bum right knee, scarred by three surgeries. Testy ever since my fourteen-mile hike on Ash Wednesday, the knee was now swelling up stiff. Pain was shooting up through my thigh and burning into my hip. It was keeping me awake, at least.

.   .   .

A long, groaning rumble from my stomach. "Why don't you eat?" James gestures at the remains of my bagel.

"Can't seem to. Maybe in a while."

I reach for my cup of hot water, begged earlier at the counter. "Sometime after midnight," I say, picking up my story, "we pulled over again for gas. Truck stop, this time. I paced the tarmac, stretched, tried to limber up. Grace wandered off toward the restroom. When I went to get back in the truck, I discovered she'd locked the keys in the cab."

James groans.

"Somebody called the sheriff for help. He got there around one-thirty in the morning. He really had to work to get a door unlocked—almost gave up too soon—but finally he got in. Grace and I climbed right into the cab, anxious to be gone. I turned the key—and there was nothing. *Nothing!*"

"What a nightmare!" James says softly.

I negotiated with U-Haul for an hour before they agreed to allow the mechanics there at the truck stop to look under the hood. The chief mechanic had a hunch, painstakingly detailed, about what might be wrong. Daft with exhaustion, I couldn't comprehend what he was saying. Meanwhile, you stood across the room in a pout, clearly blaming me for all our misfortunes. When I spoke to you or asked you questions, you'd scarcely respond.

"The repair will take several hours," the mechanic said. "Why don't you both get some sleep?"

"By then," I say to James, "it was around three in the morning. Eight hours since we'd left Columbus. We should have been in Rockford. Instead, we were spending the night in a truck stop lounge. Sleeping in orange plastic chairs bolted to the floor."

"When did you finally get going again?"

"A little before sun-up. The chief mechanic told me the truck was `a heap of junk.' He warned me not to shut the engine off before we got to wherever we were going. So we took off—" I drop my head into my hands— "and just a couple hours down the road, we got lost."

I could feel it. So close to Rockford, and now we were going the wrong way, even though you insisted we weren't. You wouldn't allow me to consult your map. With your back against your door, you stared at me non-stop, as if I were a demon you didn't know how to exorcize. I tried not to look at you. Kept my eyes on the road. The pain in my leg was torture.

In the middle of nowhere, we approached a ramshackle service station. The fuel gauge was well above empty, but I lied and told you we needed to stop for gas.

I filled the tank with the engine running. Then, inside the station, I asked the kindly proprietor how to get to Rockford.

"You'll have to turn around," he said. "Rockford's about an hour and a half back. Can't miss it."

I close my eyes, press them against the heels of my hands, trying to relieve the sting of bloodshot. Suddenly I feel like I'm dreaming. My sleep-deprived mind, playing tricks. Under the table I force my bad leg to stretch out straight. The pain makes my jaw clench. I regain my wits.

"So finally we get to Rockford. Now, Grace had told me she'd arranged to store her belongings at a Baptist church till she found a place to live. But when we arrived at the church, around ten o'clock, the staff didn't know what arrangements she was talking about. We waited for three hours till the minister showed up. He told us there'd been `an unfortunate misunderstanding.' Grace would have to find storage space elsewhere."

As I drove away from the church, still reeling from the minister's words, you suddenly presented me with a crisp $20 bill from your wad of cash. Empty as my pockets were, the money in my hand barely made an impression. After nearly twenty hours on the road, and with scarcely any sleep in more than thirty, I was in a numb fog. Beyond hungry. Beyond feeling the pain in my leg. I was just trying to drive. Every step on the brake, every press on the accelerator, every flip of the turn signal, was an act of will.

At a facility across town you rented a storage unit. Then we cruised the streets till you spotted a skinny, shabbily dressed white man, maybe retirement age, collecting aluminum cans along the roadside. You ordered me to stop and ask him if he'd help us unload. I pulled over but refused to speak for you. I didn't want any part of it. I was only there to drive.

He fell for your pitch, made with such charm through the window. "I got emphysema," he said, climbing in, "but I'll do what I can." You didn't tell him what I already knew, that you wouldn't be paying him a tip for his trouble. Just like you hadn't paid the U-Haul guy.

By the time the three of us got the truck unloaded, the man was breathing hard, coughing up thick phlegm. His insulated sweatshirt was soaked through. "That was a work-out," he gasped, wiping his forehead on his sleeve.

Back in the truck, you instructed me to drop the man off where we'd first found him. When he got out, he waited expectantly at the door. You shook his hand, thanked him for his time, and abruptly pulled the door shut.

Driving away I watched the old man growing small in my rearview mirror. He stood bent over, hands on knees, till I couldn't see him anymore. "An instrument of the Lord's will."

The $20 you'd paid me was burning in my pocket.

I slide Grace's $20 bill across the table to James, a sad confirmation of events. He doesn't touch it.

"We dropped off the truck at U-Haul, then walked a couple blocks through drizzle to the nearest bus stop, to catch a bus to the Greyhound terminal."

You stood far from me. The air was thick. I didn't understand what had happened between us, and I didn't have the energy to figure it out. Come on, bus.

Suddenly you strode over to me and waved a $10 bill in my face. "Take it!" The command like the cold snap of a steel trap.

"No, you keep it. I wasn't expecting to get paid for driving. Just a bus ticket home."

"Take it!"

"You already gave me twenty dollars."

"So?"

"So I don't need any more money. Besides, you're going to need all the money you got to start over."

"Don't take it then!" You stuffed the bill into your coat pocket. "Many people would be grateful if I tried to give them money." Your voice dripping venom.

I drew a deep breath. "Look, Grace, I'm sorry. If it means that much to you, I'll take the money. I was just trying to be helpful. I thought you might need the money more—"

"No! It is too late now. You did not want the money, so you are not getting it!"

The energy around us was crazy. I was spinning. "Grace, have I offended you somehow? Are you angry at me about something?"

"Angry?" you hissed. "Why do you think I am angry?"

"Your tone of voice. Your silences. Your staring at me in the truck—"

"This is your evidence? It means nothing. Nothing! Do you not think I am grateful to you for bringing me here?"

Your question reeked with sarcasm. Irritated, I was losing my calm. "No, Grace, I don't. You've paid me some money, but you don't seem at all grateful—"

"Stop it!" you shrieked. "Just stop it! I do not want to hear anymore. Just be quiet!"

Furious, you strutted off and stood with your back turned to me, waiting for the bus, your red coat darkening in the pelting rain.

"At Greyhound," I tell James, "she bought two tickets. She threw one at my feet, then took a seat across the lobby. I picked up my ticket, made sure I was bound for Columbus, turned it over and over in my hands. Such relief!"

"Where was *she* going?"

I shrug. "I wondered. I mean, it was almost dark. All her stuff was in storage. I don't know what she was doing."

A few moments of silence, then James asks when I finally got back to Columbus.

"This morning, around four." I lean back in my seat, flex the ankle in my bad leg. "Thirty-three hours after we left."

"Where'd you go, at that hour?"

"Nowhere. It was pouring down rain, it was dark, it was cold, my knee was sore and swollen—no way I was going anywhere. I settled into a chair in the terminal, hoping to nap till sunup. *That* was a mistake—"

Pain exploded—

Jolted from a restless sleep, I clutched with a groan at my bad knee. Somebody had just kicked it, and hard.

"Got some proof you got a right to be here?" a man's voice growled.

Dazed, I couldn't comprehend what was happening. "I'm sorry—" squinting up at the voice, I finally made out a security guard— "but what exactly do you want from me?"

"Why you here?" His eyes were like a mean dog's.

"I got off the bus a little while ago. It's not safe to just go out wandering the streets at this hour."

"Got a ticket to prove it?"

"Yeah. Here—" I dug my crumpled ticket out of my coat pocket.

"Ain't nobody picking you up?" he said, studying it. "Ain't no place else you can go?"

"No, sir. I'll be leaving as soon as it gets light."

"Make sure you do."

"I watched him go. He strolled by other sleeping people with complete indifference. Understandable, I guess. They didn't look anything like me."

Tears are bright in James's eyes. When I see them, a knot rises in my throat.

"Of all that happened on that trip," I say finally, "the thing I don't understand is the drastic change in Grace. I can't stop thinking about it. We were getting along just fine, and then—well—*something* happened. Somehow I feel betrayed."

TWO CUPS

Late afternoon, McDonald's on South High. "Could you spare two cups of hot water?" James asks the lady behind the counter, as I settle into a booth.

She pours the water and is about to hand him the styrofoam cups when her manager stops her. He tells her to charge 30¢.

"I've only got one penny in my pocket," James says, truthfully.

The lady glances at her boss, then lowers her eyes. "Sorry, I can't serve you." She tosses the steaming cups into the trash can.

CALVIN

After Einstein Bros. closes for the day, James retrieves from its dumpster the garbage bag of bagels he'd discovered this morning. Then, heading back to the riverbank, he plays Santa along the railroad tracks, dropping off bagels at various camps, leaving a few in plain sight when nobody's home.

Approaching a tent camp, he calls out, "Hello, anybody in there?"

No answer.

"Hel-*lo*," he repeats.

After a couple seconds a gruff voice says flatly, "What."

"Hey man, you want any bagels?"

A grizzled old man, in his seventies maybe, sticks his head out the tent. "What you want?"

"I've got some bagels. You want any?"

"Can't eat them. My teeth's bad."

James lowers the heavy bag from his shoulder. "I'm James. What's your name?"

"Calvin."

"Nice to meet you, Calvin."

"Yeah, yeah."

"I just built the camp down the way."

"Yeah, I noticed. Ain't there a woman with you?"

"Yeah, her name's Phyllis."

"You met Jake and Rooster?"

"Yep."

"Well, be careful. They use drugs and liquor, make lots of noise at night. I stay away from them, much as I can."

"Okay, Calvin, thanks for the warning. I'll be careful. See you later."

"Okay, bye." The tent flap drops back.

ETIQUETTE

Dinnertime. Rooster (minus Enid) and Jake (minus Sarge) have offered to cook us spaghetti. In Rooster's camp they build a fire in a deep-bellied charcoal grill, fill a dirty pot with water from a jug and set it over the flames to boil. A little tipsy, they disagree on everything—how much wood they should feed the fire, how much time they should boil the pasta, whether to put hot dogs in the sauce....

Time groans by. The day's been long. James and I silently weigh our desire for hot food against our need for sleep, while Jake, stirring a pan of spaghetti sauce, lectures us on neighborhood etiquette. "We're all in this together. Everybody watches out for everybody's stuff. Just try to keep your place neat, and don't make a big fire or the people up on the hill will call the cops. Don't use water from the river—it's damn polluted. If you scrape up enough money for a night at a motel, invite everybody to come and clean up, hang out, watch TV, that kind of thing—"

The water's still not boiling. At this rate, we'll be eating at midnight.

"Everybody out here's got a story," Jake says. "You don't need to know ours, and we don't want to know yours—"

This rule is immediately broken. Jake and Rooster start speculating, affably, on what might have brought James and me to the riverbank. James, they decide, is probably just down on his luck; me, they can't figure. With few women living along the river, they have few stock stories to choose from.

They tell us they'll soon be leaving town. Jake's wanting to avoid a jail sentence for a misdemeanor, and Rooster, in trouble with his old street gang as well as the cops, will tag along. "Got some money coming in," they say, "that'll pay our way to Florida."

They want to go up top for more beer and smokes. James and I should stay behind and keep the fire going. Rooster bends down to James's ear. "If there's any trouble while we're gone," he whispers loudly, "there's a nine-millimeter in my tent, under my pillow." He pats James reassuringly on the shoulder, then disappears with Jake into the dark.

Uneasily we tend the fire, watching the pot that never boils.

NOT FOR PROFIT

Headlights sweep. Car doors slam. Anxious voices seep down into the woods. Rooster, afraid of cops, hightails it from his camp toward the river.

"It's just them people from Take It to the Streets," Jake hollers after him, but Rooster's already gone.

I've heard of Take It to the Streets, a nonprofit organization founded years ago by Harold and Ada Martin. Over the years the local news has regularly reported the group's ministries among homeless people, especially those living on the streets. Most of its volunteers are recruits from Columbus churches. As fate would have it, James had encountered Ada Martin (aka Big Mama) and a troupe of teenage volunteers his very first night on the riverbank. Now, only two evenings later, another visit.

These volunteers, led by Sabrina Martin, daughter of Harold and Ada, are mostly middle-aged adults. They've brought us lunch-meat sandwiches, hot soup, candles, prayers. Next time, they say, they'll try to bring more blankets.

Sabrina draws me aside. "Do you have everything you need, you know, as a woman?"

STALKED

Exhausted as I am, sleep in our little camp is out of reach. I'm constantly assaulted by noise. During one short stretch, a train rumbles past, shaking our shelter; a low-flying plane drones; a police helicopter chops over; hot rods burn rubber and sirens scream on streets up top; highway traffic buzzes along on the nearby interstate…. The noise peels off in layers but never strips all the way down to silence.

Maybe you couldn't bear it, if it did.

The claustrophobia that had attacked me our first night on the streets is back again, and stronger. Little more than twelve inches separate my face from the ceiling of the shelter. The air's close. Bundled in four layers of clothes, buried beneath blankets, I feel tangled up, caught in a net. Every so often I squirm out the shelter door into an icy rain, squat and urinate in the dead weeds, grateful to breathe.

DAY 12

SUNDAY, FEBRUARY 28

WELCOME

On the way to breakfast at Central Presbyterian Church, James and I make a pit stop at the Greyhound Bus Terminal. I'm nervous, going in. The last time I was here, a security guard had kicked me.

I clean up a little in the restroom. When I return to the lobby, a different security guard, a white-haired black man, is waiting for me.

"You don't have no business being here," the old man says. Part-statement, part-question.

"No, sir, just passing through."

"There'll be no more *passing through*, you hear? Next time I catch you I'll call the cops. You don't want to be going to jail, do you?"

"No, sir. I'm sorry. I won't do it again."

"Okay. Thanks for listening."

"You're welcome."

I turn to go.

"Wait—miss—"

The old black man sidles up to me. "I'm going to tell you how to get around this here thing," he says in a low voice, "but don't tell nobody I told you."

"I won't."

"See that fast-food joint just inside the terminal doors? Them restrooms in there is public. Can't nobody stop you from going in there. You can get yourself some hot water and sit in there all day long if you want. Don't tell nobody I told you, now."

Meanwhile, in the men's room, James is in trouble. Some rowdies, up to no good, have kicked in the door of his stall, then the fellow's next to him. They taunt and menace the two men before moving on to hassle a third guy at the sink. Wild-eyed, they look like gang members who had partied all night.

James hurries to leave. Their shouts follow him out the restroom door.

Out in the lobby the old security guard immediately accosts him. "You ain't allowed in this terminal. Leave now. You got no business being here."

The rowdies spill out of the restroom. Passing by the guard, one of them sticks out his tongue. The guard turns away, says nothing.

ROBBED

Hot, thick oatmeal with milk, butter and brown sugar: breakfast at Central Presbyterian. I've never noticed how real butter spoils the palate. Now I crave it. My tongue soaks it up. Across from me, James licks his lips, grinning like a cat.

Our friend Jeff, who had inspired our move to the riverbank, pulls out a chair next to us. His glasses are cracked, the frames taped together. Tiny red cuts score a purple bruise over his right cheekbone. "Maddy got robbed last night. She always holds the money I make, but she's not smart about it. I tried to fight them off." He tosses his hands in frustration. "I just don't know what to do. We try to get our act together but this kind of stuff keeps happening. We probably shouldn't have been where we was, but you know how it is. We both like to party a little. We get stupid when we been drinking."

"Is Maddy okay?" we ask.

"Yeah, just sleeping it off."

We ask Jeff if he'd gotten the bricklaying job for which he recently applied. His eyes had been eager, telling us about the job interview. "I like physical work," he'd said. "I like using my hands. It's been hard, waiting to hear."

Now he shakes his head. "I lost out. The company didn't have no way to get in touch with me. What's a guy supposed to do when he doesn't have a phone?"

PREACHING

In his homily the priest at St. Joe's says how sometimes there's no logic, no reason to suffering; it's simply a mystery, nothing more can be said. I draw new comfort from this familiar idea. Self-pity, even a vague resentment, has

Phyllis on the front steps of St. Joseph Cathedral. The swirls of light are parishioners passing by during the long exposure.

been dogging me ever since I got back from Illinois. *Grace, why had our trip unfolded as it did? Why did you grow more hostile with each passing mile? Why can't I forget your red coat, darkening in the rain?*

Maybe "Why?" is a child's question. Give it up. Move on. Grace was there, you were there; what happened, happened. That's all.

Tired tears burn. The choir's gentle chant floats down from the balcony in a minor key. Finally, on the last chord, the song resolves tenderly to hard-won joy.

When you try to help somebody, you can't invest yourself in a particular outcome. You can't even hope for a grateful response. If you want to help, you just try to help— period. Without conditions. Without expectations, either of yourself or the other. Sometimes you'll make mistakes. Sometimes you won't be appreciated. Sometimes you might even get hurt. That's life. Still, you do it. You offer yourself up, even to be broken, like bread upon some altar—

This is what I preach to myself, sitting up a little straighter in the pew.

BROWSING

Drenching downpour. The granite frieze above the front entrance of Main Library reads, "OPEN TO ALL." James takes refuge.

Third floor, as usual. Nearby in the stacks a woman is browsing the shelves for a book. Lost in thought, she cups her hands around her breasts through her sweater.

James's eyes swell with tears. "I miss Phoebe," he whispers, nobody to overhear.

SHADOWS

A heavy evening rain drips and splats on tarp and plastic. Inside our shelter, we're dry but somber as a dark room when the fire's died out. James props up his injured left ankle, gingerly presses the swollen flesh. Tonight, crossing the tracks on his way back to camp, he'd hopped a rail, and the ankle gave.

"I've had worse sprains," he tells me, "but I sure didn't need this."

Our one candle flickers, throws petty shadows.

DAY 13

MONDAY, MARCH 1

CLEAN

Daybreak: Quickly up top to White Castle, where I use the toilet, then down a back alley to SuperAmerica to shampoo my hair and dry it briefly under the hand dryer, then back to White Castle to brush my teeth and clean up a little, maybe even wash out my underwear, if I'm lucky. Too much time spent in any one restroom spells trouble, especially if it's a single toilet. You lock the door behind you, and soon a manager comes banging and hollering for you to get out.

I'm making do with spitbaths. ("Birdbaths," our neighbor Jake calls his.) I could take a shower at one of the women's shelters downtown, but only if I put myself on a list and hang around the building till 9 PM, hoping to get a turn before the bathrooms are closed to non-residents for the night. Afterwards, I'd have to hike all the way back to camp in the dark—not the smartest thing for a woman to do, especially on the riverbank.

James has a much easier time of it. The showers at the men's shelters aren't necessarily pleasant, but at least they're available to non-resident males during daylight hours.

TRAMP

The railroad tracks, we've decided, would be a quicker way to Holy Family Soup Kitchen than our usual street route. We set off in mid-morning. Getting anywhere out here takes time; you can't just get in your car or hop on a bus.

Our legs are racking up seven or eight miles a day, especially now that we're camping on the riverbank. Ankles and knees goran, even the healthy ones.

I tramp the uneven ties north. James hitches on his sprained ankle alongside the railroad bed, grateful for the crushed coal soft underfoot, fine as black sand. We both feel a consolation, being out here: nobody staring at us, or studiously ignoring us; no traffic to dodge; little noise but for the occasional train.

"If I closed my eyes," James says, "I could be walking a New England beach, deserted in winter."

GOOD MOVE

Across the table from us at the soup kitchen are a young black man, his six-year-old daughter and four-year-old son. They arrived in Columbus a few months ago from Florida. "Things are starting to come together for us now," the man tells me. "At least, I hope so."

The girl is combing her hair with her fingers. Her young face is beautiful. I pull from my coat pocket a big pink comb I got at the women's shelter and reach it across the table. "Would you like to have this?"

Her eyes light up. She stretches out her hand.

Her father snatches the comb away. "Thanks. I can really use that."

The girl stares at the tabletop. She doesn't eat another bite of her meal.

"You have kids?" the father asks me.

"No."

"Good move."[3]

DEALT

Under the bridge south of camp, a joker lost from a card deck lies atop a pile of broken and empty forties, some of the bottles still sheathed in brown paper bags. "For some reason," James says to me, "scenes like this never make it into beer commercials."

A dirty piece of tablet paper slides down the nearby embankment, dealt by the wind's hand. "Journal Entry #2," written by a schoolboy named Michael:

> You should have the right to do what ever you want to do. like a whit person want to hang out with a black person. Other people shouldn't think about what you do they should think about what they do. *[Sic]*

Pile of empty forties under the bridge

STAYING (2)

Sundown, one to two inches of new snow on the ground. I dread this time of day. In another hour or so, James and I will say goodnight, and soon after snuffing out the candle I keep bedside, the claustrophobia will begin to stalk me down. Nothing keeps it at bay for long, once I'm in the dark—not even imagining Jihong's strong body against mine. Every night I feel him teaspooning me, more real than a memory, but this is a peculiar suffering: the enemy's in my own mind. My last defense, at the point of panic, is always to grope for a match and relight the candle. Like a pesky demon the phobia shrinks back a little from the candle's glimmer, and I sit huddled there, rocking, my arms wrapped tightly around my knees, as if otherwise my body might fly apart—

I lay prayerful hands on James's puffy ankle. The day's been agonizing, for him.

We're both hobbled a bit, but we're surviving. We have a roof over our heads. We're relatively warm enough at night, even if we wake each morning to a coating of frost on the ceiling and walls. Each day we manage to get a little rest and some food.

We've figured out the fundamentals. Wryly, now, we notice that we've even raised the bar, allowing ourselves to desire more and better than we've got. Our shelter should be warmer and dryer; our food more tasty, not so stale.

In the days that remain, I suspect, our greatest adversity might not be physical. One way or another, we'll manage to maintain our bodies. But will our minds be able to cope; our hearts, to bear up; our spirits, to resist despair? *There, you finally said it. You're feeling despair.*

"Do you ever think about leaving?" James asks, lighting a second candle for the heat.

"Of course I do. Every day. Just like you."

"How will you know if it's time for you to go home?"

"Well, I always ask myself why I'm wanting to go. Is it because I'd prefer not to be so tired and cold, so scared, so lonely—or is it because I feel compelled to leave, moved in my spirit, just like I did coming out? Asking that question always seems to put everything into perspective. I'd like to be more comfortable. But that's not enough reason to quit. Not for me."

DAY 14

TUESDAY, MARCH 2

SPECIMEN

This morning my spirit is fragile, easily wounded. As I walk along Broad Street under a warm sun, resentment surges. One minute I feel like a specimen under a microscope—stared at, mostly from cars. The next minute, being shunned by pedestrians, I feel utterly invisible. Maybe they don't look at me because my appearance disgusts them. Maybe they're afraid I'll beg. Maybe they don't want to enter my pain, and one look at me is all it would take. Whatever the reason, they do their best not to see me. My warped reflection fills their sunglasses:

I'm just a lazy bum. I want a handout, a free ride. I'm a stupid drunk, a strung-out junkie. I'm violent, I'm schizo, I'm paranoid. I don't care about anybody but me. I'm on the streets because I want to be. I'm a lost soul....

Maybe I'm many of these things, maybe none at all—what do you people know? But my worst flaws and frailties aren't so different from yours. Some of you are lazy. Some of you would like a free ride, buying your lottery tickets, going on game shows, leaping at frivolous lawsuits, obsessing over stocks. Some of you are addicts, grappling with hidden cravings, appetites out of control. Some of you are violent, especially at home, behind closed doors. Some of you are afraid, depressed, messed up in the head. Some of you are self-absorbed. Some of you have made tragic choices out of desperation, anger, overwhelming grief. Some of you feel lost, like I do.

You probably don't like admitting these things. Maybe that's why I, a lowly street person, offend you: I'm a public reminder of your own imperfections; your own shame, even. If you ignore me, maybe you can go on pretending you've got no problems.

But I'll tell you something. Whatever problems you've got, whatever problems I've got, they're not who we are. Nobody's a caricature. You and me, we're human beings. It's just we forget sometimes, and need each other's help remembering.

FLESH

This men's shelter in the Bottoms is as big as a warehouse, choked with cigarette smoke. Homeless men sit around asking each other for smokes or quarters, watching a beat-up TV, or staring at the backs of those watching TV. To James, most of them look like they're waiting around to die.

"Can I take a shower here?" he asks a staffer at the registration desk.

"I wish you would," the staffer jokes. He loans James some shampoo, a towel and a used bar of soap.

The shower room is filthy. The tile walls are almost black with dirt and mildew stains, the tile floor brown with thick scum. There are eight shower heads and a single drain.

An Anglo stands at a nearby sink, gazing into the wall mirror. He reaches into his mouth and pulls out a diseased piece of gum—an actual piece of his flesh—and sloughs it off on the edge of the basin. Another white man walks in, picks up a soiled towel and wipes off his crack pipe.

James hurries to lather up, using a stray pair of jeans as a shower mat. *In the end*, he says to himself, *even getting clean feels dirty.*

SECURITY

Seeking food for our dinner, I head south to Holy Cross Church. The food line hasn't opened yet, but seventy or eighty people have already queued up. (Before I hit the streets, a Columbus cop said to me, "You know, homeless people are just like birds. The only thing they care about is filling their bellies. They'll flock to wherever the food is, just like a bunch of pigeons.")

Weary from my walk, I slink around the corner from the church and sink onto the ground, resting my back against a tenement stoop, grateful for the sunshine on my face. Elderly men and mothers with infants pass by and ask me if I know where the sandwiches are.

"You're in the right place," I tell them. "Just go around back."

A short, thinly bearded black man saunters by, hands buried in pockets. I remember him from the soup kitchen on Grubb Street. He always wears a Civil War-style cap, Union blue. Several big, shiny badges glint against his blue wool coat.

As he reaches the corner, the man abruptly turns around. He comes partway back to me, says, "You okay?" In his get-up, he reminds me of a kindly neighborhood cop on patrol.

I smile. "Just resting."

"Okay then," he says somberly, moving on. "They'll be starting the line soon."

The food line runs through an annex to the church. Its primitive foyer is unlit and unheated. A hundred or more of us are crowded inside. At the head of the serpentine line, steps descend to a closed basement door. Impatience mounts as the crowd waits for that door to open. Voices rise and toughen; male, mostly. Laughter is shrill and mean. Arguments break out. Bouts of pushing and shoving. Then, suddenly, shouts of "Security! Security!"

A burst of laughter.

"Hey, Security!" somebody yells, "you going to save the world? How you going to do that?"

They're yelling at Blue Coat. He's surrounded by taunting, jostling men. His Union cap is all I can see. "Hey, Security, where'd you get all them badges? Let me have one!"

I can hear his silence, can somehow feel the fierce battle he's waging with himself. It's a battle he can't win. Finally he lashes out, his voice fire and brimstone, his words a crazy babble. He isn't mentally stable, that's clear, and the bullies, delighted to have broken him, egg him on. Many in the crowd laugh hysterically. Others shrink back, lowering their eyes, covering their ears—

Blue Coat is saved by the basement door, opening at last. The head of the line surges down.

SAME DIRECTION

Meeting Calvin near the railroad tracks, I introduce myself. James has told me about this neighbor of ours: his tent camp, his teeth too bad for bagels, his warning about Jake and Rooster.

"Where you headed?" I ask, since we're walking the same direction.

"Don't like people asking me where I'm going," he says. "'How're you?' or 'How's it going?'—that's okay. But when people ask me *where* I'm going, I say, 'Straight to hell, if I don't straighten out!'"

TREASURE

Before sleep, a comforting ritual as rain pelts the shelter. James and I each hold a votive candle, naming simple things that brighten our life out here: a treasure found in the trash, sunshine, the affection of an animal, the smell of spices or fresh bread, a lucky penny on the sidewalk, soap, a good bowel movement, a loved one's voice on the phone, the singing of birds at dawn, a cup of water when we're parched, hot water when we're cold....

DAY 15

WEDNESDAY, MARCH 3

OCCUPANCY

God, it was cold last night. Once I crawled out to pee in the bucket and found two or three inches of new snow on the ground. Wind whipped my bare bottom.

Fonder of warmer climes, Jake and Rooster left town this morning for Florida. Saying goodbye to them, James and I had mixed feelings. Selfishly, we'll miss them as neighbors—though we've only lived here a week, they've been kind to us—but certainly we wish them a better life down south.

Jake told us that his roomie Sarge will continue to live at their shanty. Rooster, with no mention of "his old lady" Enid, urged us to move into his tent.

We have no interest in relocating, but this afternoon I do go over to claim Rooster's grill. On the path leading into Rooster's camp, I almost collide with the Professor. Our bespectacled neighbor from further downstream has a reputation for being able to answer any question put to him, no matter how trivial. Apparently he's quite the reader. James and I often see him studying in the library.

The day that we scouted the riverbank for a campsite, we passed by the Professor's place: a refrigerator tipped on its side in the woods, a pair of shoes marking it as a home.

Now the Professor tells me that he's taken up residence in Rooster's tent. His days of sleeping in a refrigerator are past.

"Good for you," I say, instantly abandoning all thoughts of the grill, in case he needs that, too.

DAY 16

THURSDAY, MARCH 4

WAR ZONE

6 AM. Shivering at the counter in White Castle, James pulls an empty styro-foam cup out of his coat pocket and asks an employee if she might please fill it with hot water. He's half afraid of her answer.

"I'm not allowed to accept cups over the counter," the woman says, "but I'll take care of you."

I'll take care of you: so comforting to hear those words from a stranger. He'll bundle them up, carry them with him all day.

He joins me wearily at a table. "Last night," he says, "I dreamed I was a soldier in World War One. Got shot in the knees. Got to go home. I was so excited to go home that I woke up—but I was still on the riverbank. My knees were throbbing *really* hard.

"This," he tells me, his eyes full of the streets, "is a war zone of a different sort."

ENEMY

The railroad tracks are quiet, contemplative, under fresh feathering snow. With my head bent I trudge into the stiff wind, tripping now and then on the snow-covered ties. Left boot down, right boot down. Left, right, left. I watch my plodding feet as if they belong to somebody else.

The wind is just the wind.
The snow is just the snow.

The cold is just the cold.
Don't make them the enemy.

I almost step on it before I see it: a dead dog, glazed with snow, decapitated by a train.

BACK OFF

The crowd at Holy Family Soup Kitchen is thinner today, as it has been all week. Government checks are out. For the moment, there's less need. Some people without permanent addresses have their government benefits deposited directly in a bank account; others have them sent to a P.O. box, or to a shelter or social service agency.

James and I begin stockpiling food for the weekend, when this place will be closed. We fill empty eight-ounce yogurt containers with goulash, wrap bread and cookies in napkins and stuff them into our coat pockets.

As we work, an Anglo on crutches hobbles by our table. Soup's sloshing on the tray he's trying to carry. I leap up, offering to help.

"Will—do—it—myself," he growls through clenched teeth.

I back off. It's so easy to presume too much.

Ready to leave, James heads up a side aisle to return his tray to the stack, only to have his way blocked by a burly black man sprawling in a chair between the table and the wall. He's noticed this fellow here at the soup kitchen before—he always wears an oversized army coat, and he always looks mad.

"Excuse me, buddy," James says.

The man pretends not to hear. Others at the same table tell him, "Scoot up, man! Let the guy pass!" He ignores them.

As gently as he can, James says again, "Hey, man, can I please get by?"

Teeth clenched, the man glares up at him. One good eye, one eye crossed, both glazed like cubes in a bar drink. Tension mounts till it's almost unbearable. Finally, with a sneer, the man shifts an inch or two toward the table, just enough to let James past.

NO JOKE

Homeward bound through the downtown. The workday has ended. Thousands scatter. Our ears catch bits of stock talk, job blues, dinner plans. Outside the upscale City Center Mall, a smartly dressed black man of retirement age tells three black teenage boys in baggy hip-hop jeans, "These streets ain't no joke." Overhearing, James thinks of the joker he saw lying atop the beer bottles under the bridge. *Kids, listen to the man,* he pleads silently. *Take the old guy's words to heart.*

JACKPOT

Bathroom emergency on First Avenue. A three-mile walk to a Twelve-Step meeting has churned James up. Passing a church, he tries every front and side door. Locked up tight.

Around back, cars are pulling into a full parking lot. The rear door of the church is busy. He strides into a buzzing, smoky auditorium: bingo night. Hundreds of people at the tables, waiting for lucky numbers, packs of smokes stacked beside their game cards.

He lunges for the men's room.

BELOVED

Despite the extreme cold and the merciless drafts in our shelter, I'm burning only one votive candle, rationing our supply. We have only one tapered candle and two stubs left.

Breath hangs in the air. I shiver beneath the blankets. The shelter would be warmer if both of us were here.

I prop *Cry, the Beloved Country* against a stray shoe. Serious fiction is difficult to digest from the underside. These past nights I've been rummaging around in this book as if it were a trash bin, scrounging for whatever scraps of sustenance might be inside, not thinking too much about the story at large. It's too much to bear.

"There's only one thing," I read now, "that has power completely, and this is love. Because when a man loves, he seeks no power, and therefore he has power—"

My eyes leave the page.

We're so quick to say that love is patient, and kind, not envious or boastful or rude. It never ends, we say; it bears everything, it believes and hopes and endures—*everything.* But mustn't we also say that love is sometimes impetuous and tough, desirous and brazen; that sometimes it does end, or is at least transmuted; that sometimes it buckles because not yet mature, doubts because there's good reason, despairs because it doesn't yet know how to do more, be more; that sometimes love does in fact give up? Let there be power in confessing: yes, we know love, and not only as children do. We know it in all its glory, but also in its weakness. It's as much heartache as ecstasy. It demands our life, and won't let us go....

This afternoon, to escape the rain, James and I went to the Agora and asked if we could volunteer at the day-center for homeless families. Soon we were washing down grubby plastic chairs. The place was full of children: infants, toddlers, grade schoolers. Among their parents, we recognized Appalachian hillbillies by their accent, Somalis by their dress. Most of the families were huddled around a huge TV screen, eyes glued to *The Princess Bride*, a fairy tale spoof—entertainment for some, English lesson for others. *Who knows about happy endings?*

Take It to the Streets pays me a call, bringing dinner. Tonight's volunteers are a youth group and their adult leaders from First Community Church. Though nervous, the teenagers seem more open, less inclined to dictate the action, than many of the grownups who have visited our camp.

"It's so *cold* out here," they say, "and the weather's been rotten, so why don't you stay in a shelter?" When I tell them why, they say it's a familiar story, heard in other camps around the city.

I tell the kids, too, about the significance of seemingly small things, like the simple kindnesses of the railroad crewmen who offer us supplies, and wave at us, and sometimes toot a greeting. "Everything you do *matters*. Like your coming out here, and taking time to talk to me, to treat me with respect even though you don't know me and maybe are a little scared of me—these things *matter*." Listening, the kids dig their gloved hands deeper in their coats, breathing clouds. They don't look away from me. I feel in their gaze a rich consolation, and tell them so.

They're gone now. I pick up my book again:

Cry the beloved country for the unborn child that is the inheritor of our fear. Let him not love the earth too deeply. Let him not laugh too gladly when the water runs through his fingers, nor stand too silent when the setting sun makes red the veld with fire. Let him not be too moved when the birds of his land are singing, nor give too much of his heart to a mountain or a valley. For fear will rob him of all if he gives too much.

DAY 17

FRIDAY, MARCH 5

BLUE

Along the railroad tracks north of camp, under a gunmetal gray sky, James and I meet up with a black man. "Name's Blue," he says, reaching out to shake hands. "I've got a shack in the woods, over there. There's another shack, back of it, not being used. You guys can stay there if you want."

"Thanks," James says, speaking for us both, "but we've got a place further down."

Together the three of us walk the tracks. Every so often Blue stoops down, picks up a stone from the gravel, examines it briefly, then either tosses it aside or pockets it in his jeans. As a boy, he tells us, he loved hunting for rocks. He'd take them home and carefully clean them with a toothbrush and baking soda before polishing them with varnish.

Listening to him, I'm reminded of my own childhood, when I'd scour plowed fields for pieces of sandstone and quartz, fool's gold and flint. I'd carry my treasures home, coat them with clear nail polish, and glue them into flat cardboard boxes for display. "I'm going to be a geologist when I grow up," I announced to my parents, as certain as a schoolgirl could be, and for my next birthday they'd bought me *The Illustrated Guide to Rocks and Minerals*.

I wonder if anybody was there to encourage Blue, all those years ago, but before I can ask him a locomotive horn blasts up ahead.

We've just started across a trestle from the south side, and now a slow train's about to cross from the north. James and I, both hobbled, want to turn

The railroad trestle

back, get off the tracks and let the train pass, but Blue shouts, "We can beat it!" He begins to run.

Stupidly, or with a little faith, we hitch along behind him as fast as we can on our sore legs. The train brakes sharply. The trestle shakes. The air pulses with deafening sound.

You can't hear him, but Blue's laughing hard.

MAKING IT

Leaving Holy Family Soup Kitchen, we slouch through the Bottoms with a fellow named Morris. James asks him how he makes it on the streets, day in and day out.

"The Man Upstairs," Morris says. "*He* keeps me going. You know, just one foot in front of the other." A pause. "Lord, I wish spring'd hurry up and come."

GETTING OUT

Passing by Rooster's old camp, James and I hear a voice holler, "Hey guys, come on back!"

It's not the Professor. Of all people, it's Jake. He should have been in Florida by now.

"We never got out of town," he tells us in a hangdog voice, feeding a big fire in the grill. "Rooster's money didn't come through. Actually it was his old lady's money—you guys ever meet Enid? Whatever. The money didn't come. We got a couple nights at a motel though. Got cleaned up a little."

Tonight the Professor's back in his refrigerator.

ROUNDS

James and I dig a small firepit and set into the hole a small grill we've scavenged from the woods. Having already gathered a supply of kindling, we ignite a wet-wood fire with a railroad flare. Red flame hisses and smokes. Purgatory.

At last there's a strong blaze. "Smells like home," I say wistfully, laying on another piece of brushwood. We enjoy the fire's lively sizzle and pop till a light rain chases us inside.

Some time to write, then we put out the candle. We snuggle down beneath our blankets to the sound of rain on plastic.

Maybe ten minutes later, a car horn blares, not far away. Then we hear somebody running in the brush—a series of yells—

"Who do you think it is?" I whisper.

"Don't know. What should we do?"

"Don't know."

We hear more yelling.

"Cops?" I suggest.

"Maybe those gangbangers after Rooster. God, I hope not!"

Footsteps outside the shelter.

"Hey, guys! You in there?"

Jake. We groan in relief. He tosses two brownbags of food through the door. Harold Martin, he says, is making rounds of the camps, delivering cold meals in the rain.

DAY 18

SATURDAY, MARCH 6

SENSE OF STYLE

Dotting the railroad tracks are little dunes of white sand, used to improve a train's traction on the rails. During a lull in the rain, James and I lug some of it home in a five-gallon bucket (our toilet) and scatter it around the campsite to help cut the mud. Then we lay a stray sheet of plywood over the sloppy ground directly in front of the shelter. Finally, we rig more plastic over the door to protect against the weather.

I step back to study our little home. "So, Irishman, what do we call this architectural style?"

"Evolved crude."

PROPERTY VALUES

When it's open, Main Library continues to be our best daytime refuge from inclement weather, and we're not the only ones who seek it out. In fact, even more homeless people pass time here than we originally thought. It's as if some of them exist in infrared, and you can't see them till you put on night-vision goggles.

Today James runs across an article in the *New York Times* about St. Francis of Assisi. Born in the twelfth century to wealthy merchant parents, he lived a spoiled, carefree life till a stint in the army, followed by imprisonment and severe illness, transformed him into a mystic and mendicant. Thereafter regarded as a fool, he solidified his reputation when he stole the expensive

Statue of the Buddha in a frozen meditation garden

cloth from his father's warehouse and sold it to fund the repair of a tumble-down church. Ordered by the local Catholic bishop to restore what he'd taken, Francis stripped off his own rich garments and handed them over. Walked away naked. For the rest of his life, he wore a tunic of rough brown cloth. Poor man's cloth.

"This change in dress," the article says, "was certainly a signal, made centuries earlier by the Buddha, that doing without had been elevated to an existential option...."

James and I rouse ourselves from poorly disguised naps to attend a performance in the library auditorium by the African-American Youth Choir and Storytellers. The participants range in age from four to thirteen years. Some of them radiate immense energy. My aching feet, sweating in my clodhoppers, marvel at the children's stomping and leaping and stepping out to the rhythm of deep-bellied drums. They throw their bodies with abandon, laying claim to the dances of their ancestors, while the drummers, an old woman and a young boy, let fly their hands.

SWANKY

In late afternoon we step out the door of Main Library into snowfall. The flakes are so huge and wet we can hear them dropping onto our coats. The air's turning colder by the minute, but for now, in the quiet of snow falling on snow, the world feels gentle.

We take the German Village route home, wandering a maze of alleyways. German Village is a restored neighborhood south of downtown. In the mid-1800s its biergartens and narrow cobbled streets were crowded with German-speaking brewers and bakers, bricklayers and tanners, storekeepers and hausfrauen. Today its residents are no more German than Greek, and its property values, ever climbing, are considerably more than working class.

The architecture here is conservative, solid and plain. Clean red brick dominates: tiny brick cottages, larger brick Italianate and Queen Anne houses, brick rowhouses, brick carriage houses and sheds, brick privacy walls with black wrought iron fences, brick restaurants and giftshops and churches. Beneath our feet, designer-brick sidewalks.

In a cobbled alley behind a red-brick garage squats a snow-crusted couch, in good shape but out of style, apparently headed to the landfill. What luck! Its hefty foam-rubber cushions, joined together to form a mattress, will be both softer and thicker than our paper-stuffed garment bags. In the space of one night, those pillowy garment bags had flattened into bedrock.

We each set two cushions atop our head. Steadying them with our hands, we continue on down the street. As we pass a swanky German Village restaurant, the sight of us seems to amuse the diners at window seats. James manages a wave. A man and woman at a table for two exchange a smile.

"I miss making people smile," James says.

SPLURGE

In consumer culture, there's only one thing to do when you doubt your place in the scheme of things: Shop. Spend. Buy. In my heart I don't believe in the gospel of consumption, but hearing a weak jingle of change from my coat pocket, I'm suddenly a feel-good convert. We still have around $15 left from Grace's $20. I confess to James that I've been feeling stingy, carrying it around, reluctant to spend even a penny for fear we might need it later. I don't like playing the miser.

"What would help?" he asks.

"Well, what would you say to a splurge?"

He grins.

So we're agreed. Tomorrow we'll blow a couple bucks. Probably we'll buy something outrageous to eat: two slices of Chicago-style pizza, or a pint of Homemade Brand ice cream, or a chocolate torte from a German Village pastry shop. Thoughts of the food inspire pleasure; thoughts of the purchase, a peculiar consolation.

GOLD

On the corner of Kossuth and Front, a bottle of Cuervo Gold Tequila lies in a puddle, three shots left in the bottom. *A good drunk,* James says to himself, headed for a Twelve-Step meeting, *would never leave a drop.*

Back in the old days, tequila had been one of his drinks of choice. At $16 a bottle, it would always give him a boost, then knock him out so cold he could have fallen face-down in a gutter of rainwater and stayed there till he drowned.

Since he's been on the streets, he hasn't drawn the usual inspiration or reassurance from Twelve-Step meetings. *Maybe the reason,* he admits to himself as he reaches the door of tonight's meeting, *is that I don't go to be real. I go because I can walk in, no questions asked, and be warm for an hour, maybe hear a good joke, drink some coffee—beyond this, I have no expectations. To make real connections with the people, to experience the power in their stories, would require me to let my guard down and be vulnerable—I can't do that. Not out here. If I did, I'd totally collapse. Too much grief lurks under the composure. Too much. I need to be strong—so strong—*

"I'm James," he says to the roomful of eyes, "and I'm an alcoholic."

MUSTER

Well into the evening, an army of volunteers arrives. Alone in camp, I yank on my boots, then crawl out of the shelter and stumble up the path to greet the people, lighting my way with a guttering candle. For now, the heavy snow has stopped.

A wave of troops surrounds me, all adults. They present me with a flashlight and loose batteries, plus two bags of food, just as a breeze snuffs my candle.

An older black man steps up, introduces himself as Harold Martin. Now I have a face to go with the name. When he asks to see our camp, I lead him to it, followed by maybe a dozen volunteers.

"Somehow," Harold says, "I had the idea James and you was further down the river." He lifts the plastic over our door and flashes his light inside, then circles the shelter, inspecting its construction. Apparently it doesn't pass muster. "We got a tent you can have. I'll bring it out, next time I come."

"We're doing fine," I say. "Please give the tent to somebody who truly needs it."

Harold's insistent, but I'm stubborn. To accept the tent would be like taking up beds in a city shelter. It doesn't feel right. Finally I seem to convince him that James and I are staying warm enough, and dry.

After presenting me with yet another bag of food, the volunteers join hands and start to pray. A rambling, if passionate, prayer. Not wearing a coat, I'm soon shivering uncontrollably. My grip on Harold's hand is a vise. Finally he breaks into the prayer and ends it. "You're cold," he says. "Get on back inside."

MILLENNIUM

Harold and his troops head out, but before I can retreat into the shelter with my bags, two more women start down the path into camp. Worried lest they trip in the dark, I go to meet them. Dorothy and Maybelle, elderly, black. Dorothy invites me to her church. "You people could teach us a few things, you know."

"Oh? Like what?"

"We're very concerned about the turn of the millennium, Y2K and all. You know, like how we're going to live without water and heat and all. You people could really tell us a few things."

I rest a hand on her arm. "There's only one thing you need to know."

"What's that?"

"Don't be afraid." I lean in close. "Don't *ever* be afraid."

Her eyes widen in the moonlight. Then, very quietly, she says, "That's right, isn't it?"

For a moment the three of us women stand together in silence, the cold and snow forgotten.

"Can I give you a hug?" Dorothy asks suddenly. She pulls me and my bags into a long bear hug against her bulky camel-hair coat. Her perfume reminds me of fresh rosemary leaves. I wonder how ripe I smell.

"It's a good night for angels," I call after the women, as they begin making their way back up the path.

Dorothy stops, glances back at me. "You're the angel," she says, and I laugh.

FARCE

Before the women are all the way up the path, yet another wave of volunteers starts down. I'm already juggling three bags of food, a flashlight, loose batteries and a candle—and now two full-size blankets, a New Testament, and a large trash-bag about to burst with assorted bedding, clothes and window treatments *(yeah, window treatments)* are deposited in my arms. As the volunteers clasp hands and plunge into yet another prayer, I fight like Lucille Ball in a comedy classic to hold up my clumsy load.

Once the prayer's over, a bearded man who has visited before steps up. "I've been thinking about you guys every day. Is there anything you need?"

His asking is kind, but my arms are weakening. I summon the patience to answer. "As a matter of fact," I say, pinning down the New Testament with my chin, "we could use more candles. The flashlight you brought tonight will be helpful, but candles give off heat."

He nods. "Yeah. Besides, it's a different kind of light."

I smile faintly. That much he understands. I shore up my sagging load with a knee. My balance is precarious.

"Look," the man says, blind to my predicament, "I work at a food pantry. I'll try to get some more canned goods and bring them out next week with the candles. All I could bring tonight was canned peaches and salmon. Government food."

He slips the handle of a bulging plastic grocery bag around three fingers of my left hand, the only place left to put it. "Hope you can carry all that," he says with a grin as he leaves.

DAY 19

SUNDAY, MARCH 7

PEACE

During the opening hymn of mass at St. Joe's, a powerful voice seizes my attention. Not quite on key, but impassioned, colored by a European accent. I locate the singer across the aisle, a few pews up: a wispily bearded, balding man, gaunt, sagging on metal crutches. He and the crutches look long acquainted.

The old man knows the hymn lyrics by heart. He sings them voraciously, with only loose regard for the pipe organ's tempo. Sometimes his head tilts back as he sings. As I follow his gaze up into the vaulted ceiling, my tiredness lifts.

At the Passing of the Peace, I leave my pew to shake the hand that belongs to the voice. "Peace to you," I say to the old man. "You sing with a full heart." His bushy gray eyebrows shoot up quizzically. Then, he smiles.

For James, as for me, the Passing of the Peace is one of the highlights of mass. The handshakes are telling. He gets some firm ones today. One man, in the next pew up, is clearly surprised by James's smile and hearty grip. The woman with him doesn't bother to turn around. Her uneasiness in our presence was plain from the moment they sat down in front of us.

Another, older gentleman has been glancing repeatedly at James throughout the service, casting scowls. Now, during the Peace, at the last possible moment, he turns around to shake hands. As he and James touch, the man's face brightens, and he breaks into a smile that seems full of relief, even joy.

CURRENCY

On a downtown sidewalk, a full pack of Newport Menthols. James picks it up, puts it in his coat pocket. Every day Jake and Sarge search the ground and the streets for half-smoked butts. Tomorrow they won't have to.

Out here, cigarettes are a currency of good will. In our other life we don't smoke, but out here we try to pass them on when we find them and accept them when they're given.

FREEDOM

It's time for our much-anticipated splurge on food. Yet, as James and I consider our epicurean options, the greatest pleasure for the cheapest price, we're totally, helplessly, stumped. Having granted ourselves the freedom to indulge, we seem unable to exercise it. Weighing the possibilities demands too much energy. The appeal goes flat as a slashed car tire. Finally we decide to go home.

On our way back to camp, we browse in German Village trash. Tomorrow must be collection day: full garbage cans line the street, many labeled "RESI-DENT USE ONLY—VIOLATORS WILL BE PROSECUTED." Lifting their lids, we joke that we surely qualify as "residents," given the amount of time we spend digging in such receptacles.

German Village trash is upscale. It rarely disappoints, and today's no different. From an industrial-sized dumpster outside Thurn's Bakery and Deli, James pulls two liverwursts, Gold Medal Brand, still sealed in their wrappers. He holds them up with a triumphant grin, like a mountain man who's bagged a critter for supper.

Now, from Einstein Bros., yet another trash-bag full of day-old bagels. Laughing at our luck, we sniff one bagel after another—garlic herb, sundried tomato, blueberry, apple cinnamon, whole wheat, cracked pepper…. Tonight we'll feast on bagels spread with liverwurst and grilled over a smoky fire. For dessert, government peaches. Splurge for free.

REMOVED

In the glimmering of a candle I pick up *The Crucible* by Arthur Miller, a paperback I salvaged from a cold rain. I read this play once, long ago: a tale of testing, and tragedy; of outrageous suspicions, false accusations, rigged trials,

German Village trash can: "RESIDENT USE ONLY"

punishments without mercy. Neighbor is set against neighbor, husband against wife, parent against child—even the heart itself is riven.

The pious seventeenth-century folks in Miller's play, whose fear of witchcraft swiftly becomes hate masquerading as faith, consider the woods outside Salem the Devil's last preserve. I smile sadly at this. James and I seem not so far removed.

MERCY

We go up top, just before bedtime, to use the restroom and payphone at Wendy's restaurant. By the time we return a half hour later, some angel of mercy has deposited two brownbags of munchies, sandwiches and fruit on the roof of our shelter, plus some slightly used candles, and two more blankets. We laugh till we hurt.

From a pamphlet left with the food:

Jesus was homeless. Rejected by his family, accused of being a drunkard and thought to be crazy, Jesus walked from town to town, spending most of his time with people out on the streets. He was criticized for associating with poor and dirty people, and often was in trouble with the authorities; he occasionally got run out of town. He knew what it was to be hungry, thirsty, and tired....

DAY 20

MONDAY, MARCH 8

SPREE

Anxious to replace my cumbersome boots, I ransack through a foul-smelling box of used shoes at JOIN. Most are children's sneakers or women's high heels, but finally, an ugly pair of canvas and leather hiking shoes, size nine, with reinforced ankles and deep tread. They're three sizes too big but probably manageable if I stuff wadded paper in the toes and continue to wear three or four pair of socks. They're not waterproof like my boots, but I can tie plastic bags around my stockinged feet to serve as a lining.

Inspired by my luck, James visits JOIN with me later in the day. He scrounges a pair of construction boots, one size too big but much better, he believes, than his white Salvation Army sneakers. Those, slashed by his knife, he throws away.

Meanwhile, up at the service window, a young Latino is trying desperately to make himself understood. He speaks only a smattering of English; the volunteer, no Spanish. In the end they both give up, frustrated. The man moves slowly toward the door, hanging his head.

"Buenas días," I say, as he passes.

His head jerks up at my greeting. "Buenas días! Habla español?"

He wants to know if I speak Spanish. "Un poco," I say, apologetically. *Only a little.*

The man erupts in a torrent of Spanish. I drown in an instant. Waving my hands, shaking my head, I tell him I'm so very sorry—"Lo siento, lo siento!"— wishing I'd taken high school Spanish more seriously, all those years ago. "No comprendo," I tell him, "no comprendo." *I don't understand.*

The man hands me a piece of paper. A legal document, in English. Skimming, I learn he's just been released from jail on his own recognizance; for what crime, I don't need to know. I hand the paper back to him with a helpless shrug.

The man's calmer now. Somehow he makes me understand he has nowhere to go. I want to help him, but how?

He's wearing only a windbreaker. Today's temperature probably won't rise above freezing, even if the sun manages to shine. If the guy has nowhere to go, at least he can go nowhere in warmer clothes. I tug on his sleeve. "Muy frijole!" I say, pulling the Spanish out of the air, hoping it means "very cold" but half afraid it's nonsense, or an insult.[4]

I slip out of line, grab a shirt from a clothing rack and hold it up. "Free!" I shout, as if the man were deaf. Maybe this English word can cross the divide.

"Uno?" he asks, raising one finger.

"Mucho!" I say, handing him a grocery bag. "Mucho, mucho!"

He stares at me in disbelief, then takes the bag, walks over to the racks and begins to shop.

KGB

Standing nearby is a striking older woman. Her silver hair is beautifully styled, her cosmetics skillfully applied. If not for her clothes, clean but worse for the wear, you'd expect to see her strolling through City Center Mall with a designer shopping bag slung over her wrist. "Olga," she says her name is, after I introduce myself. Her accent betrays European roots. When I inquire, she tells me that she was born in Czechoslovakia but has lived in the U.S. for decades. "You know, my dear," she says, her term of endearment a caress to my ear, "I speak seven languages."

Now that Olga's started talking, there's no end. With rolled Rs and staccato Ts, she launches into a very articulate but mostly unintelligible conspiracy story about KGB death threats, U.S. government plots, the disappearance of her millions, a life spent on the run from secret agents. The deeper she goes into the story, the lower her voice drops. "The KGB came for me in the middle of the night," she murmurs, tears pooling in her eyes. "They strung up my woman friend in the basement, but I got away—I broke my ribs jumping through a window, but *I got away*. I was still wearing my nightgown. They will never take me. *Never!*"

Beside her on the floor rests a worn leather valise and a battered suitcase. Close against her body she clutches a large handbag. From this she draws a worn heirloom Bible. Tucked inside its gilt pages are scrawled notes and crumpled documents from lawyers, banks, government agencies. These papers are her life. She displays them to me one by one, trying to explain.

"They say I am *dead*. They say my money is *gone*. They say I cannot *prove* that I am alive. They do not *want* me to be alive. They would rather have my millions."

Tears spill down her powdered cheeks. She dabs them away with a lacy kerchief. "Thank you for listening, my dear," she whispers. "I have to let this out sometimes. Otherwise I explode."

Her story is either tragic or mad, maybe a little of both. I want to listen, I want to give her the space she needs to vent, but her energy has become so intense, every word a suppressed burst, I feel my spirit draining away. She's like a black hole sucking up light.

"The KGB is closing in," she says, under her breath. "I must leave right away. That is why I am here, to get a bus ticket. To Detroit. I will be safe in Detroit."

Suddenly she becomes calm. She glances around, checking to see nobody's listening. "You know, dear, I am writing a book about all of this."

The space between us collapses.

"My dear," she asks, "do you need a pencil?"

I disappear in her. "I can always use a pencil," I struggle to say.

"Here." From her handbag she digs out a long, black pencil with a red pen-cap over the lead. "I do not need this. The woman who gave it to me thought it was an eyebrow pencil, but it is not."

I notice now: her eyebrows are expertly drawn. No hair there to entangle with the brows of the ancestors. That old Zen saying, my Ash Wednesday prayer, turns to sad lament.

"The KGB," she says, "tried to kill me by setting a fire, and my face was badly burned. You would never know it now, except for my eyebrows. My eyebrows have never grown back."

SHOE SWAP

Around suppertime Jake stops by camp to chat. He happens to mention that Enid, Rooster's companion, has no boots. Take It to the Streets brought her a pair to try once, but they were so big she couldn't wear them.

"What size is she?" I say.

"Don't know. Real small."

"Here, give her my old boots to try. Size six. Maybe they'll fit."

An hour or so later, he returns, carrying a pair of men's leather workshoes, size ten, almost new. "Enid thanks you for the boots. These are the shoes they brought her some time back. Probably won't fit you, but they'd sure keep your feet dryer than the ones you got on."

Once Jake leaves, James and I build a fire in our firepit. When the flames are burning easy, he rests the toes of his "new" construction boots on the grill's edge, letting the heat warm them through. "You know, I could swear I've seen these boots before."

"How's that?"

"A construction worker staying at the overflow shelter had them on one morning when he asked me if I could spare a pair of socks. My first reaction was, `Sorry man, I need them.' Then I glanced down at his boots—*these* boots. Bare black ankles were sticking out the tops. Obviously the guy needed some socks. I gave him one of the three pair I had on.

"Now I've got his shoes. I wonder what *he's* wearing."

CRAZINESS

Jerk myself awake—nightmare—can't remember—

Slow down—breathe—

"James—"

Shake his foot—

"James!"

"Wha—what's up?"

"Need your help—"

"What's going on?" He props himself on an elbow, shielding his eyes from my flashlight beam.

"Sorry to wake you—needed to hear a familiar voice."

He stares at me. I'm crouched low on my knees, totally panicked, like a muskrat caught in a steel trap, ready to gnaw its leg off.

"What happened?"

"Nightmare. Can't get calmed down. I want to get out of here bad, but Jake and Rooster's going at it out there."

We listen to the commotion outside, our neighbors arguing ugly. Minutes pass. Finally I can't stand it anymore. "James, I've got to move, burn some of this adrenaline. I'm going up to White Castle. Maybe I can steer clear of the guys."

"I'll go with you."

Into our coats, our shoes. Out the shelter, up the path. We're just to the field, thinking we're clear, when we bump into Rooster. "Don't be alarmed," he tells us, "if you hear a ruckus later. It'll just be Jake getting what he deserves!"

Craziness. we stumble on toward the tracks.

It's after midnight when we sink into chairs at White Castle. The brisk walk and nippy air have calmed me down some. We small-talk. We stare out the windows. We wait. For what, exactly, I'm not sure; some sort of resolution.

James is sagging in his chair, almost asleep, when all at once the nightmare rushes back into my mind, swift as a flash flood: Olga, standing directly behind me, insane as a prophet. She leans in over my right shoulder and whispers a dreadful truth, her breath hot in my ear, hot on my skin. What she said I can't remember—such things in dreams you can never remember, they're far beyond your grasp—but the monstrous thing is still there, angry and sick, pounding away in my chest.

I begin to weep. There's a sad relief in the veil having lifted, if only this much. Ever since leaving JOIN, I've been haunted by Olga; all day long I'd carried her through the streets, like a worn leather Bible stuffed full of terrible secrets. Time now to lay her down.

DAY 21

TUESDAY, MARCH 9

SINKING

You waken before dawn, by some miracle having managed several hours of deep sleep, and emerge from the shelter into steadily falling snow. A bank of white, muffling all sound. The wind's down, at least for now, the air moist and warm. Anxious to use a bathroom and to get warm, you slog through five or six inches of wet powder toward White Castle, following the railroad tracks. The rails, glistening steely black against unbroken white, disappear not far ahead into snowy haze. For all the world it looks like the sky has fallen.

To get up top, here at the bridge, you have to leave the tracks and take a footpath up the steep embankment. You're the first person up, or down, since the snow started. Sinking into snow up to your ankles, you climb up a few steps, slip on buried forties, land on your belly, slide down till you stop. Grabbing hold of dead weeds, you pull yourself to your feet, dig in a toe, take a step up, ease forward, take another step, slip on more bottles, land hard on your bad knee, go sliding down again with a groan. You're completely covered with snowdust now, and sweating, but this is your only way up: to crawl over the waste of other people's lives. You feel like you're stepping on bodies.

ENID

By mid-morning homeless feet have packed a narrow trail through the deep snow along the tracks. Tramping the line back toward camp, I meet Enid. I step aside into several inches of fresh powder to let her by. Her tiny feet, I notice, are swimming in my old sixes.

TORMENT

Headed up the railroad tracks toward Grubb Street, I swing my right leg from the hip, my bad knee refusing to flex. James walks ahead of me, leaning into a northerly wind, his feet chugging like steam engines, breaking the deep snow to make my going a little easier.

He says that his "new" construction boots are pure torment. "It's an old story, I know," he complains, "but they absorb water like sponges, they chafe my bad ankle, there's no padding left in the soles.... I can't bear to wear them much longer.

"What's that old proverb—" he says, "`Don't judge a man till you've walked a mile in his shoes?'"

Beneath an overpass we pause to catch our breath. On one of the walls are two graffiti in close juxtaposition, the first spray-painted in bold block letters, the second in a trembling scrawl:

SAGE

Evil Never Dies

From my pocket I take the pencil Olga gave me yesterday; the pencil that could never redraw her missing eyebrows. Kneeling, I gently press it down into a low drift of fresh snow that's blown under the bridge.

May you walk hand in hand with the ancestors, Olga.

CITIZENS

Snow has fallen throughout the day like flour sifting from heaven. Schools have been canceled and civic events postponed, but thankfully the federal district courthouse is still doing business. That's all that matters, to me. This afternoon, almost twenty years after he left China, the land of his birth, my husband will be sworn in as an American citizen.

Approaching the federal courthouse, I spot Ron, a dear old friend, clumping up the sidewalk in his rubbers, shoulders hunched against the wind. Braving the weather and hazardous roads, he and his wife will be among those attending the naturalization ceremony. Overjoyed to see a familiar face, I wait at the courthouse steps, scarcely able to contain myself. But he walks right by me, as if I weren't there, and starts to climb the steps.

"Sir," I say, "do you have a quarter you can spare?"

Graffiti beneath a dark overpass

He turns back. Peers at me. "Is that *you?*" he exclaims.

Once through the doors and metal detectors, Ron and I hurry to join other friends in the hall outside the courtroom. I imbibe their good will. Everybody's excited for Jihong, already seated inside. Loved ones of other citizens-to-be are clustered around us, laughing and chattering in a babble of languages.

A court official ushers all the spectators into the courtroom. My eyes scan the crowded seats. Jihong's up front, in the second row of immigrants, looking dapper in the black double-breasted wool suit he wore at our wedding, five years ago. Seated with him are forty people from twenty-one nations, each of them a story, each of them making a new home.

How far this federal courtroom seems from that Ohio State classroom where Jihong and I first met. Though he already held a doctorate in chem-

istry, he'd enrolled in a composition course I'd been assigned to teach, wanting, he said, to improve his writing skills. During the term, I gradually,
unwittingly, fell in love with him, seduced by his essays about his childhood,
sometimes funny, sometimes sweet, always thoughtful and fluent. Now the
boy who had celebrated the Chinese new year by engaging in firecracker
battles with his friends, lighting the wick of each pao-zhang with the glowing
tip of a cigarette—that boy stands here a man, raising his right hand on what
was once the alien side of the world.

No firecrackers in my pocket today, Sweetie, but a small American flag found in a
dumpster. Welcome to freedom.

BOSOM

Everywhere, ponds of street slush. Dirty snowdrifts have clogged the sewer
drains; the salty runoff has nowhere to go. Careful as I am, watching my every
step, my socks are wringing wet. So much for plastic-bag liners.

Coming to St. Mary Catholic church in German Village, James and I slip
inside to rest, reflect, and lay prayerful hands on our ailing bodies. The sanctuary is empty. We sidle into pews halfway up the aisle, remove our hats, our
gloves, our coats.

Silence.

Yank off our shoes.

Silence.

This isn't like the silence of a library—you feel the difference profoundly.
Silence in a library has to do with absence: the absence of noise, of outward
distractions. It's built on rules, on submission to custom and its custodians,
those kindly librarians who *shhhhh!* at you over their reading glasses like
serpents licking dust. If you were somehow to find yourself alone in a library
after closing hours, everybody else gone home, you'd break this silence
without much thought, muttering to yourself as you searched the stacks,
reading a poem aloud with verve, exclaiming at an insipid editorial, even
grinding your new pencil down to a stub in the sharpener, just for the grating
sound of it.

In an empty church, like this one, on this late Tuesday afternoon, the
silence is different. It's all about presence. Presence you can't name for what it
truly is; presence you can't see, but you can feel, if you bring your heart across
the threshold from the world outside the door.

This church could just as easily be a synagogue, or a mosque, or a temple—
any place you consider holy—it isn't a religion that you meet here, necessarily,
but yourself, and that inexpressible Mystery which lies beyond you, of which
you're the merest of parts. This presence requires reverence, not obedience.
There's no need for rules, no need for enforcement. You're alone, nobody's

around to hear—still you don't talk, except in the barest of whispers. You don't walk around, except to go and kneel at the shrine, and light two small candles, though you've no donation to make but your prayers. Prayers for things beyond words and even thought. Prayers of the open heart.

This silence is alive. It creates itself, one moment to the next, and makes possible a change.

Silence—

Two people meet for the first time. Maybe for the only time. What fills the fragile space between them? What do they offer each other in the silence—absence, or presence? Reverence?

Afternoon light is dying. Above us rises Mother Mary, in stained glass, hands crossed over her bosom.

DOMESTICITY

Tonight is laundry night; our first in three weeks. Pinching our pennies, we should be able to afford one load of laundry a week from now on.

In a dingy laundromat on South High, we play avoid the roach while stuffing our gamy clothes into a washing machine. The small tub won't hold all of them; we could easily make three or four loads. Time for hard choices.

The machines eat our quarters like slot machines, but finally some of our clothes are clean and dry, sparking with static. Domestic joy bubbles up as I sort and fold.

DAY 22

WEDNESDAY, MARCH 10

NO NEED

Yesterday afternoon, with eight inches of new snow on the ground, my spirits were as low as they've been since my first night on the streets. I asked James if the weather was affecting his mood. He said no, and for the rest of the day I leaned on his strength, as he sometimes leans on mine. Rarely are both of us depressed at the same time.

This morning I'm much better. All things pass.

Living in the outdoors has made me more attentive to things from which I'm insulated, or distracted, in my other life: a few degrees' drop in temperature; a slight shift in the wind, or its lying down a little; the one cardinal trilling amidst a squabble of crows; the way a gray sky modulates from slate to smoky to mottled to pale; how the sun doesn't rise all at once, but slivers over the horizon, just when the cold is coldest; how cold in your body can begin to burn like heat; how when your fingers slip from tingly to numb, suddenly you can't distinguish cold from wet—

In any one day are many days, in any one hour many hours. No need to be patient, waiting for change to come. It's already here.

LEGAL TENDER

According to our sometimes unreliable "Street Card," an information sheet for homeless people obtained from the library, three medical facilities in the city will provide health care at no charge. Maybe one of them will supply an elastic wrap or brace for my ailing right knee.

I'll use the phone here at JOIN, where local calls of three minutes are permitted, free. Arriving before the doors have opened, I sit wearily on the floor of the crowded foyer. Before long an argument breaks out between a homeless guy named Winfield and a sequined cross-dresser who delights in provoking him. I haven't seen the cross-dresser before, but Winfield shows up nearly every morning at McDonald's on Broad, toting a leather satchel full of photocopied documents and handwritten notes. Pages and pages. I've heard him say that he's on the run from the feds and the tobacco companies, who he believes have put out a contract on his life. He spends his afternoons in the law library at Ohio State, researching his rights.

With a linebacker's body, an attorney's intellect and a black preacher's tongue, Winfield isn't somebody you soon forget. You're just not sure he's sane.

In their battle of words, the two black men notice me listening. (In the cramped foyer you can't *not* listen, but everybody else is pretending not to hear.) They begin to play up to me. I haven't a clue what they're arguing about; it's the intensity in their eyes, their voices, that has me hooked. Sometimes, though, a whole sentence, or even a cluster of thoughts, sneaks through the crazy bombast, making complete, even elegant, sense.

Now the cross-dresser says to me, "Life's all about money, don't you agree?"

I gesture helplessly.

Winfield pulls out a dollar bill and snaps it smooth in front of my eyes. "What does this say? Do you *see*, miss? `Legal Tender.' *Legal. Tender.*" He laughs scornfully. "As if anything we're asked to do for money is *tender*. Sometimes it isn't legal, either. Just ask the tobacco companies. All for this!" He waves the bill dramatically, then stuffs it deep in his pocket.

"But here's the thing, miss." He points the silver grip of his cane right at my nose. "Human life is far more valuable than money. *Far* more. Money can always be retrieved if you lose it. Life—it's just plain *gone*."

Several streets away, James is circling a puddle of slush. He notices a $20 bill floating in the gutter. Picking it up by a corner, he shakes off the water and glances around for a pedestrian who might have dropped it. Nobody.

Helplessly he stares at the wet bill. For four weeks he hasn't had more than a couple bucks on him at any one time. Now he doesn't know what to do.

Finally he puts the money in his pocket. Walking up the street, he imagines the look on my face when he shows it to me. He pictures us in a High Street drugstore buying elastic wraps for his ankle and my knee. He fantasizes about buying tickets to a movie, one night when it's whipping cold; maybe even getting a big tub of hot buttered popcorn; maybe even hopping a city bus to the theater and back....

DOCTORING

I dial a hospital, the first number listed on my Street Card. A recording tells me to call back between certain hours to arrange a rendezvous with a mobile medical unit. *Too much bother*, I decide, *for them and for me.*

The second number is a free clinic at the Columbus Health Department. "The clinic's only open," I'm told, "on Monday nights." *What day is this?* I wonder. I decide it must be Wednesday. Almost a week's wait.

I dial the last number on my list. A nurse informs me that no elastic wrap or brace can be dispensed without my first seeing a doctor. Would I care to make an appointment?

I thank the nurse for her time and hang up. I don't want to answer a doctor's inevitable questions about who I am, why I'm on the streets, what happened to my knee.

I guess I'll have to follow James's lead and doctor myself from a dumpster. Every morning he wraps his sore ankle in a length of blue plastic discovered in somebody's trash.

MEAT

Over full food trays at Holy Family Soup Kitchen James and I chat with Morris. My acquaintance with him dates back to McDonald's on Broad, that morning after my first night on the streets. I didn't know his name then; he was just a graybeard with glasses who thought it wise to take life one day at a time. Soon after, James met him at the Bexley shelter. These past weeks, we've eaten with him several times here at the soup kitchen, but we haven't seen him in a while. Today he's full of stories, not all of them easy on the ears. We struggle to listen without passing judgment.

"I'm sorry, what's your name again?" Morris asks James, for the dozenth time since they've met. When James reminds him, Morris smiles through his beard. "Oh, that's right."

My name he always remembers.

"This beard," he says, "sometimes I get tired of it, but I just don't look like me without it. I shaved it off once and my family didn't know me. Besides, my granddaughter likes to play with it."

"Do you see your family often?" James asks.

"No, not really."

James pushes back his chair and leaves the table to use the restroom.

Morris watches him wend his way through the crowded cafeteria and disappear into the hallway.

Now, from across the table, he fixes his gaze on me. For a long minute neither of us speaks. Somehow I sense what's coming. I work harder at buttering my dinner roll.

"There's something I want very much," he says finally, his voice like putty, "but I don't have the money right now."

I bite into my bread. He waits. Finally I'm tired of the feel of his eyes. "What's that, Morris?"

"A nice young woman like you."

I chew, refusing to say a word, or even to look at him. He begins to fidget. The silence thickens till at last he seems to realize he's overstepped. "But—I want—I want you to know," he stammers, "that I appreciate your—and James's—company very much."

"Thank you, Morris." Now I look him straight in the eye, just as James returns to the table.

This isn't the first time I've rebuffed a man since hitting the streets. Here at the soup kitchen, where there's maybe one woman to every nine men, I often feel like a side of beef hanging from a meat hook, prepared for inspection by wolves. James and I are assumed to be a couple, and this affords me a measure of security. When he isn't with me, the stares become more brazen, the comments more suggestive, the brushes against my body more frequent, less accidental. Still, James isn't with me to be my bodyguard. Coolly, deliberately, I try to keep my distance from every man I meet. This is probably the best course, but I can't help feeling ambivalent, knowing how easily prudence can turn into hardness of heart.

LIGHTPROOF

James sits under a busy overpass, changing the photo paper in his pinhole camera. On the walls all around him, Fuck Yous and garish demon faces. Fear lurks here, waiting to pounce on shaky confidence and bland hope. His fingers fumble in the lightproof bag.

PAIN AND WONDER

Thumbing through a back issue of the *Columbus Dispatch*, I run across a comment attributed to a director of one of the city's homeless shelters. She maintains that if you aren't mentally ill when you hit the streets, you soon will be. At first her statement offends me. Then I think of how I've been beset by claustrophobia and panic attacks, and how bouts of depression sometimes drag James and me down—

An Anglo struts across the room. The back of his jacket reads "PAIN AND WONDER, Athens, Georgia." The name of a business, probably, but "pain and wonder" is also an apt description of our experience, living in the between.[5]

MODESTY

This evening I meet Ada Martin for the first time. Sitting in her Blazer, she looks younger than her forty-nine years, and fairly robust, considering how ill she's been. According to the *Dispatch*, this well-known angel to the homeless needs a heart-lung transplant.

"You doing okay?" she asks sweetly. "There anything you need?"

We talk tampons. I have little modesty left.

DROUGHT

My body's in drought. I've never felt such an intense longing to be touched. To be comforted by even just an arm around my shoulders, a hand to hold, or fingers stroking my mussed hair....

DAY 23

THURSDAY, MARCH 11

CRAVE ZONE

6:30 AM. Hardly slept last night. Yesterday's *Dispatch* had predicted the overnight temperature would drop to fifteen degrees. It might have gone even lower. My bladder complained, sent me five times out to the bucket.

Street people are traipsing into White Castle to get warm. Posted all around us are bright ads, reminding us (as if we need reminding) that we're in "The Crave Zone." I open the morning paper.

In my other life I rarely read a newspaper. There's no need, the important news still seems to reach me. But out here I want the paper. Reading its pages seems a basic necessity, a tenuous connection to a larger world from which I feel terribly removed. Every morning I hang around this joint, hoping some customer will leave a *Dispatch* behind. Today somebody did. Actually this same customer, a distinguished older black man who keeps the sections in order and refolds them precisely when he's finished, has let me have his newspaper the last two days. This morning he even walked across the room to hand it to me. Smiled, didn't say a word.

I twist in my seat, trying to get comfortable. On my way here I took a bad fall on glare ice, landing squarely on my tailbone. My body is taking a beating.

Two articles in today's *Dispatch* warrant more than casual attention. In the first, concerning Operation Feed, an annual food drive benefiting local pantries and soup kitchens, I learn that while the Columbus metropolitan area has a booming economy and a record-low 3% unemployment rate, it also has a 17% poverty rate. Lots of jobs, in other words, but too low-paying to meet the bills. Most of the higher-paying jobs are concentrated in the suburbs, far from the people who need them most; so far, in fact, that the city bus lines don't even run there.

The second article reports on a recent survey of homeless families. Asked to identify the primary causes of their plight, they most often cited eviction, loss of income, relationship problems, and lack of affordable housing. The basic reason for homelessness, according to this study, is poverty—not, as commonly believed, mental illness or substance abuse, which affect homeless people only at about the same rate as the general population.

TRASH

Opening the lid of a dumpster at the corner of Naghten and Church, James finds it nearly empty of trash, so he crawls in and lowers the lid after him. He doesn't like to change photo paper out in the open. Too conspicuous.

A sliver of light penetrates the crack under the dumpster lid. Inspired, he and his wide-angle camera play with that little light as if they're best friends. He experiments with various exposures and angles, bracing the camera first between his knees, then against the side of the dumpster. Leg muscles cramp. Butt and hips fall asleep.

After each shot he must change the photo paper—a time-consuming process, but worth the effort. He likes the symbolism of light, especially since hitting the streets. If he's lucky, one of these shots will actually be usable, but using pinhole photography, the odds are against it. In a week's batch of twenty-five or thirty negatives, only two or three ever turn out.

Propping open the dumpster lid just a tad, he notices an American flag billowing in the wind across the alley. What a vantage point from which to shoot it! He holds his camera for an exposure of around twenty seconds, not daring to move lest he blur the image. As he waits, stock-still, he reflects on how often he's been treated like trash since hitting the streets. Now, lounging atop the few trash-bags in this dumpster, he's surprisingly comfortable, and safe from eyes that skewer—

Suddenly the dumpster lid opens. A woman is ready to toss in her garbage. Clumsily he rises to stop her, stammering an apology. She jumps back with a scream and runs, spilling her bags on the ground.

FRAMES

James calls the workplace of one of his darkroom assistants to arrange a photo swap. The two of them rendezvous every couple weeks so he can exchange his new negatives for the prints she's produced from his earlier shots. These prints he'll study carefully, evaluating the performance of his cameras.

At the moment his darkroom assistant is away from her desk. He asks the receptionist on the other end of the line for directions to their office building.

"We're located in German Village," she says, "near Wasserstrom, near Banana Joe's—"

Given their general location, he must walk past these establishments almost every day, yet he can't place them. His frame of reference, his landmarks, are totally different from the receptionist's.

"Where's your office from the Salvation Army?"

PATRONS

A small, third-floor reading room in Main Library, with a window view. Outside, a white-out.

Alone in the room, James and I take off our shoes so our burning feet can breathe. As I seat myself at the lone table and pull *The Crucible* from my pocket, he lies down on the floor with an anthology of Pablo Neruda's poetry, propping his sore legs on a chair. His bad ankle is throbbing and tight; the ball of his foot, tender. He reaches to probe it, ever so gently, and his right shoulder pops. It's been doing that a lot lately, with noticeable pain.

A security guard appears, purposefully, as if he's been dispatched. "I'm going to have to ask you to get off the floor," he says to James, his tone flat.

As James rouses himself, the guard, a stocky black man, looks from our stockinged feet to the book in my hand, then back to our feet. I can see he's of divided mind. Our casual behavior has violated library custom. He should make us leave the building, but....

Show him you're a responsible patron, I tell myself. I lower my eyes to my book and conspicuously turn a page.

The guard makes his decision. "Both of you put your shoes back on," he says firmly, then moves on, giving us a break. He casts an uneasy glance at us over his shoulder.

SPOTLIGHT

Back at our shelter, James and I are about to blow out our candles for the night when we hear voices carrying down through the woods. They're calling our names.

"Take It to the Streets. Has to be."

"Shouldn't visiting hours be over by now?"

Neither of us is anxious to get out of bed. With reluctance James pulls some clothes over his long johns and starts slipping on his workboots.

Now, from right outside our door, Harold Martin's voice. Startled, James lifts the plastic flaps to crawl out of the shelter, only to be blinded by a cluster of dazzling lights. Screening his eyes, he struggles to his feet, bewildered.

"Hi, James!" says a chorus of voices.

Long seconds pass. James senses expectation in the air, as if he might perform some sad song and dance. He waits, unmoving, in the glare of the lights. Finally Harold Martin clears his throat and begins reading a list of supplies the group has brought us tonight, including two gently used ski suits he's very proud of.

"Where's Phyllis?" he asks then.

"Lying down," James says, still wondering about the lights.

Harold calls in to me, says he'd like me to come outside. Frustrated, James leans down to lower one of the plastic flaps over our door. "She's tired. It's late."

Harold hesitates, then slips James a small paper bag. Tampons.

Suddenly James notices a small red light next to one of the big bright ones. Now he knows. Anger rises hot. He's being videotaped, "homeless man being helped on the riverbank." Part of him would like to smash the camera he still can't see against a tree.

He swallows hard and holds out his hands for the supplies and ski suits. Then, mumbling some quick Thank yous and Good nights, he hastily retreats into our shelter.

DAY 24

FRIDAY, MARCH 12

DREAMS

At a nearby table in White Castle, Jake and Rooster are mulling over the classifieds. No longer fighting, it seems. They hope to scrape together enough money soon to rent a cheap apartment. Florida's a dead dream.

"I'm tired of this shit," Jake says to me. "A person just can't keep living like this. Hell, I've lived all over. Always on the move. But you get tired of not having the simple conveniences—a phone, a shower, a stove, a fridge, some heat. You end up losing your self-respect." He tips his head in my direction. "*You* know what I'm saying."

"You and James," Rooster says, "you make sure to move into my tent once I'm out. Then the Professor can move into *your* place. You guys need to be warm. Need to be able to stand up and move around." He says nothing about Enid, his "old lady." Maybe she's no longer in the picture.

"Let the Professor have your place," I say. "James and I are warm enough. Besides, our shelter's *cozy*."

Rooster and Jake exchange a glance, then laugh loudly. I blush.

They toss me the rest of their newspaper. An article on the effects of welfare reform explains how difficult it is for poor people to obtain health care coverage. No longer covered by Medicaid, they can't afford to self-insure, and they rarely receive benefits at work. Those who suffer most, as a result, are the children.

The children.

Fact: If you're a child in this country, you have a one in five chance of growing up poor. More than fourteen million American children live in poverty, and that number's rising.

Fact: If you're a child living in poverty in this country, you're four times more likely to die from disease than a child who isn't. You're also much more likely to suffer from malnutrition and other serious health problems. In short, you need medical attention more than most, and you're among the least likely to get it—

The children.

The other day, in the restroom at Holy Family Soup Kitchen, two little girls were talking in the stall next to mine. One said to the other, "My family's got a place now—it's got an upstairs and *everything*! We're going to have so much fun!"

AARON

Two guys sitting next to James in the soup kitchen are rapping about their struggles with alcohol. The black guy says how he's staying away from the booze now. The white guy wants to quit, too. He says he's been sober for three days and is feeling pretty good, but he's still afraid he won't make it.

The black man leaves the table. To the Anglo—short, finely bearded, maybe in his fifties—James offers a pamphlet listing Twelve-Step meetings held all over the city.

"What's this?" the fellow says. "Some kind of book? I can hardly read, man."

"These are meetings for people who want to quit drinking. Meetings have helped me a lot. You ever gone to one?"

"Oh yeah, I been to some." He's not convincing.

James briefly describes what it's like, working the Steps. Then, on inspiration, he asks the man where he plans to go, now that he's finished lunch. The fellow says he wants to get a bed for the night at a nearby shelter.

"I'm headed that direction, too," James says. "Let's go!"

He sees me throw him a guarded look, as if to say, "Slow down, don't push it." But he's too wrapped up in the prospect of helping the man to catch himself.

Once he's out the door, he says, "I'm James, by the way."

"Aaron," the man replies, shaking hands.

TREES

Aaron is limping badly. "Got hit by a car three weeks ago," he tells James. "Least, that's what they told me when I come to. I got to go see the doctor—

the shelter's getting me in to see somebody in a couple days. Should have been killed, the way that car hit me."

"Sounds like it wasn't your time."

"Yeah. I ain't ready to go yet. I want to see my granddaughter. My son don't want me around her till I clean up my act."

"You know, Aaron, I used to drink. I was a mess. But I haven't had a drink in over two years now. I just needed to believe there was something greater than me that could help."

"Myself, I believe in Jesus. But I ain't so right with him now." Aaron thinks a minute. "Could a tree be something greater?"

"As long as you can find strength in it."

He brightens. "A tree. Yeah, I know some big old trees that's been around longer than me."

"Aaron, if you go to those meetings in that pamphlet, they can help. I can help you, too. But you got to want to stay sober."

"Yeah, I want to."

"You don't have to go through this alone. There are lots of people who've been where you are and made it through. They'll help you out."

By now they've reached the homeless shelter. "Think about it," James says. "If you want, I'll come by sometime and talk to you some more. Take care, buddy."

"Yeah. You too."

Walking away, James is so charged up that he scarcely notices the drug dealers working the corner.

BROTHERS

James's latest fashion: black Everlast sneakers, culled once again from a box at JOIN. Lightweight, an exact fit. Walking's a cinch now, but he'll keep his construction boots, just till he's sure.

Back on the riverbank he strolls over to Jake and Sarge's to ask if we might borrow a pan. Their campsite is very neat and organized: one trash-bag for empty bottles, another for paper and garbage. A small grill sits between two plastic chairs puddled with rainwater.

He raps on the door of the shack. "Hey guys, it's James."

Jake invites him inside. Sarge clears away some clutter so he can sit down. The place smells like an old station wagon—musty, lived-in, stale with cigarette smoke. Jake and Sarge each light a cigarette on the flame of their gas stove, and soon they're bantering like brothers, needling each other, poking fun. James feels good, laughing with them and getting better acquainted, especially with Sarge. Up till now, he's struck James as not so friendly, but now he just seems rather shy, even oafish, with a droll sense of humor that catches you by surprise.

James asks how they built their place. Sarge rolls his eyes.

"It was a bitch," Jake says, with a smoker's yellow smile.

SOBERING UP

"I've got to slow down with Aaron," James tells me, warming leftover noodles from Grubb Street for our supper. "I was too excited today, too zealous, as if in an instant I might get him to turn his life around."

Getting sober hadn't taken James very long. Naturally he wants the same for Aaron, so this afternoon he'd leapt in with both feet, trying to help. He says he'd even considered the possibility of becoming Aaron's sponsor and leading him through as many of the Steps as possible before we go home on April 4. But for most addicts getting sober is a long and torturous process. Nobody can force the change, or speed it up. "Everything's up to Aaron," he says. "While we're together, I'll be as present to him as I can. Beyond that, I'll hope, and I'll pray, but I have to let go of the outcome."

Compassion requires dispassion—we talk about this at length. The deeper our compassion, the more our efforts to alleviate the sufferings of others are grounded in calm, impartial concern. We're neither excited by success nor disappointed by failure, being detached from the outcome of our actions. We have no expectations. We don't interfere, or impose our will. We don't rush, don't grasp, don't force, don't pry. We give nourishment without trying to grow the plant. We give guidance without trying to take over the journey.

Being present to another person, having compassion for him, doesn't mean living his life. We have to set boundaries in the relationship; otherwise, our spirit bleeds out, and his seeps in, till neither of us has a center from which to choose or act. But what boundaries are appropriate? Where does the wisdom and energy come from to maintain them?

There are no ready-made answers. Even good intentions won't ensure we'll act for the best. So we must practice, practice, practice. Day by day, we must try to cultivate more integrity, empathy, courage and smarts, gaining from our errors in judgment, our fumbles and muffs. Day by day, we must learn to walk with people instead of trying to carry them, disciplining our minds to recognize the difference and our spirits to live it.

Compassion, in this deep sense, might seem more a spiritual ideal than a livable ethic, but we've have known a few individuals who have grown to embody it. They're not perfect—they still make their share of mistakes—but they're utterly devoted to the well-being of the world. They enter the suffering of others with neither pity nor pride. Their caring is tireless and humble. They have nothing to prove, no goal to reach, no timetable to follow. They've learned to listen when it seems time to listen, to speak when it's time to speak, to march when it seems time to march, to sit still when it's time to sit still. Everything in its season.

Such people are our spiritual elders. We follow their light through the dark dark wood, stumbling over what remains hidden.

DAY 25

SATURDAY, MARCH 13

HOME MOVIE

Today has turned out to be family day, organized by Jihong. James's father is flying in from New York City. My parents are driving in from Kentucky, five hours south, and my younger brother is coming from two hours north with his family. All of them, plus Jihong, will be at the Statehouse during noontime meditation. Afterwards, we'll have a reunion behind closed doors at the Agora.

James and I both feel ambivalent about seeing our relatives; the inevitable questions, the impossible answers, all mingled with terrible longings for which we have no words. We'll still be the loved ones our families remember, yet in many ways strangers, too, just as they'll be to us.

Scenes of the impending reunion play like a jiggly home movie across the screen of my mind, all in black and white: the touches, the hugs, the hand-holding, the searching eyes—and then somebody says, "Haven't you had enough? Isn't it time to come home?", and I have to muster the strength to tell them, "No, the Thing isn't done with me yet."

UPSCALE

James is waiting in McDonald's on South High for his father. They've arranged to meet privately over breakfast. He's leafing through some stray sections of the *Dispatch* when, to his dismay, our neighbor Calvin settles down with his own newspaper at the very next table.

Calvin looks intently at the pages, but his eyes don't move. He doesn't seem to be reading; more like he's acting a part, wanting to fit in. Every so often he glances nervously around the room. He isn't in a hurry.

James's father arrives promptly at 9:30. "Hey, Turks," he grins, leaning down for a hug, but James jumps up and quickly leads him past Calvin's table and out the door.

"Sorry, Dad, but we need to get out of this neighborhood. I know too many people."

Once in the rental car they exchange a quick embrace. "Your nose is red," his father says. "You've got that 'homeless boozer' look."

"It's from the sun and wind."

They drive to Katzinger's, a faddish deli in German Village. Nobody will recognize James here. Too upscale. The place is warm with the aromas of baked goods just out of the oven and specialty coffees, freshly brewed. Standing in line at the counter, James's father wants to buy him breakfast, as well as food for later. Though grateful, James declines his offer and instead purchases a cup of coffee with street change. He and I had asked family members and friends never to bring us money, food, supplies or other forms of help while we were on the streets.

"What do you *do* with yourself all day?" his father asks, once they're settled at a table. "You must have a lot of time to *think?*"

James smiles a little. *How familiar, he thinks, your tone of voice, your pattern of speech. I've missed our talks—missed you—more than I realized. Out here, I've tried not to think much about you. Thinking about anybody I love just makes the distance between us more painful.*

Now, how to tell you what you want to know? How to tell you that most of my time and energy, every day, goes just to walking—to a gas station to clean up, to the soup kitchen to eat, to the library to get warm? How to tell you that I don't spend too much time reflecting, because I'm just too tired, too hungry, too raw? How to tell you that I'm gradually losing myself—that I see ghosts of me hanging around the State-house, the alleyways, the churches, the tracks—I can't call those ghosts back home, and I can't scare them off—I don't know who I am—

SCORCHED

For me, the reunion's over. All the touching, all the tears, all the catching up on family news, all the questions—over. I'm dried up. Scorched like a tea kettle left too long on the stove.

Back at camp I replenish our pile of kindling and build a slow fire. Then, using a jagged piece of brick, I work at scraping the charred remains of last night's noodles out of our cookpot. The labor is simple, requiring attention but not thought. Just what I need.

I'm nearly finished when Jake shows up, drunk, with an armload of fire-wood. Clumsily he deposits the pieces on our modest woodpile. They're just the right size for our grill.

Waving off my thanks, he makes a move to go, then turns back. "You know," he says, in a sweet tipsy slur, "anytime you want to get warm or anything, just come on over. Me and Sarge, we got a little propane heater. Gets real toasty. Besides, I don't want to scare you or nothing, but I worry about you being alone over here. If you ever get scared, just come on over and sit with us."

"I appreciate that, Jake."

"I *mean* it. It's rough out here. You know that, well as anybody. It's good, you sticking by your man through thick and thin. I know it's a little thin right now, but if you hang in there, it'll get better."

"Thanks, Jake." *You're a brother.*

"So if anybody ever bothers you over here, you just holler, and me and Sarge'll be right over to chase them off. You remember that."

SOLIDARITY

Well after dark, four carloads of volunteers begin to make their rounds of the camps. Hungry, waiting alone by the fire, I grudgingly realize that I've begun to depend on these food drops, made mostly on Thursday and Saturday nights. The volunteers are usually under the supervision of Sabrina Martin, daughter of Harold and Ada. Sometimes her parents show up, too, but they can't be everywhere at once. Their organization delivers food all over the city.

Tonight, Anglos from an evangelical church. People from this same church come every Saturday, always with the same bag of rations for each of us: Christian literature, a pair of socks, two Nutri-Grain bars, a large bottle of vitamin C tablets, several four-ounce cartons of both fruit drink and expired milk. For the most part, these are things we don't need. Tomorrow, as usual, we'll throw out the sour milk, then consolidate the remaining contents of our two bags of goodies and tote them to a soup kitchen. We'll quietly leave them there on a hallway table for others to claim.

"Is James looking for work?" one of the men inquires now, offering me a pack of cigarettes, which I refuse.

"Yeah. I am, too."

"So what kind of work's he looking for?"

"Honest."

The group erupts in laughter. When they calm down, they pray briefly for James's quick success in finding a job.

"Will you guys be at next Saturday's camp-out?" somebody asks after the Amen.

I stifle a laugh (*isn't every day a camp-out?*). "What camp-out do you mean?"

"Harold and Ada's sponsoring an overnighter. All the street people and volunteers are going to spend the night together at Mad Dog's place, on up the tracks. There'll be food, and a bonfire, and a big-screen TV—everybody's invited. Even some TV people."

"Is that so?" I'm wondering if anybody had consulted Mad Dog before planning this shindig. Whoever Mad Dog is.

"Yeah. It's supposed to give us volunteers a taste of what it's like to be homeless, and also allow us to express our solidarity with people like you."

"Uh-huh." I glance around the group. "So, you all going to be there?"

The confessions start rolling out, all the reasons they won't be able to make it. Scheduling conflicts. "Such short notice, you know." Some in the group seem genuinely regretful, others appear relieved.

"Well," I say, "James and I probably won't make it either. We're not into crowds."

THIS IS HOME

A stout white woman traipses down the path and introduces herself as Kate. Quite the cook, she has baked some homemade lasagna, served up with dinner rolls in foam containers. She has also prepared a special box of supplies for James and me: peanut butter, pork and beans, baby sausages, tapered and votive candles, two glass candle holders, four rolls of toilet paper, a tube of Colgate, tampons, several disposable razors, shaving cream, feminine body wash....

"I've been thinking of you two all week," she says tearfully, "wondering what I could bring you."

Her thoughtfulness moves me deeply. Many of these supplies James and I will actually be able to use. "Are you with the same church as the others?" I ask, making conversation.

She bristles. "*No, I'm not!* I don't even like being *associated* with them. They just *barge in* on folks, not knowing what kind of mood you're in or anything, and then they're upset when one of you gets *mad*." She stares at our shelter. "I mean, *this* is your *home*...."

DAY 26

SUNDAY, MARCH 14

COME AS YOU ARE

Five minutes late for breakfast at Central Presbyterian. This serving line for poor and homeless people runs on strict middle-class church time, not come-as-you-are street time, but the scowling door monitor admits James and me anyway. We hurry to the serving windows in Fellowship Hall, trying to catch our breath, faces bright red. White ladies with silver-gray hair ladle sausage gravy over hot biscuits, adding extra when they hear how far we walked in the bitter cold to get here.

At least we weren't plodding through snow. The weatherman had predicted a big storm overnight. Counties just south of the city are socked in under eighteen inches. Here it's nippy, but not a flake.

Over breakfast we sit with our neighbor Blue and his new friend Elena. She's been staying with him in his shack up the tracks since being beaten and robbed four days ago. If I don't look at the bruises on her tanned face, she closely resembles an old friend of mine—her eyes are soft but bright, her middle-aged body earthy and lithe, her presence full, even now, under the influence of alcohol—but of course I can't look at her face and not see the bruises.

Blue's tender with her, and protective. She touches him with affection. The sight makes my heart ache. You don't see many people touching each other with tenderness out here. You don't see many people touching.

Elena says, with great calm, that she's used to roughing it; that not so long ago she was living in the mountains of New Mexico with no running water, no indoor plumbing, no heat. Her voice is gentle, like an old love song.

A youth group is visiting from a suburban Presbyterian church. While we eat breakfast, one of their members wanders among the crowded tables like a minstrel, strumming a mellow guitar. Then, to begin worship, the group leader reads the gospel story of the rich young man who goes to Jesus, says he's been keeping all the commandments, asks what else he must do to have eternal life. Jesus tells him to sell his possessions, give the proceeds to the poor, and follow. Not exactly what the guy wanted to hear.

Ordinarily at this point the minister would tell us "congregants" what the scripture passage means. But this morning he isn't here. The visiting youth group invites a discussion instead. Several homeless people venture opinions about the text, arguing its implications with the vigor of seminarians. The exchange is refreshing. For a change, nobody seems in a rush to leave.

"God isn't opposed to people having possessions," says a passionate young black man named Michael, getting in the last word. "God's opposed to people *losing* themselves *to* their possessions. It isn't materials but *materialism* that gets in the way of our faithfulness."

Prayers, now. With no minister to speak on our behalf, the young people encourage us to pray aloud the prayers we want to pray. The petitions are few, brief, simple, poignant. Elena's voice is so soft, her prayer seems hardly meant for hearing by human ears. "Our loving Father," she pleads, each word measured and grave, "I ask you for guidance. Show me which direction I should go."

The tables empty. James and I stand up, don our coats, shake hands with Blue and Elena. But for Elena, shaking hands isn't enough. She hugs me, hangs on, sags. I struggle to hold her up. One of her tears moistens my lower cheek.

Blue reaches out, gathers her in. I struggle to let her go. "Got to take care of each other," she mumbles as Blue shores her up and leads her slowly toward the door.

So many of the folks we meet out here say the most tender things; some, even as they're killing themselves, slow as gin.

On a car parked outside the church, a vanity plate: HUMAN FRM.

TRACES

Tonight I've thrown some lumps of coal into the fire; another gift from the railroad tracks. They've finally begun to glow. You smell the sooty burn before you see the smoke.

I'm writing on photocopies of old birth certificates. My dirty fingers leave black smudges on the paper, tiny lines that swirl; ephemeral prints of a body, a person, a life.

I felt very emotional today, very raw, like a wound when its scab has been torn away. At morning mass, where the priests were wearing rose-colored chasubles instead of the usual purple (a reminder, they said, that we've now entered the second half of Lent), it didn't take much to prompt my tears: the wafting frankincense; a word, any word, in the first hymn; a fleeting thought of my father, now probably back home in Kentucky, planting his new rose bushes; a priest who, shaking my hand before the service, said, "How're you doing today?", as if he genuinely wanted to know—

It doesn't take much.

James and I now have more days behind us on the streets than lie ahead. Till lately I haven't let myself think much about the end of this ordeal, but here by the fire my thoughts drift to our last day like smoke to heaven. I do so look forward to not having to struggle for everything I need; to not being deep down in the bones tired; to not being filthy; to not feeling invisible, or despised. This scant dose of anticipation I permit myself, an indulgence made possible by my life of privilege. After all, leaving home on February 17 had been entirely my choice; going home will be, too. But what of those people who have no real home to return to? To what do they look forward tonight?

Is anybody missing *them*?

Fire crackles. Overhead, a honking gaggle of geese flies in elegant silhouette across the orange-streaked lavender sky. A blue heron too lifts in flight, and suddenly I'm back in childhood, behind my family's house on the east bank of the Blanchard River, where long-legged herons, wading in the shallows, would wing away if you got too close. The sight, or the memory, makes me lay down my pen.

I'm so happy, out here, for the company of birds....

BON APETIT

James enters camp and kneels beside the fire I've kindled in the grill. Like rabbits from a hat he pulls from a sack two rounds of focaccia bread topped with cheese, tomato sauce and spices, courtesy of the Einstein Bros. dumpster. Laughing at our luck, I plop them on the grill to warm.

We're terribly grateful for any food that we can forage, or that we're given, out here. Like the biblical loaves and fishes, no matter how little we possess, somehow we always seem to have enough. Still, we feel a poverty around food that has nothing to do with quantities. It has to do with intimacy. We want more affinity with what we eat.

I want to decide what food I'll fix, and how I'll prepare it. I want to scrub and mince and dice and chop, almost slice my finger. I want to overcook the pasta and overbake the bread. I want to set the table, sit down with somebody I love, and eat slowly by candlelight, savoring each bite. Then, at meal's end, I want to clear the plates and let my hands wrinkle up red in hot, soapy dishwater....

Out here, our connection to food is almost entirely animal. We consume it to stay alive. Gratitude, yes—we feel it profoundly, and this might set us a little apart from vultures and wolves—but without apology we confess: we still desire pleasure.

This too, I believe, might make us less the beast.

ROBIN HOOD

"Jeremy! *Jeremy!*"

"Is that Rooster?" James says, with a dozy groan. The hour must be after midnight.

I prop myself on an elbow. "I think so, but who's Jeremy?"

The yelling draws closer. Rooster's crashing through the woods.

"James, he's calling *you*—he's just mixed up the names. Probably been drinking."

"Jeremy! Hey, *wake up!*"

Rooster's outside our shelter now, stomping around, hollering nonsense at the top of his lungs. Closer than James to the door, I stick my head out the flaps. "What's up?"

"Where's Jeremy?"

"If you mean *James*, he's sleeping—"

"Well *hell*, tell him to get out of bed and come on out here, see this shit I brought!"

I shove my feet into the nearest pair of shoes and crawl out, making excuses for James. As I stand up, Rooster proudly dumps a garbage bag full of packaged meat onto the frozen ground—hot dogs, sausage links, processed hams. He dances around the pile, snorting and whooping in the moonlight.

"Yessirree," he squeals, "I'm a goddamned Robin Hood! I steal from the rich, give to the poor! Going to feed every motherfucking homeless person out here!"

Apparently he's robbed a convenience store.

"I tell you, that bag was *heavy*." He flexes a bicep. "Proved to myself I'm still a young man! Hey, I'm going back for more—you guys want steaks? Old Robin Hood will get some for you—"

"Rooster, we don't want any steaks. I appreciate your thinking of us, but —" I stop in mid-sentence, not knowing how to finish.

"I'll come by later," he says, "and pick up the meat I want. How much should I leave for you guys? What'll you eat?"

"To tell you the truth, we don't need any of it. Besides, the critters—"

"*Hell*, if the critters get into it, they need it worse than you do. Look, I'll just leave you some steaks, and some hot dogs, and one of these here ten-pound hams—"

DAY 27

MONDAY, MARCH 15

LOOT

James and I want it to have been a dream, but in early morning Rooster's loot is still lying in a heap outside our door. Thankfully, no steaks.

Presumably Rooster came back last night for the meat he wanted. We stare at the remaining forty pounds, wondering what to do. Finally we bag up as many packages as we can carry and set off on the long march to the nearest soup kitchen.

JABBERWOCKIED

Walking through the downtown I'm a scarecrow in the wind. My steps seem almost to miss the ground. I don't know how to use my feet. Deliberately I pick one up, stamp it down, pick up the other, stamp it down. Carrying myself used to be so easy.

Vanity plate on a hot red sports car: ABOUT ME.

My spirits, James's too, have been low ever since Saturday. To reunite with our families, we had to pass like Alice back through the looking-glass; everything that used to be so easy and familiar there was now jabberwockied, but we stayed as long as we could, happy at least to feel loved—

Then, all at once, it was over.

The emptiness that remains is crushing.

Across the way, a shaggy mutt lies chained and dispirited in muddy snow. In the same yard two guys shoot hoops, no net on the rim. A threesome deals drugs on the corner, while a woman stares wistfully out the first-floor window of her ramshackle house, watching for a parade that will never come.

Outside police headquarters a cruiser lurches back and forth, back and forth, the cop trying to parallel park.

I walk to St. Joe's Cathedral for some uninterrupted quiet. Its lofty nave, especially when empty, never fails to soothe, lifting my spirits above the cold streets. In the vestibule, I'm dipping my fingertips into the holy water (I don't know what it means, exactly, to touch this water to my forehead, but it's customary here, and somehow a comfort) when I notice a flimsy cardboard box resting on the floor, wrapped in plastic. The box contains a few muffins and dinner rolls, and a deli bun thickly spread with chicken salad. It's the kind of food somebody might carry away from a generous soup kitchen. Whoever it belongs to must be in the nave.

I go inside, seat myself in a back pew, glance around. Nobody.

My stomach growls.

The ceiling soars.

Over the next hour or so, several parishioners come and go. After meditating I simply rest, drawing consolation from the cavernous silence and the solitude, the streets so near, so far.

Footsteps approach from the chancel. I open my eyes to see "just Sam," who, weeks ago, had given James and me sandwiches at the rectory's back door. He looks taller than I remembered.

"How are you?" he asks.

"Okay. You?"

He grimaces, moves on as he says, "Oh, you just can't *trust* some people...."

After a few minutes, he's back. "You know, there's a box of food in the entry."

"I saw that. I thought it probably belonged to somebody who'd come in here, but nobody was around."

"Tell you what, if you go out and get that food right now, it's yours."

"Really?"

"Really."

"Well, okay, but only if you remember one thing."

"What's that?"

"You can trust *me*."

He smiles a little. "I'm counting on that."

Now he tells me that "something valuable" has just been stolen from the sanctuary—"again." "You try to keep the place *open*," he says as he walks off, sounding dejected, "and this is what happens."

Watching him go, I can't help suspecting that the food James and I will eat for our supper was left behind by a thief.

Georgie, surrounded by gifts

OUR GEORGIE

James and I hike to Greenlawn Cemetery, hoping to visit a grave recently featured in the *Dispatch*. We're not prepared for the cemetery's size—four hundred acres, says the man at the cemetery office. He produces a map; more than 160,000 graves and crypts, the earliest dating to 1848. Buried among the magnificent old trees and gently curving lanes are such notables as the preacher Washington Gladden, the aviator Eddie Rickenbacker, the humorist James Thurber, and of course, George Blount. That's who we've come for. The cemetery man quickly marks the route to the boy's grave.

George Blount, 1867-1873. Died from a fall at the age of six. Perched up high on a granite chair, facing west, the boy wrecks your heart even from a distance. Tiny Tim in stone.

For years now, according to the newspaper, some lady has been dressing George Blount against the cold of winter. This year she's decked him out in a blue knit cap and matching scarf. Around him lie various offerings: pacifier, doll baby, teddy bear, box of crayons and coloring book, Christmas stocking bleached by the sun. One of his hands is full of pennies, some shiny, others copper-green.

Way over in German Village, the bells of St. Mary's are tolling, faintly. I hear but neglect to count the hour.

A foot marker reads "Our Georgie," yet the boy seems to be alone; no parents, no siblings buried in adjacent plots.

I go up to him and remove his blue cap. The elements have worn him into an old man, bald and blind. The north side of his face is dark and pitted; the south, light and smooth.

James kisses Georgie's cheek. I replace his cap, making sure his ears are covered. Whatever brought us here remains. God bless us, every one.

WORLD BEAUTIFUL

James and I are resting by the river when Rooster happens by, clean shaven, dressed up and smelling of cheap cologne. He swigs a brownbagged bottle and announces he's going to church. Somebody from the congregation will soon be picking him up.

Earlier, I'd run into him by the tracks. He was still high from last night's misadventure. "I'll be stopping by your place to pick up the rest of my meat," he told me.

"Gosh, I'm sorry, Rooster. James and I thought you'd already taken what you wanted. The meat that was still there this morning, we gave away."

"You didn't keep *none?*" He tugged his knit hat low over his eyebrows. "Well, I guess that's okay, if somebody really needed it. By the way, I'm sorry I didn't get you no steaks, but when I went back to the store, the cops showed up. I had to sneak out a window and climb up on the roof to get away."

The river invites contemplation. I perch on a boulder a little ways off from the guys, gazing on the water. Rooster, meanwhile, has James's ear.

"Dead bodies been found all around these parts," he says in a guarded voice. "They found a black guy on the other side of the river, decapitated, wearing his boxers. A couple weeks ago, a woman's body washed ashore after she jumped off the south bridge. Some fucked up shit around here."

He's been in jail twice. "The first time was down in Kentucky. I killed this teacher—a child molester. Walked right into the classroom and told all the kids to leave, then I closed the door and shot him. Called the police myself. Didn't run, you know. He deserved it. That shit just ain't right.

"The second time, some guy was robbing Enid. Nobody's going to mess with my woman. I gutted him with his own knife. A SWAT team come down here to get me—"

He breaks off the story, studies his bottle. "You know, I'd kill them both again. My dad, he told me women and children's what makes this world beautiful. Got to take care of them. Hell, if I ever raised my hand or voice to a woman, my dad, he'd come down from heaven and shoot me hisself."

HOUSEPLANS

The evening's too brisk for a fire. James and I crawl into bed, pile on the blankets, light a candle, eat a cold supper. We're jotting down notes, hoping they'll make sense the next time we read them, when car doors slam. More volunteers.

James wants to stay in bed, and I'm tempted, but at least one of us should go, out of politeness. "My turn." I'm tying my shoelaces when Harold Martin's flashlight pokes in through our door. I ask him to please wait outside.

He's brought a group from a suburban church. The volunteers hand me two styrofoam boxes. James and I aren't hungry, but in this deep-freeze weather, food keeps.

Harold's excited. "We've got a hut for you."

"What do you mean?"

"We're building you a hut. We're going to set it up next week."

Déjà vu. Last time I saw him, he was trying to give us a tent.

"Harold, please believe me, James and I are satisfied with our shelter. Give the hut to somebody else. Ask the Professor if he'd want it. He's living in a *refrigerator.*"

"We're going to give you a little heater, too," he says. He ignores all my efforts to dissuade him. "We'll talk about it later," he states finally, and leaves.

I never thought I'd be working so hard, begging somebody *not* to help.

Back inside the shelter, James and I mull things over. When did we forfeit the right to choose our own home, the kind of place in which we'd like to live? When did we become subservient to the good will of others, compelled to accept whatever they want to give us, or do for us, or make of us?

"To stop this," I say, "maybe we're going to have to lie."

We can hardly think of a time on the streets when we've told an outright lie about ourselves. Sometimes we've tweaked the truth a little, but mostly, till now, we've just allowed people the right to their assumptions about who we are and why we're here. Considering the circumstances, though, we now need a story of our own, as true as possible, that will help us deflect help we don't want in the direction of somebody else—starting, of course, with Harold's hut. By candlelight, we improvise, finally settling on a simple "come-up" tale, spun of just enough truth to salve our uneasy consciences. Since it's often presumed that, of the two of us, only James is seeking employment, we make him the story's hero: "I have a line on some work up north," he'll say. "We'll probably be leaving soon, so please give the hut to somebody who can use it more."

We'll tell the Martins our good news, next chance we get.

DAY 28

TUESDAY, MARCH 16

HANGING BY A ROPE

On our way to Grubb Street for lunch, James and I pass a crew of railroad men realigning a short section of rail. Though the change looks to be subtle, it's measured in straining muscles and the gritting of teeth. Like one's life, this track, wherever it leads, demands not only routine maintenance but careful attention and respect. Otherwise, disaster.

Further up, we cross a trestle over the river. On the south bank, suspended in a harness from a tree, a railroad man is using a chainsaw to lop off limbs grown too close to the bridge. James and I exchange a glance, recalling our first day on the streets, when city workers in Worthington were trimming saplings. That day we identified with the trees. Today we identify with the railroad man, hanging by a rope in mid-air over a swollen, muddy river, out here where nobody can see him. *What if you were to fall?*

GALLERY

Roaming back alleys in mid-afternoon, James comes to an abandoned warehouse, recently torched. The barred windows are ringed by soot. Peering into the building through a vent, he sees charred beams crisscrossing the floor, light spilling from holes in the roof. The way the stark light illuminates the space makes him want to take pictures. He shoulders his way through a stubborn door.

Melting snow drips from jagged edges of roof, creating pools of liquid sunshine on the blackened floor. The reflected sky is brilliantly blue.

His steps are measured and slow. Hardly a sound. *Careful,* he tells himself —*you might not be alone.*

A small room off to the side has been used as a shooting gallery. Syringes and crack pipes litter the floor. A tourniquet hangs off a wobbly table, like a dead man's arm off the side of a gurney.

Despite its scars, the place has an ethereal feel; captivating now, but dangerous after dark. James manages three photos before shadows creep in and send him hurrying out through the stubborn door.

BUSTED

We take the railroad tracks south out of the downtown, James shooting pictures on our way to camp. We're almost home when we spot Jake up ahead, waving his arms to get our attention.

"Hey guys, the railroad cop's coming!"

We exchange an anxious glance. *There's a railroad cop?*

We turn to look in the direction Jake's pointing. A white jeep is headed our way, bumping along over the coarse gravel between two sets of tracks.

We step off the railroad bed and walk a little ways off, trying to appear casual, pretending we're not scared of being busted.

"What should we do?" I ask James.

"Don't know."

We smile and wave as the jeep rolls up. The cop waves back, drives right on by.

We look at Jake, relieved. He's grinning, ear to ear.

"Yeah," he says when we catch up to him, "the railroad's got some cops. They drive through every so often, and if they see you walking on the tracks, they'll arrest you. Usually they give you a warning first. They especially don't like you walking over that trestle to get to Grubb Street—I been busted there. Got to be careful. It's best to walk alongside the tracks, if you're going to walk them at all."

So much for the one place we felt totally free.

PICK-UP LINE

We're almost home when another vehicle approaches us from behind. With a low western sun glinting on glass and metal, we can't make out the driver till he's right on us—Harold Martin. Ada's in the passenger seat.

"Hey," Harold says, "you want to go somewhere, maybe chill out a little?"

"We got a house," Ada says, "where we sometimes take people. Why don't you come on? You can get a bite to eat, clean up a little, watch some TV. "

Dead tired, we hesitate.

"You guys can even take showers if you want," she says.

Showers? Hallelujah! We open a rear door and climb in.

Up top, Harold stops at a gas station. As he's filling the tank, Ada twists around in her seat to say, "Oh, by the way, there's going to be some TV people at the house. You don't have to talk to them if you don't want to."

Dread spills through my gut. "I really don't want to," I say, with an emphatic echo from James.

"That's okay. I just wanted you to know they're going to be there."

Soon we're zipping through traffic. After ponderous weeks of walking, I'm unprepared for speed. I grip the handle of my door, white-knuckled. Harold turns right, veers left, shoots into the far lane, then back across, and suddenly we're out on the freeway, headed east. I blink. *How far are we going, anyway?*

"You sure you don't want to talk to the TV people?" Ada asks over her shoulder.

STORIES

"Where you from?" Ada wants to know. "How long you been on the streets? Are you on welfare? SSI? Are you looking for work? What kind?"

"Ada," I say, trying to change the subject, "how do you keep going, with all this work you do?"

"Well, of course it's the Lord, it's *always* been the Lord, but—" And now she launches into the story of all she and Harold have accomplished the past seventeen years. Much of the story is familiar. Articles have run in the paper, coverage has aired on the news, word gets around on the streets. It all started just before Thanksgiving, 1982, at a downtown skating rink that no longer exists. Harold spotted a homeless man stealing a skater's shoes, and he intervened, giving the man his own sneakers, socks and coat.

The Martins fed that man for several days. Then he disappeared. When they went looking for him, they couldn't find him, but they found many other people in the same straits. All these years later, they work with volunteers up to six nights a week, delivering food to homeless people in different areas of the city. They also collect toys for homeless kids, line up jobs for the unemployed, hold memorial services for people who have died on the streets, and run a halfway house that helps homeless people make a transition to stable housing. That house is apparently where we're headed.

"Homeless folks are *my* people," Ada says more than once. "They're my *family*. Harold and I, we don't make *any* judgments."

Harold, a factory worker, has been married to Ada, a civil service retiree, for more than thirty years. He admits wishing sometimes that they could have more time alone, especially now that they both have serious health problems, or that they hadn't spent so much of their own money on homeless people. "But then," he says, "I'm always thinking, `What if *I* was homeless? What if it was *me*?'"

"By the way," he says to us after a while, "we're going to get you guys a TV and hook it up to run off a car battery. We'll get you all set up."

I look at James, he looks at me. "Thanks," I say to Harold, "but we don't want a TV."

He stares at us in his rearview mirror. "What do you mean, *you don't want no TV?*" He shakes his head.

NAKED

Clear over on the east side of the city, in working-class Whitehall, Harold pulls into a driveway. The house itself makes no impression, I'm so anxious to be clean, but I do observe, thankfully, that we've arrived before any TV crew.

Once inside, James and I are introduced to Charles and Theo, two black men, formerly homeless, who reside at the house. Charles escorts me to an upstairs bathroom, where he provides me with a bar of hotel soap, shampoo and a towel before I finally, eagerly, close the door.

So relieved am I to strip off my dirty clothes and be naked in the heat of this room, I begin softly to cry. Nothing to hide here, and no need to hurry. I stand in front of the mirror: long straggly bangs, dark circles beneath my reddening eyes, face sunburned, windburned and pimpling, cheekbones starting to jut, lips chapped and peeling.... My vanity's shot to kingdom-come.

I lean into the glass to look closely. Scarcely any light in my eyes. That scares me a little.

I'm even thinner than I used to be; the mirror doesn't tell me this, but the vague way of my body in air. It feels light and empty, yet coarse, like a dusty burlap sack after its feed has been dumped in a hog trough.

In a downstairs bathroom, James stands naked before a cracked mirror. He hasn't seen his skin in two weeks or more. His face is red from the elements, but the rest of his body is yellow gray.

He stinks. Bad.

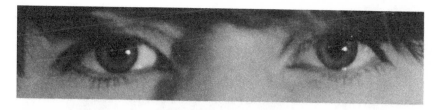

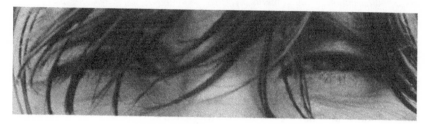

Light lost from the eyes (photo credit: Jihong Cole-Dai)

He can hear my shower running upstairs. Reaching into the tub, he turns the water on hot, then grabs a bottle of Prell from the vanity. Peeling back the cheap shower curtain, he steps into steam.

The water pressure surges and sinks; the temperature runs cold, then hot. He doesn't have a washcloth, but the water, *oh, the water....*

PRACTICALITIES

A knock on the bathroom door. Hurrying to finish dressing, I open it to Theo. He holds out a pair of high-heeled boots, flare-legged jeans and a tight sweater, all suitable for a sorority girl. Wherever they came from, they'd be impractical for the streets. He frowns when I turn them down.

"Don't worry," I tell him, laughing at the dirty clothes I'm wearing, "it's almost laundry day."

Downstairs, James has no towel. He squeegees his body with his hands. Then, still dripping, he leans down, picks up the fuzzy teal bath mat from the floor and begins to wipe....

ALIAS

I descend the stairs slowly. Channel 4 News has arrived. In the adjacent living room, bright lights are being adjusted by a cameraman. Ada's talking in low tones to a woman, heavily made up, whom I recognize as a feature reporter. Instantly uneasy, I consider retreating to the second floor, but before I can make my escape the reporter spots me on the stairs. She walks over and says she wants to interview me on camera.

"I don't want to be interviewed," I say. *So this is the reason for the change of clothes. They wanted you to look more presentable. More stylish. More like a respectable woman, for the camera.*

"This is *very* important." The reporter draws me down the steps and into the living room. James, his hair and beard dripping wet, is already sitting on the couch. The reporter stands between us—a classic "divide and conquer" tactic. "Don't you know why we're here?"

"I'm here to take a shower," I say.

"Well, let me tell you why we're doing this segment. We want to help Harold and Ada. They have to raise forty thousand dollars in the next two weeks, or this house will be repossessed by HUD."

Ada is directly behind the reporter, her eyes wide open and fixed on me, her palms pressed together as if she's beseeching the Lord Almighty. *Please, please, please,* she mouths. I understand her desperation, but James and I *did* tell her no interviews. Told her not once but twice.

"All we want the two of you to do," the reporter says, "is tell us how important this place is to you. What it means, knowing you can come here—"

"But we didn't even know this place existed," James says, "till a couple hours ago—"

"More than two hundred people have lived here," Ada pipes in, as if prepping us. "We helped get them off the streets. Other folks come here, too, like you done tonight, just to chill."

"We *really* need you," the reporter coaxes.

James shoots me a *what-have-we-gotten-ourselves-into* look. I shoot it right back. If only the Martins had been straight with us. But then, we haven't exactly been straight with them. Maybe you reap what you sow.

Spirit does move in mysterious ways. Some good might yet come of this. I draw a deep breath. "Okay, I'll help, but on certain conditions. I don't want my face shown, I don't want my real name used, and I won't answer any questions about my past or my personal life. All I'll do is talk about what I know—that it felt great to come here tonight and take a shower."

The reporter agrees. She retrieves a memo pad and pen. She wants background. "Where are you from? Why are you on the streets? How long have you been out?" Amazed at the effrontery, I respond to her questions only vaguely, reminding her, more than once, that she'd agreed to respect my privacy.

"What's your name?" she says.

"Phyllis," I say, noticing that she hasn't bothered to introduce herself, "but like I told you, I don't want my real name used."

"What name should we use then?"

I smile to myself. Just this afternoon Jake had christened James and me Mister and Missus Ingalls, after the characters on *Little House on the Prairie*. "That was one of my favorite TV programs as a kid," he'd said. "Yeah, the *Ingalls*. Rooster and I thought that name fit, because you guys don't smoke, you don't drink, you don't party—you're kind of, like, the *good* couple." The three of us had laughed.

"Use the name Ingalls," I tell the reporter. "Mary Ingalls."

LIGHTS

Harold escorts James into the kitchen. After setting out some chips and salsa, he asks James if he'd like some soup.

"Yeah, okay," James says weakly, wondering how I'm holding up on camera.

Harold opens a can of Campbell's chicken noodle and dumps it in a pan. Smoking a cigarette as the soup heats, he repeatedly begs James to do a straightforward interview. "You got to let them see your face. *Please* show your face, man. Come on! *Please*—"

James is beyond disturbed. Not that he doesn't want to help; he just feels pressured, and betrayed, as though the promise of a shower, the goodnatured chitchat and now the food have just been meant to buy him off. He protests, but Harold whines like a spoiled youngster in a toy store till he breaks down, sick at heart, and agrees to show his face on camera.

When the TV crew finishes with me, Harold ushers James back into the living room. Pulling his knit hat down over his eyebrows, James slumps on the sofa. "Call me Jonathan Ingalls," he tells the reporter. Every ounce of him wants to get up and walk out the door, but he has nowhere to go. On the verge of tears, TV lights hot on his flushed face, he answers the questions put to him, never looking directly into the camera.

The interview is a blur. Finally the reporter says, "We've got enough." She gets up and walks away, but the cameraman keeps rolling, pretending he's not.

News at eleven.

DERAILED

Around 10 PM, more than four hours after they picked us up, the Martins drive us back to the riverbank. On the way across town Ada sermonizes about

"Show your face": James (photo credit: Jihong Cole-Dai)

how she must be "faithful to the Lord" in her life and work in order to be successful. Her words are bewildering to hear after the events of this night. As we get out of the Blazer along the tracks, she reminds us that "we're family, and will always be family."

"Three hours ago," James mutters, as we stumble through the darkness toward camp, "those words meant something. Not now."

We fall into bed, totally spent. We feel like passengers on a train that derailed after somebody secretly switched the tracks.

The night's surprisingly warm. We open the plastic flaps over the shelter door, but the fresh air doesn't help us sleep. We're both restless. So many unresolved feelings: regret that we ever got into the Martins' vehicle; resentment, even anger, at being exploited; guilt over our own imposture; fear of being exposed; hope, despite everything, that these strange doings might yield some good. The showers we took are all but forgotten. The price we paid was too high.

Grown weary of tossing, I light a candle and pick up *The Crucible* where I'd left off. The curtain's about to fall on Act II. John Proctor is in a helpless rage. "We are only what we always were," he cries, "but naked now. Aye, naked! And the wind, God's icy wind, will blow!"

DAY 29

WEDNESDAY, MARCH 17

KINSHIP

Walking alongside a train, just after dawn. It's coasting on the rails in the same direction I'm going, at the same unhurried pace, with scarcely a creak or groan. I feel an easy kinship with it that's getting harder to feel with people. Maybe a train's easier to trust.

6:40 AM. Take-out customers in White Castle stand in a long line at the counter. Street folks occupy a few scattered tables. In the booth next to mine, a wild-haired Anglo wearing a ragged army coat is grumbling in an ugly tone, now to himself, sometimes to the rest of us. I've never seen him before.

I try to make small-talk with him. Gradually his tone begins to change, losing some of its hostility. Following his lead, we discuss American history since the Civil War, McCarthyism, recent discoveries in physics, Hillary Clinton's service as a KGB agent, how he'd like to hone his carpentry skills and move to Vermont, or go to Scotland and become a fisherman, or get lost in the heart of New Zealand....

The Philosopher (as I think of him) slips outside to smoke a cigarette. Soon he's in passionate conversation with the air.

There's an ongoing debate, a *Dispatch* article reports this morning, over how to deal with the city's "Homeless Problem." With the redevelopment taking place in and around the Bottoms, just west of downtown, certain shelters will have to be relocated, but nobody seems to want a new shelter established in their neighborhood. One Franklin County commissioner would like to present homeless people with a choice: "Either get your act together, or we'll give you a bus ticket out of town."

From across the aisle a well-dressed black woman starts telling me about her husband of eighteen years. He lives on the streets. She can't remember the last time she saw him. Sometimes, when she has a free hour, she hangs around here in case he drifts in.

"He's an alcoholic," she says with a sigh, "and he uses drugs, but he raised all our kids before he left. He was a good father. He was *real* good about *that*."

I ask the man's name. *Who knows, our paths might cross.*

"Name's Luther. He probably goes by some other name now, but how would I ever know?"

BAGPIPES

Today, the Irishman reminds me, is St. Patrick's Day. He wants to see the downtown parade, scheduled to step off from St. Patrick's Church at 11:30 AM. I don't have any blarney in my bones, but even I have an itch to hear some bagpipes. Somehow they'll match my mood after last night's fiasco with the Martins and Channel 4.

James's pace quickens as we near the crowded parade route. At the corner of Broad and High, he flops down on a spare patch of curb, a good Irishman looking for some better luck. Next to him is a young woman with a stroller. The infant inside is wearing a green bonnet. James smiles at the child's bright blue eyes and rosy cheeks till the woman notices and protectively turns the stroller away.

The parade approaches: the standard assortment of shamrocks and leprechauns, the slow march of pipes and drums. The bagpipes wail, echo. James rests his chin on his knees; his eyelids droop, close.

I might not be Irish like James, but I do know that St. Patrick's Day celebrates the life of a remarkable man. Despite the legends, he didn't drive all Irish snakes into the sea, and he wasn't the first to bring Christianity to the shores of the emerald isle, but he *was* the first person in recorded western history to condemn slavery. He was also one of the few early church leaders who respected and upheld the dignity of women. A tireless prophet, he demanded justice for all poor and disadvantaged people. So on this, the feast day of Patricius, the Brit who became patron saint of Ireland, I carry in my pocket a wee bit of Kelly green, paper from somebody's trash.

ANONYMITY

Our route out of the downtown in mid-afternoon takes us past the Columbus

"JUSTICE": billboard in the downtown

Health Department. Two staffers in neckties smoking on the back stoop hail us and say, "You guys looked good on TV last night! That *was* you, wasn't it?"

So much for anonymity.

We find a payphone. I call Jihong. Yes, he says, James and I were on the 11:00 news last night. A few of our friends, most of whom rarely watch the Channel 4 broadcast, called to tell him they'd just happened to have it on.

Maybe the news segment will help Ada and Harold obtain the required funds. Maybe not. We hope for the best, but we aren't attached to the outcome. It isn't difficult to let go of something you weren't invested in from the start.

It's the questions we can't seem to let go of. Why us? Was our involvement in all this mere happenstance, or something more? Had the Martins, desperate for donations from a predominantly Anglo viewing audience, drafted us because we're white? Is that why Harold had pressed James to show his face on tape? Is that why the reporter had chosen *not* to interview two black residents of the halfway house, and instead begged *us* for paper-thin testimonials?

Amid all our questions, only one thing is certain: last night's events would never have happened if we hadn't come out on the streets in the first place and kept our identities a secret. Who knows? Maybe all of us—including the Martins and the reporter—had just been doing the best we could.

DAY 30

THURSDAY, MARCH 18

HOME IMPROVEMENTS

We're always looking for ways to improve the shelter. James is especially creative. This morning, on the ground near a utility pole, he finds a glass insulator; in the trash at the bottom of the bluff, a rusty bedspring.

Back at camp, he stretches the bedspring into an inverted cone, sets the insulator upside-down into the coil, and hangs it from the ceiling. Perfect for holding a votive candle.

What helps best is often humble.

LOST

Still bleary-eyed after a tough night, James and I wait at a table in Holy Family Soup Kitchen for the serving line to open. Suddenly we hear a familiar voice.

Maddy. We're thrilled. We haven't seen her in weeks.

She tells us the cold and snow eventually got the better of her, and she gave up camping with Jeff. Luckily she got into a shelter, then into a short-term rehab program, hoping to detox.

You can see in her eyes she's not making it.

"It's hard, isn't it?" we say.

She nods, tearing up. "I want to get straight," she says, looking broken, like the spine of a book too long mishandled. "I know what I got to do, but I can't seem to do it. Sometimes I think knowing you're a drunk is worse than being in denial."

She tells us for the first time about her children, who live hours away. She's lost custody. She doubts that she'll ever see them again.

"Sometimes," she says, "I cut myself."

"You cut yourself?" I say, making sure I heard her right. She's beginning to mumble, as if drifting off to sleep. She nods, then mutters something about suicide. Stunned, James and I make her promise not to hurt herself. We try to offer encouragement.

She begins to weep. "You two," she says weakly, "are my kind of people."

MAKE-BELIEVE

In late afternoon James and I pass by a German Village art gallery now closed for the day. On a table in the window, a slim gray tiger cat with white spots lounges in a last splotch of sunshine. Through the glass we scratch her forehead, tickle her paws. *Make-believe.* She rolls over, exposing her belly, then jumps up and rubs against the pane. Gloves now off, we stroke her back, smearing fingerprints. After a while she draws back on her haunches and stares at us, as if mystified. Finally she rises abruptly and butts her head hard against the window. She wants our touch as badly as we want to give it.

GODPARENTS

Rooster and Jake surprise us with a strapping Rottweiler pup, maybe three months old, a stray they've "rescued from the streets." She lies on her back, very calmly, in the cradle of Jake's arms, already his baby, trusting him completely. Her short black coat is soft and sleek, her body rippling muscle. Her paws, limp in air, fill the palms of our hands. She's absolutely adorable— likely not a stray, of course, but James and I don't ask any questions. We're just grateful to touch her.

"I'm calling him Dog," Rooster says. "That's it. Just plain *Dog.*"

"How about you guys being godparents," Jake says, "just in case something happens?"

A SINGLE CANDLE

James and I rest in a back pew of St. Mary's Church. Parishioners straggle in and out. When the sanctuary finally empties, James lies down on the carpeted floor. This church is about the only good place he's found to do his yoga stretches and release some tension—lots of room, no guards, no snow, no cold, no dirt, no mud.

I rise and go to a shrine. I light a candle for Elena, now disappeared ("I couldn't help her," Blue said, "she liked the bottle too much"). I light a candle for Maddy, who feels so cut off from the world that she slices herself with razor blades. I light a candle for Enid, feet tiny as a ballerina's. I light a candle for Sweetness *(is she in her new apartment?)*, for Cindy *(may you soon be in Texas)*, for Toots *(know you're free)*—

I make myself stop. If I keep on, there won't be a single candle left.

A small placard requests a donation. I offer my goodwill. Not everybody who needs to light a candle can afford one.

HAUSFRAUEN

Walking along the tracks near camp, I come up behind our neighbor Enid, standing with her arms crossed, staring south as if expecting Yahweh himself to appear. Beyond a few bald facts (she was born in Germany seventy-six years ago, was once a nurse, is now a panhandler, is living in Rooster's tent), she's still a mystery. I've rarely seen her, never up close. We've never spoken.

"Guten abend," I say as I pass, wishing her a good evening, my tongue testing my recollection of college German.

"Guten abend," she returns perfunctorily, as if she and I were two hausfrauen meeting on a street corner in Berlin. Then, suddenly, she seems to realize where she is and what's just happened—

"Guten abend!" she exclaims.

I smile at her over my shoulder. Her mouth is hanging open.

DUST

Jihong once told me that the Chinese character for human being is 人 , two lines supporting each other. In other words, no human being stands alone. Just as a house is made up of studs and joists, wiring and pipes, who we are as individuals is largely constituted by a network of relations, both intimate and vast. Not only am I wife, daughter, sister, friend, neighbor, colleague; I'm also a conspiracy of sunshine and rain, soil and trees, gravity and genes.... On and on, out and out, down and down the web of relations goes, spun without beginning or end. By virtue of it, I'm located in space and time, and just as truly I'm blown away, a particle of dust. I'm everything, and nothing.

On the streets I have trouble sensing the intimacy, trusting the depth, of these relations. Most of the time I feel remote from them. The house is gone, you might say, and home with it: I seem to stand alone, a nobody, a match lit in breeze.

Then somebody sees me. Bothers to look, and sees me true. Their eyes penetrate mine with the recognition that I matter, and suddenly it washes over me, all that I've fallen out of touch with. In that instant, I feel restored. Significant.

WALKING THE LINE

Per the usual schedule, James and I were expecting a visit tonight from Take It to the Streets, but nobody showed up. As we spoon down a little government peanut butter with cold canned salmon, we second-guess ourselves for not having packed out some provisions from the soup kitchen.

This night's hunger, though slight, is a good teacher, revealing just how much we now rely on the Martins and their volunteers. By stressing how happy they are to tend our needs, and at times even tending needs we don't have, they clearly invite this dependency, and from relief we've fallen right in. We're much more lax than we used to be in seeking food elsewhere.

The line between accepting somebody's help and becoming habituated to it is a fine one. When you're dead-tired and depressed, you walk that line like a drunk.

DAY 31

FRIDAY, MARCH 19

GRUDGE

Crusty snowdrifts in the downtown are melting fast away, except on the north side of buildings, where they're out of the sun's reach. There the snow refuses to thaw, stubborn as an old, old grudge. In some places, despite the springlike days of this past week, it's still piled up to the eaves.

On busy Front Street Harold Martin drives past in a rusty red pickup. Seeing us, he brakes to a stop, then backs up alongside the curb. "We'll be working hard on the hut today," he says, holding up traffic. "Next week, it's all yours."

The hut. Of course. We'd forgotten all about it.

Harold's face is bright as he gives us a parting wave. The truck sputters off.

"Something's happened," I say to James.

When we reach the Statehouse, shortly before noon, Jihong is waiting. Meeting us briefly in an out-of-the-way spot, he informs us that an anonymous donor has pledged to purchase the Martins' halfway house from HUD for $40,000, the exact amount needed. Channel 4 updated the story last night. Ada Martin was shown, live, receiving the good news from the same reporter who had taped the appeal.

James and I are pleased. We wonder, though, if the donor would have been as anxious to help if the halfway house were located in an upper-class suburb like Bexley instead of blue-collar Whitehall. According to the *Dispatch*, a recent effort to transform a three-story Bexley building into supervised housing for a dozen homeless men has met with strenuous neighborhood opposition.

FEAST DAY

In Roman Catholic tradition St. Joseph is the protector of anybody who calls on his name for help. Today is his feast day. To honor the saint for his patronage, the Cathedral is hosting a special luncheon for the homeless in its undercroft.

The dimly lit rooms of the undercroft, with their arched doorways, brick floors and stone walls, remind me of vaults in a mansion's wine cellar. In one room several tables have been spread with white linens and adorned with silver service. White tapers flicker in silver candelabra above crystal platters overflowing with homemade bread, chunky chicken salad, deli meats, cheeses, fresh fruit and sweets.

In an adjoining room James and I sling our filthy coats over the back of two chairs, feeling a little out of place. Only a half dozen of us among the twenty or thirty people present look remotely poor; the rest, dressed in Sunday finery, are chitchatting about church matters, family concerns and business affairs.

At the buffet table we're happy to run into Sam.

"Did you ever find what you—uh—*lost?*" I say, referring to the recent Cathedral robbery. He shakes his head.

James and I sit down with mounded plates. Against the far wall the mustached monsignor, dressed in a black double-breasted cassock and purple sash, stands stiff as starch, saying little, hands tightly clasped.

Another, older priest, sporting a collar but in casual clothes, hollers a greeting to us across the room. Last Sunday, I remember, he offered us donuts after mass. Now he compliments the size of my sandwich, chicken salad heaped high between two slabs of homemade bread. I laugh, making no apology.

After the tables begin to clear, somebody from the church remarks on how few homeless people showed up for the meal. Sam mentions that last year none came at all.

"The luncheon isn't advertised like it ought to be," says a streetwise Anglo who often hands out sandwiches at the rectory door. "Homeless people are just trying to make it from one day, or one hour, to the next. You can't just advertise a meal like this a whole month in advance and expect them to remember. They're not going to be writing it down in a date-book.

"Besides," he goes on, "who would have known about the luncheon in the first place unless they read it in the church bulletin? We got to do a better job getting the word out. We got to think the way homeless people think. We got to take the news to where they are."

FRECKLES

In Deaf School Park James and I collapse spread-eagled on the ground, thrilling in the sun's warmth. Within a few minutes, a policewoman appears across the way, mounted on a magnificent chestnut horse with a braided tail. She snaps the reins, and the horse begins a slow saunter in our direction.

"We *are* allowed to lie on the grass, aren't we?" I say to James with alarm. Asking the question seems absurd, yet necessary, considering all the anti-homeless laws on the books in this country. Besides, when you've been rousted as many times as we have, and can easily be charged with vagrancy by anybody not liking the looks of you, the absurd seems more possible than not.

The cop reins in just a few yards away. Deciding to take preemptive action, I jump up and walk over to her like we're old friends.

"Can I pet your horse?" I ask.

"Sure," she says, smiling. "His name is Freckles."

ALL SMILES

A woman in her twenties with a full head of long, red curls bounds out of a doorway to her car, parked curbside.

"Nice hair," James says.

"Thanks!" she replies, with spirit, turning to look him straight in the eye. Then, to us both, dirty and ugly as we are, "You guys have a *great* weekend!"

We're all smiles, ready to burst.

DAY 32

SATURDAY, MARCH 20

GRAVITY

In the field above camp I'm hailed by Rooster, standing at the edge of the woods near his campsite. On the ground at his feet slumps an old man, head bowed. "This is Joseph," Rooster says as I walk up. "Joseph, this is Phyllis, one of our neighbors."

Joseph stares vacantly at the ground.

"He's eighty-six years old," Rooster says, pride in his voice. "Full-blooded Indian. His picture used to be in all the papers. He'd lead all them big Indian dances, you know, out west. That was a long time ago, now."

"How long?" I say.

He gestures toward the woods. "Since those big trees were small."

The old man can't be warm, clad only in a thin shirt and a lightweight coat, zipper broken. Dried blood stains the front of his dirty khaki pants.

"Old Joseph escaped from the hospital last night," Rooster says. "Somehow he made it all the way out here. I let him spend the night in my tent, but he can't stay. Got to get him some help." He tells me Jake's gone off to retrieve a wheelbarrow from his shack.

Joseph won't be easy to move. He's big-framed, well over six feet tall, bloated from drink. Dead weight. I lean down to rest my hand on his shoulder. "Are you warm enough? Do you need a drink of water?"

"Oh," Rooster cuts in, laughing, "Joseph only drinks alcohol, says water rusts his pipes."

Joseph lifts his head for the first time. High, square cheekbones. Dark eyes, boring into mine. "What I could really use is a cigarette, if you got any."

"I'm sorry, Joseph. I don't."

His eyes soften, drift.

Jake's wheelbarrow is small and rusty, with a flat tire wobbling loose on the rim—discouraging, but it's all we have, and probably better than nothing. Jake and Rooster get on either side of Joseph and hoist him off the ground with throaty grunts. I maneuver the wheelbarrow in behind him. I see now that the old man has soiled himself. I think again of the blood on his pants. *Why were you in the hospital last night? Why did you run away?*

Jake and Rooster lower Joseph as gently as they can into the wheelbarrow, but sometimes gravity is cruel, and at the end he drops hard, with a moan, onto the shabby lawn-chair cushion Jake's put in the bottom. I ease the back of the barrow down. Joseph's legs hang over the front, the tips of his shoes almost touching ground. Under his weight, the tire's splayed flat beneath the wheel's rim.

Jake says they'll haul him south along the tracks. Once under the bridge, they'll go up top to call Netcare, a county-wide agency that provides emergency services for persons with substance abuse or mental health problems. A squad can carry Joseph up to street level on a stretcher, then transport him to a hospital.

Joseph's muttering, trying to say something. Rooster kneels beside him. The old man draws a shuddering breath. "Don't want to go," he says, in barely a whisper.

"You don't want to go?"

Joseph shakes his head. An awkward silence. Then he says, "Guess I got to."

Rooster gets to his feet, steps a short distance away, turns his back. Hands on hips, he digs at the ground with the toe of his boot. At last he tips his head back, as if staring straight up into heaven, and doesn't move. Not for the longest time.

When finally he turns around again, his face is flushed deep red and tears are streaming down his wind-burned cheeks. "Joseph," he says, his voice cracking, "I just can't take care of you. Not like you need. Not out here. Understand?" He wipes his cheeks on his sleeve. Joseph doesn't say a word.

Rooster circles behind the wheelbarrow, grabs the handles, lifts, and shoves. The wheel doesn't budge. The barrow teeters. Jake throws his weight against it to keep it upright.

"She ain't going to roll through the field," he says. "We'll have to pull her."

"What can I do?" I ask.

"This ain't for you," Rooster says, not without kindness. "Jake and I'll manage."

Reluctantly I stand aside. "Okay, but if you guys get stuck and need another pair of hands, come get me. I'll be at camp."

They promise they will, but I know they won't. They're both protective of me, Jake in his sweet, almost brotherly way, and Rooster with a machismo that sometimes seems exaggerated for my benefit. "This is a good thing you're doing," I say to them, as encouragement.

The guys each grab a wooden handle and at the count of three begin to drag the barrow behind them through the dead weeds. Momentum's slow to gather, the going clumsy, till finally they hit the smoother ground alongside the railroad bed. There they start to push the barrow on the flat tire. Joseph bumps along, chin resting almost on his chest, straight gray-black hair tumbling over his shoulders, shoestrings untied and dangling.

If only you'd had a cigarette.

James, returning to camp from up top, meets the wheelbarrow along the tracks. "You guys need help?"

"Yeah," Jake says. "This here's Joseph. He ain't doing so hot."

Joseph rolls his head toward James, opens one eye. "Hey, you got a cigarette?"

"Sorry, Joseph. I'm all out."

The three men take turns shoving the old man on the rim, all the way down to the south bridge. Sometimes the barrow gets bogged down in a dip and won't budge. Then it takes all of them to lift.

"Joseph, you big dummy," Rooster jokes during a break, panting for breath, "if you didn't eat so much, you'd be able to get out of here on your own."

Back at camp I yank off my coat and throw down my gloves. I pace, now and then kicking the ground. I pick up long sticks and smack them against trees till they're only stubs in my smarting hands. Finally, tears come, powerless and angry—angry at Joseph for drinking himself down, angry that we couldn't have moved him with a little more dignity, angry that Jake and Rooster might end up just like him—

Yet Jake and Rooster had bothered to do what they could. For this I feel keen gratitude, and respect. There's joy, even, for those tears on Rooster's face (tears he'd wanted no one to see), and for that seedy cushion Jake had thought to put in the bottom of the wheelbarrow.

Sometimes hope screams.

COUNTING

Occasionally during our noontime meditations at the Statehouse, James observes passersby stopping to contemplate the Statue of Peace. Some people, like this business suit wearing loafers shined to a high gloss, seem to be interested in the statue itself. Others are apparently more curious as to why two street people should be resting on the ground within the shadow of its wings. Whatever the reason, their gazing at the angel, their considering the word PEACE engraved below, always fills James with a quiet satisfaction.

Not today.

Today, after Joseph, the strain's too much—

You look at the angel, he says silently to the businessman, *while all around you there are terrified human beings—can you bear to look at them? Do you want to know they're here? So many men and women, all around you, trying hard not to remember anything good that's ever happened to them, anybody who's ever been kind to them—they don't dare remember—remembering just reminds them of what they don't have, and feel powerless to get, anymore—just makes them want to tip a bottle—*

So many people—without a home—afraid—grieving—lost—

Who keeps those statistics—

Who does the counting—

Who counts—

Who—wants to know—

LETTERS HOME

On the east end of the Statehouse is the Ohio Veterans Plaza, dedicated in August of last year. Inscribed on limestone walls are excerpts from letters that soldiers scribbled home to their loved ones from trenches and jungles, foxholes and tents, hospital beds. This afternoon, while James goes off to shoot photographs, I linger on the plaza, reading the soldiers' words. I'm surprised sometimes to hear them speaking of things close to my own heart, here on the streets:

"The place I sleep is my home."—Brad, during the Gulf War. *The Professor, sleeping in his refrigerator.*

"Perhaps soon I can tell you just where I am. Even after I tell you, you probably won't know where I'm located."—Joe, war not specified. *Elena, whereabouts unknown.*

"I am really anxious to get out and get home and stay there and live like a human."—Clyde, writing from Japan, end of World War 2. *Jake, wanting his own apartment, telling me, "A person just can't keep living like this."*

"How are we going to get home? Perhaps on the wings of angels."—Gail, the Gulf War. *Maddy, separated from her kids, fantasizing suicide.*

"We could not help but think of the ones who will never know the joys of this day.... They too dreamed of their homes."—Ralph, end of World War 2, remembering his fallen buddies. *James and I, when we finally leave the streets, aware of those we're leaving behind.*

Life on the streets isn't war. But it *is* a pitched battle, waged against the elements, hostile powers, even your own body and mind. However you come to be on the streets, you won't leave them unscathed. That's guaranteed. And if you leave them alive, that won't be proof you survived. Veterans know: You can be dead and still walking.

LIFESAVERS

An Anglo is digging feverishly in a small dumpster. At his feet is a growing pile of assorted snack goods, vending machine fare. Amazed at the man's luck, James walks over and peeks into his treasure chest.

"Mind if I grab some, too?" he asks.

"Yeah man, go ahead." The fellow stuffs his haul into two grocery bags and leaves.

He was thorough. Any remaining goodies are now at the very bottom of the dumpster, and most appear to have been nibbled by mice. James leans over the edge of the bin, his feet sticking up in the air, and scavenges the only snacks whose wrappers are still intact: two granola bars, a pack of gum, a chocolate bar and a roll of Lifesavers.

At a big dumpster behind an upscale bakery in the Short North, I smell the yeasty bread even before I lift the lid. The bin's empty except for a dozen or more large, golden loaves of bread, down in the smutty bottom; crusty Italian bread, unwrapped but relatively clean. I'm tempted to climb in and retrieve them, but without some trash to stand on, I don't know how I'd ever crawl back out of the bin with my bum knee.

In the very next dumpster I check, behind an apartment building, I find a single loaf of the same bread within arm's reach, fresh as you'd ever want to eat. Letting out a howl, I toss it into a Lazarus shopping bag and loop the handle over my wrist.

In another trash bin, not far away, are cosmetic cases containing a woman's toiletries. Lotions, tweezers, powders, lipsticks—did she move across the country and not bother to take them? Did a jilted lover throw them into the trash? I don't speculate long. I'm just happy now to have a few things that used to be hers: aloe vera gel, sunblock and chapstick, for my sun- and windburned face, plus a small cardboard box, probably from her desk, chockful of pencils and pens. One of the pens is glittering gold, stout, inlaid with tiny diamond-shaped mirrors. In my grip it feels like affirmation.

WITNESS

I'm walking along Broad Street opposite the Statehouse when a police car squeals to a stop in the far lane, lights flashing, right in front of the Statue of Peace. Two cops jump out in pursuit of a tall, lanky black man, who is apparently unarmed. He's barefooted, wearing only bib overalls.

A white family, touring the capitol grounds in their heavy winter clothes, scurries out of harm's way as more cruisers scream up and kill their sirens. Six squad cars, by now. Mother and children huddle within the father's circling arms, gawking as the cops quickly hem in their target.

This being a weekend, the square is fairly empty of pedestrians. Something tells me to stay put and serve as a witness (*would anybody listen to* you?) in case the cops—at least ten of them, all white—should use excessive force on this black man. By now they've trapped the fellow on a wheelchair ramp near the Statue of Peace. He's immediately across the street from me, drumming the handrail as he fantasizes an escape, guns trained on him from all sides. *Don't be foolish.* The cops tighten their noose, trying calmly to reason with him. *Please don't be foolish.* At last he tries to leap the railing and flee, but one of his gangly legs doesn't make it over. He flops headfirst into low evergreens. Easily apprehended, he's frisked and cuffed and hustled into the back of a cruiser.

Across the way the white children stare.

WAITING TO BE SEEN

Tonight is the Take It to the Streets camp-out at Mad Dog's, up north along the tracks. Wanting to avoid the news cameras we know will be there, James and I treat ourselves instead to a televised basketball game at Columbus Community Hospital. March Madness is well underway, and the Ohio State men's team, after a rash of losing seasons, is in the midst of a surprising tournament run. Tonight OSU battles St. John's in a regional final.

The game's already on when we enter a waiting room adjacent to the emergency department. Feeling conspicuous at first, we soon relax. Nobody's paying us any attention. Relatives and friends of patients brought in by squad shuffle in and out. Even the most distraught visitors watch a little of the game till white coats finally come to confer with them in hushed tones. Gradually the room empties.

After a couple hours, a nurse walks in. "Is anybody in here waiting to be seen?"

James and I exchange a smile. Waiting to be *seen?* If only she knew.

DAY 33

SUNDAY, MARCH 21

ANSWERS

Early morning in White Castle.

James: "I dreamed that you and I were back home, and everybody was asking us questions—'What's the solution to the Homeless Problem?' 'What should be done about overcrowded shelters?' 'How can you help people who won't help themselves?'

"We didn't know what to say. We didn't have any answers. We'd never been *looking* for answers—just came out here to *be*—and nobody could understand that. Questions flew at us from every direction till finally all we could give, in reply, were tears."

STINKING

James and I are walking into the downtown for breakfast at Central Presbyterian Church. The Sunday morning streets are practically deserted, so we're surprised to see a van parked in the middle of the sidewalk, up in the next block, and an Anglo climbing onto its roof from the rear. He aims a pressure washer at a store awning and starts hosing it down. Mist travels all the way down the street to greet us.

As we approach the van, the guy on its roof thoughtfully turns off the spray so as not to drench us. Smiling up at him, James yells, "Hey man, I need a shower. Can you hook me up?"

The man grins and playfully points the nozzle at us. "Sure, I'll get you—"

We all laugh. Another guy sticks his head out a van window. "We got *hot* water, too!" he says with a wide, toothless smile.

All kidding aside, we do need showers. Bad. As James is fond of saying, "There's nothing wrong with stinking. The problem is when you know it's you."

TIGHT SHOT

Along the railroad tracks north of camp is a gigantic billboard, visible to the freeway—a tight shot of a white man's eyes, staring down. They're the kind of eyes you'd rather not have looking at you; the kind of eyes we see every day. Wanting to photograph them, James shinnies halfway up a utility pole with a pinhole camera. Hanging on as best he can, he squeezes the box between the post and his belly to keep it steady, then barely breathes through a roughly ninety-second exposure. He's climbing back down when he notices a cluster of homeless people under a nearby overpass, huddled around a big bonfire, watching him like he was a circus act.

Uh-oh, he thinks. *How'll you ever explain yourself?*

Quickly slipping the camera into his duffel, he walks over to join two men and a woman, all Anglos, their cheeks rosied by the heat of the fire. Amazingly, he's never seen any of these faces, despite passing through here practically every time we go to Grubb Street. The trio has seen him, though. "Almost every day," they say, "you walk by with your woman."

Initially guarded, the group soon starts to open up. The younger guy introduces himself as Don; the older man, Mad Dog; the middle-aged woman, Susan. They offer James potato chips left from last night's Take It to the Streets camp-out, held around this very fire. Lots of volunteers came, they say, and a TV crew from Channel 4, but only ten homeless people they can think of. Harold and Ada Martin hooked up a big-screen TV so they could all watch the OSU-St. John's game while eating burgers from White Castle.

Don jokes and raps with James as if they're old buddies. He's incredibly big, as is Susan; a rare sight on the streets. He brags about his weight, says he's around three hundred pounds.

Susan picks up the theme. "The first month I was out, I had lots of trouble finding food. Dropped from two-hundred-fifty-six to a hundred-ninety-eight." She throws more wood on the enormous fire. "Where you from, James?"

"New York."

"Me, too. I'm a tough girl from the Bronx. Used to own two construction companies. Then I got a three-thousand-dollar-a-day dope habit and lost it all. Two times since then I almost starved to death. Once I almost froze.

Tracks that James and Phyllis walked almost every day, stared down by billboard eyes

"Those three times I broke the law to stay alive, and ended up in the state pen. I'm not a criminal. I just wanted to live."

The four of them talk together for a good half hour. Nobody ever asks James what he was doing up the pole.

RAP

James is walking along the railroad tracks, just coming up to the bridge south of camp, when a chorus of Hey yous rains down. On the bridge are three young black boys on bikes.

"Hey, you poor?" they shout down to him.

"Yeah."

"Where do you sleep?"

"In the woods."

"Where your mom and dad at?"

"Back east."

"You cold?"

"Not bad, today."

"Where you going?"

"To hang out with a friend. Where you all going?"

"To jump our bikes in the park. Do you ride trains?"

"If they're slow enough."

Excited, they talk among themselves, voices floating down. "I want to ride some trains." "Me too, man." "Yeah, cool."

Maybe fifteen minutes later, James comes upon the same boys in the White Castle parking lot. They're all wearing football jackets—Ohio State, University of Miami, Dallas Cowboys. "Hey," they say, "you the dude we just saw down on the tracks. How'd you get up here?"

"I walked."

"You broke?"

"Yep."

"You don't have no money to get a drink or a cheeseburger?"

"No."

"You hungry?"

"No."

"Where do you eat?"

"Churches, soup kitchens, dumpsters."

"What'd you eat today?"

"Bologna sandwich for lunch, oatmeal and a biscuit for breakfast."

"*Big* bowl of oatmeal?"

"Yeah."

The leader of the trio leans back on the seat of his bike, grinning. "Yum, you making me hungry—we ain't been home *all day*."

MAN OF GOD (2)

Early on, the afternoon was sunny, breezy, temperature in the forties. Now, with the sun disappeared behind ominous clouds, it's getting cold fast. I beg a cup of hot water and collapse in a corner booth of White Castle. I stare out the window at the darkening day, grateful to be out of the bullying wind.

A few minutes later, Harold Martin rousts me from my reverie. He has a sack of burgers in his hand. "You need anything?" He pulls his wallet out of a hip pocket. "Want a cup of coffee? How about a sandwich?"

"No thanks, Harold, I'm fine."

He flips a dollar bill onto the table. "There. Get something for yourself."

He leaves. I stare at the bill for a minute, then pick it up with both hands and touch it to my forehead. "When a man of God tries to give you something," David said, that first night, "you don't say no."

Wind beats against the window.

STAYING (3)

"The Thing's got me," James says tonight, out of a long silence.

I wait for him to explain.

"To be honest, till these past few days, I think I've stayed on the streets not because I felt a deep sense of call, but because I had enough *reasons*. For one thing, I was searching for spiritual lessons, and I didn't want to miss something important by going home early. I'd also made a commitment, and I like to finish what I start. Then, well, you know, I'd look weak if I went home early. If nothing else, I did have my pride.

"But now the Thing's got me. Just when it got me, or how, I can't say exactly, but it has, and now all those old reasons don't matter so much anymore. Being here, staying here—it's not about reasons. It's about Joseph in that wheelbarrow. It's about Susan, Don and Mad Dog, huddled around that bonfire. It's about Maddy, missing her kids. It's about those boys, riding their bikes. It's about—*presence.*"

DAY 34

MONDAY, MARCH 22

BOLDFACE

Alone at camp in early morning, James lies in bed, lazily browsing a recent issue of the *New York Times*, rescued yesterday from a German Village trash can. Nonchalantly he turns a page, and instantly bursts into laughter—

ANALYZE THIS

It's a movie title, printed in huge boldface letters on a full-page ad, but it might as well be heaven's idea of a bad joke: "Yeah, man, your being on the streets is absurd. Analyze it all you want, but you won't ever be able to explain it to anybody. Not really."

Still laughing, he props up the ad in plain view just outside the shelter door, then scrambles back into bed.

Some time later, I return from my morning toilet at White Castle. Spotting the ad front-and-center, I chuckle. "Well, Irishman," I holler inside, "I can tell *you're* in a fine mood this morning!"

We enjoy the levity while we can. It won't last. It never does. Out here, nothing's that funny. Laughter is just your soul struggling to survive. One minute you're rolling in a fit of hilarity; the next, you're spent, wanting to cry for no reason.

TRESPASS

Before the serving line opens at Holy Family Soup Kitchen, a volunteer staffer usually leads everybody in the Lord's Prayer. The crowded room quiets. Voices join. Not the words we say, exactly, but the act of our saying them together, around these tables, creates some semblance of fellowship. That sense of fellowship might be fleeting, lasting little longer than the Amen, but it's worth something.

The Lord's Prayer is practically in my genes. I grew up reciting it. But the words have never resonated like they do out here. Especially "Give us this day our daily bread." Especially "Forgive us our trespasses as we forgive," a petition so poignant on the streets, where "NO TRESPASSING" signs glare at you from chainlink fences, utility poles, dumpsters, doors; where you have no claim to the trash you're digging in, to the land you're squatting on, to the money you're begging; where just your standing where you're at, if not your very existence, is an offense to many....

ZIPPERS

The zipper is working loose from James's coat. Zipping and unzipping is an exercise in mindfulness; if he's the least bit careless, he widens the tear. To ease the stress on the remaining stitches, he carries less in his pockets. On warmer days he lets the coat hang open. Not today.

As the stitching unravels, so does his mind. Hallucinations, now. Seeing things that aren't there. Not seeing things that *are* there—or, at least, not being certain they're real. Delirium without the fever.

Uneasiness comes and goes in waves, prompted by nothing specific. One minute he's fine, the next he's full of anxiety and confused emotions, his insides roiling like whitewater. In such moments, faith disappears. He feels utterly alone, unable to cope. He forgets to ask for help, almost as if he never knew how.

Sometimes the spell passes quickly.

LUCK

The last few days have yielded more than our share of lucky pennies. The thing about lucky pennies is, they show up when you're not especially looking for them. Else they wouldn't be lucky, I suppose; just found. That's the secret: Don't try to find them—they'll find you, so long as your eyes are open.

Sometimes, though, you forget what you know. Just now, I had my eyes glued to the sidewalk along State Street, searching for lost change, and I walked smack into a low-hanging tree limb.

MOTHERLODE

In an industrial-sized dumpster next to a derelict gas station, James hits the motherlode: some photographer has apparently cleaned house. Excited, he picks through outdated darkroom equipment and other spoils. He packs into his duffel a Polaroid camera (*maybe it still works*); some *American Photo* magazines, for evening reading; a portfolio of black and white pictures, for browsing; and a sage smudge stick, still in the wrapper. For that he has special plans.

Rummaging further, he uncovers a box containing a hundred or more lightproof photo bags. Amazing. On the streets he's been storing his photographic exposures in bags like these, then passing them on to his darkroom assistants. His supply is nearly depleted. Now, more bags than he'll ever be able to use.

DAY 35

TUESDAY, MARCH 23

NEANDERTHAL

White Castle, 4:35 AM. Terrible night. For the first few hours, the most peaceful sleep I've had in weeks. Then, out of nowhere, a panic attack. Instantly awake, I fled out the shelter door. I stood staring up at the empty sky. At that moment, it would have been so easy to quit and go home—if only the Thing had given me up.

City lights were reflecting off the clouds, making it difficult to judge the time. Surely, though, it was almost daybreak. *Go up top, wash your hair, wait for dawn. You always feel better at dawn.*

When I got here, the wall clock read 4:20.

Now, hair dripping dry, I sip hot water, exhausted but relieved to be out of the shelter. I'm amazed at how Neanderthal the mind can be; how in dark, close places it can twist and wring your perceptions till you cry out and run. No matter how you try, you can't reason away the fright.

Never in my life have I felt so powerless.

The attacks of fear are more severe when I'm in pain—this I've begun to notice. Limping up to eight miles a day on concrete and asphalt, my legs ache almost constantly, and my bad knee burns. By nightfall, muscles are knots, from hip to ankle. As soon as I lie down in bed, they start to throb, then to scream for space, for stretching out, and there's no room. There's just the darkness clutching in from all sides, and eventually the cramps, and finally a mind crazy for escape.

Got to stay awake. Got to keep your head up off the table, or you'll get rousted.

At the counter, a few people straggle in to carry out. Most of the business is drive-through, though. Odds on a newspaper at this hour are slim to none.

A while ago a *Dispatch* delivery truck dropped a stack of papers at a store cross the street. The store's still closed. The bundle sits innocently on the stoop. *Who'd know if you took a copy? Who'd it hurt?*

No. Sleep is what I need. Maybe I should go back to camp.

Maybe you could go to St. Mary's, lie down on a pew. It's a long way over there, and the doors might be locked, but maybe you could break in—

That homeless woman James met under the overpass—what was her name?—Susan, I think—she said she'd only commit a crime if her life depended on it.

But the church would be so warm—

This is crazy. Since when do I think about stealing newspapers and breaking into buildings?

Since when can't you spell? Since when can't you do simple math? Since when can't you talk without mixing up your words or losing your train of thought? Since when can't you walk down the street without forgetting where you're going? Since when do you get urges for whiskey, or pills, anything to get you through the night—

But none of that is me.

Maybe it is you, sunk low. Broken.

"It takes a lot of courage when faith is hard to find"—a line from the middle of some love song, radio music being piped into the joint. Funny what you hear, sometimes, when you don't know you're listening.

DISAPPEARED

5 AM. Traffic on the streets is picking up a little. Out on the curb sits a young man who looks homeless. Maybe he just walked up from the riverbank. Is he anxious for this night to end, too? What's he waiting for at this hour, out there in the cold?

An elderly couple settles in at the table next to mine. There's comfort, for me, in their being here, starting their day. The man looks like a farmer; he and the woman remind me of my grandparents sitting in a small-town diner. I'm happy not to be alone in the tables.

The young man's gone from the curb. *How quickly you can disappear.*

LINES AND CIRCLES

5:30 AM. A line of carry-out customers, now. A black cop. A jaundiced old white woman, hair in bristly curlers. Delivery men. A Latino cab driver. City of Columbus employees, in pairs. A black security guard. Another white woman in curlers, around my mother's age. A homeless Anglo, gaunt, wearing

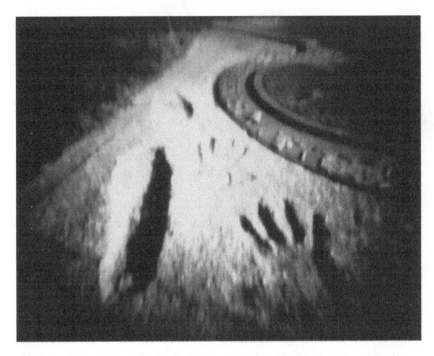

"How quickly you can disappear:" Footprint and handprints near a manhole cover

a pony tail, counting out change, coin by coin. A construction worker in Carhartt overalls.

Some of the customers greet each other by first name. Men shake hands, slap each other's backs, ask after wives and work, tell bad jokes, gripe about the government, the war. Most of the women quickly leave.

Outside my window, it seems darker than it was. Dawn's on its way but so is bad weather. I shiver in a draft from a ceiling vent.

James shows up, heavy bags under his eyes. Water he just splashed on his face in the restroom drips from his beard onto the tabletop.

"Guess I'm rubbing off on you," I say. "You're never up this early."

Wearily he flashes that Irish grin. "If I start menstruating, too, I'm going home for sure."

WOE

6:15 AM. We decide to spend 50¢ on a *Dispatch*. Today's edition is woefully thin, but it'll occupy us till the sun comes up. "Kosovo Still A Stalemate," the front-page headline blares. A band of refugee children—toddler to maybe ten years old—walks hand in hand away from the violence, no adults in frame.

Sometimes you're so alone....

SIGNS OF TROUBLE

Mid-morning, we run into Jake and Sarge, all of us headed for Grubb Street. Hands buried in pockets, we walk the tracks togethe toward the soup kitchen, our pace slow, no reason to hurry.

We ask Jake where Dog is.

"Gone. Just couldn't keep him."

Sarge doesn't have much to say. He rarely does, especially when Jake's around and in the mood to gab, as he is now. Jake confesses that one of Enid's Social Security checks was to have paid his and Rooster's way to Florida. A second check was to have set them up in an apartment here in town. Neither scheme had worked out. "I'm not proud of taking the old woman's money," he says, "but that's what we were going to do."

Will James and I ever properly meet Enid, our tiny neighbor from Germany? Now and then we catch glimpses of her, but only rarely have our paths crossed, in such bad weather nobody wanted to stop and get better acquainted.

As Jake tells it, she used to be a nurse. Over the years she'd accumulated a nice little nest-egg, even owned her own home, but then somehow she met Rooster. Now he's conning her, love for money. After sweet-talking her into living out here on the riverbank, at her age, in a leaky tent, he's spent nearly every penny she had on booze and crack. She spends her days panhandling at the top of a freeway exit ramp. "Riches to rags," Jake says. "That's what it is, for her."

As for him and Rooster, they've had a serious falling out. "I got to get away from him," he says. "He's crazy. Going to bring down the heat. Wouldn't be surprised if he don't kill somebody out here."

ELDERLY

The day's an ugly duckling turned swan, sunny and calm, temperature in the high forties. For many people here in German Village, the workday is over. Infected by spring, they gather in Schiller Park, warming to the languid breeze.

Dogs freed of their leashes chase preening ducks off the banks into the fishpond; collies stop at water's edge, retrievers leap in headlong. Watching the action, toddlers prance and squeal within arm's reach of their parents. On the sidewalk, bicycles whizz by, roller blades whir. Not far away, on a blanket spread over grass, a middle-aged man and woman kiss. Lips linger. A hint of smoke wafts from a distant cigarette.

I take off my shoes off. Then, on impulse, I peel off my many socks, too. The pale skin of my feet, exposed to sunlight, is tinged yellow gray, like that of a new corpse.

I feel old. Feeble as a tottery grandmother. But why should this surprise me? Life on the streets forces you to contend with many demons faced by old people—physical deterioration, lack of mobility, loss of self-sufficiency, weariness, loneliness, a sense of not being needed, of no longer being somebody who matters; fear of the unknown. Little things now seem big, nothing works well, everything's an effort—

You suffer. Even being here by choice, you suffer.

Still, as many elderly people will say, there's also a part of you that can detach from the suffering of your body. It can watch from down deep, or hover above you, serving as impartial witness to whatever's hurting in you, and changing, passing away piecemeal. That part of you, I suspect, you mustn't lose. If you do, the light fades in your eyes, and once it's completely gone, even the greatest of loves might not be able to bring it back.

GONE

James has been quieter these past few days than I've ever seen him. Tonight in camp he seems especially far away. I ask him where he's gone. "Not sure," he says.

The words he spoke aren't quite true, though. He knows exactly where he's gone. He just doesn't know how to tell me.

Where he's gone is deep into desolation. He feels completely self-absorbed, utterly collapsed upon the ruins of what he'd thought himself to be. This is his hell, an ice-cold pit of self-pity. The longer he stays in it, the more normal it seems, and the harder it is to try and pull himself out.

DAY 36

WEDNESDAY, MARCH 24

MISSING

There's a spot up top, overlooking the tracks, where homeless men often sit together, drinking beer. Last night Bobby was up there, drinking alone. White, in his mid-fifties, he lives in a tent camp somewhere downstream. Calls himself a river rat. Almost every morning I see him at White Castle with his sister Jan, a farmwife who drives into the city to eat breakfast with him.

"See you *early* tomorrow," he hollered down last night, as I walked the railroad bed.

"Why's that?" I shouted back.

"It's going to be *cold*, girl. Cold and rainy. Big storm's coming."

"Maybe it'll go around us."

"Yeah, maybe." He laughed. "I'll see you *early*."

Now it's shortly after 7 AM. I'm in White Castle. Up at the counter, there's brisk business. Bobby should be here by now. He's *always* here, by now.

Across the aisle from my table, his sister Jan says to a friend, "I've got a bad feeling about this."

My old paper-buddy, the black gentleman of the meticulous folds, is back this morning. It's been a long time since I've seen him. Patiently I wait. Finally he folds his newspaper, pulls on his coat, dons his hat. Crossing the room, he makes a hand delivery to my table, a slight smile creasing his lips. He never says a word, isn't interested in my thanks.

A song lyric plays over the radio:

I believe in you
and all I wanna do is help you
believe in you

"I've got a *really* bad feeling about this," Jan says again.

I share her anxious vigil from behind the pages of the *Dispatch*. In Kosovo, NATO has ordered airstrikes. An estimated 25,000 ethnic Albanians have fled their homes in the past few days. *25,000.* Foxes have holes, and birds have nests, but the children of God have nowhere safe to lay their heads—

"I'm worried someday they'll find Bobby face-down in the mud." Jan absently stirs her coffee. "He takes coumadin, you know. Bloodthinner. Could easily freeze to death. That's why he has to have a heater in his tent, despite the risk of fire."

An hour drags by. Another homeless man, a friend of Bobby's, comes into the restaurant. He tells Jan there was some fighting along the river last night, down near Bobby's camp.

"I *knew* it!" she cries. "I could *feel* it!" She buries her head in her arms. The man tries to console her, saying he'd surely have heard by now if "anything bad" had happened.

We wait. After another hour, Bobby's still AWOL. Reluctantly I rise from my seat. I have to head back to camp. It's almost time to leave with James for Grubb Street.

When the door closes behind me, Jan's pacing around empty tables.

FRIENDS

Aaron, our friend who was hit by a car some weeks back, hobbles up to us in the soup kitchen like a saddlesore cowboy. He seems somewhat stronger and more centered than the last time we saw him, but he's still suffering with his injuries, and now he has a bad cough. When I reach out to shake his hand, he warns me off. "Better not—I don't want you catching nothing."

I offer him the baggie of vitamin C tablets I always carry in my coat. Tomorrow, I promise him, I'll bring a bottle of 250 pills. Take It to the Streets brings both James and me a bottle, every week.

James tells Aaron that he'd like to visit him at the men's shelter later in the afternoon.

Aaron smiles. "Good."

At Volunteers of America an obliging staffer lets James have a used copy of *The Big Book*, the basic text of Alcoholics Anonymous. He removes its torn dust jacket, then opens the hardcover and scrawls inside, "To Aaron, One day at a time. Your friend, James."

Aaron's shelter is in a tough neighborhood in the Bottoms. On the corner just outside the building, twenty or more residents mingle with drug dealers. As James reaches the crowd, a dust devil swirls up, forcing everybody but him to shield their eyes. He's unaffected, wearing engineer shades that he'd found along the railroad tracks. He walks straight through the parted sea of crack and goes inside.

Aaron is sitting at a card table, staring into space. He smiles to see James, pulls out a chair and offers him a smoke. "You're my friend, you know." He smells of liquor, now. Looks half buzzed.

"Yes, Aaron, I know. You're my friend, too."

"I been drinking, James. There's only so long I can stand it, sitting around here doing nothing. Some guy tells me he's going to the store, and my mouth starts to water. I think, 'One little drink won't hurt.' Once I start, I can't stop."

"I've been there, Aaron. I know what you mean."

"Friends are hard to come by out here. You're my friend, James."

"You too, Aaron."

"You know, I went to church yesterday. I'm not right with God yet, but I'm working on it. Got to start crawling before I start walking." He leans in close. "That's a cop-out, you know. I got to get on the right path *now!*"

James places *The Big Book* in Aaron's hands. Aaron brightens. "You *told* me you'd get me a book, and you did. It'll go in my locker, with a lock." He smiles a broken, buzzed smile. "James, we're the same kind of people, you and me. I wish you could meet my son—he's a good kid."

"Maybe someday, Aaron, but I'll be moving north in a couple weeks to find some work."

"Sorry to hear you'll be leaving. Friends are hard to come by."

KEEPING WATCH

Jake stops by camp, needing some candles. I pull a box of six white tapers from our stash. The volunteers have been generous.

Jake's in a chatty mood. I invite him to sit with me by the fire, but he stands a short distance away, dodging woodsmoke. He tells me he's landed a temp job, starting Monday. "Last job, I blew it. Drank too damn much. But I haven't had a drink in two days now. Just water. Lots of water.

"You know, I really got to slow down, change my life. If I don't, one day I'll be an old man walking around with a bottle. Got to stay away from the crack, too. I like the stuff, but you got to know your limits.

"I really made a mistake, falling in with Rooster." He's talking to the ground. "He's dangerous, you know, especially when he's been drinking or doing crack. Gets real mean. You never know what he's going to do."

The fire pops. He raises his eyes to meet mine. "He won't bother *you* guys, though."

"How can we be sure?"

He shrugs. "You just being who you are."

He says Rooster's dealing drugs and leaning hard on him to sell. "I won't lie to you. I was at a crackhouse with him, night before last. I like my crack now and then. But I don't want to be selling."

With his new job, he says, he'll be just a few paychecks from moving into the YMCA. Maybe he'll even take Sarge along, if he wants to go.

"By the way, Sarge wants you guys to have this—" He hands me a digital watch-face, scratched and battered. "You guys were saying how you don't have a way to tell the time. Well, this ain't no Rolex, but it should do the trick. It's yours to keep."

CALLUS

Scrap of paper. Pencil stub. *What happened today? What can you say that will help you remember?*

Memory continues to atrophy. James and I are losing any sense of continuity with even the recent past. Today must be written tonight; tomorrow might be too late. Yesterday seems little more than heavy mist; we reach out for it, and our hands come back wet but empty. We feel cut off. Less than human.

What if you got used to feeling this way? What if you gave up wanting to remember?

By candlelight James examines one of the *American Photo* magazines he found recently in a dumpster. This issue contains "The Most Powerful Photographs of 1993"—images of war, flight, famine, poverty.... The editor believes these photographs will break through "the emotional callus" of whoever looks at them, making him or her less numb, less indifferent to the world.

"That's what I want my photography to do," James tells me. "Help break through the callus. My own, especially."

DAY 37

THURSDAY, MARCH 25

OFFENSIVE

Today we're bombing Yugoslavia.

TRAPPED

Jeff, walking the tracks with us toward Grubb Street, urges us to "try and hold our heads high." "It's hard," he says, "but you got to hold onto your pride. Sometimes you feel trapped. I know *I* do. When you've got a past, it keeps catching up with you when you're looking for a job."

He's worked low-paying temp jobs for more than a year, and he isn't making it. He wants steadier, more gainful employment. Wants to sober up, too. "I work as hard as I can, but I drink more. Can't seem to stop. Wish I could."

DICTATORSHIP

The volunteer in charge of today's crew at the soup kitchen is short. In inches. On kindness and patience. It isn't that he's having a bad day, unless every Thursday (his usual shift) is a bad day; either his heart isn't in the work, or he's afraid to let it show. In my private world I call him—rather meanly, I'm sorry to say—"the little dictator." Bespectacled, he always wears a carefully pressed off-white business shirt and bland brown tie, and a full apron, tied just so. His manner reminds me of an accountant who lives for his books, whose entire universe is arranging numbers and justifying columns and decimal points. We're his pennies and nickels, and he wants us in perfect order.

Now, in condescending tone, he instructs the room on procedure. "There will be a prayer. After the prayer the line will form, numbers one to seven. I repeat, one to seven, *not* one to ten. You will proceed to the line by sevens, *not* tens, when your number is called by the gentleman with the megaphone. You will take no more food than you can eat. You will carry your tray to the back of the room to collect your drink and your dessert—you will not be served drinks or desserts without a tray. When you have finished eating, you will push your chair back into position before leaving the table. You will walk to the service window at the front of the room, toss your trash and empty your garbage into the can, then pass your dishes through to the volunteer. You will exit in orderly fashion...."

Once the speech ends, the prayer begins. Foregoing the customary Lord's Prayer, the man invites us into a time of silence, then concludes with a prepared text: "Let us be thankful for those who donated this food, for those who delivered the food to this kitchen, for those who have prepared the food, and for those who now serve it. And Lord, please forgive those who sin, for they are only human."

I feel slapped. No need, apparently, to be thankful for those of us who will *eat* the food. No, for us, there's only a need to plead forgiveness.

I peek at James across the table. His face is screwed into a scowl.

"In Jesus's name we ask it—"

On the Amen, chairs scrape back. One to seven dash into line. "It's going to go slow today," James says, "counting by sevens—"

Suddenly there's an eruption of noise, and a surging mass of bodies, up toward the front of the room. A volunteer standing nearby freezes, says, in understatement, "Hey, we've got a problem!"

A brawl—women on women, men on men, everybody else up and trying to see, tense, the whole room could explode, the fight's spreading, nobody's moving to intervene, the servers are still scooping green beans and doling out chicken thighs like nothing's happening—

Adrenaline rushes the room like a tidal wave. A guy in front of us yells, "Hey, not in a church!" and though this isn't a church, exactly, he's got the idea, if only somebody would listen. The little dictator reaches out for a tray, ladles some noodles, hands the tray along, takes another, sneaks a look at the brawl, ladles more noodles, the swarm's out of control—*God, let there not be knives, let there not be guns—somebody do something—somebody!—*

Men shout, "Call 9-1-1!" James and I consider crawling under a table, then decide to hang out near a door to the hallway.

A few down-on-their-luck middle-aged men, employed part-time to run the line, throw themselves into the fray. Finally they manage to break it up. As they escort the toughs out of the cafeteria, the air curdles with obscenities and threats.

Crisis resolved, people return to the business of eating. Cops eventually appear in the hall.

I toy with my food, not hungry, now. One of our friends at the table complains about the lack of security. "I don't want to be afraid to come here."

James and I, when we manage to speak again, wonder aloud if the fight would have broken out, had the prayer not ended as it did.

PRIVILEGE

Every day James and I experience a profusion of moods. All of them pass, except for gratitude. Always gratitude.

Clearly we're on a downhill slide; we keep hoping for the ground to level off, but the grade only seems to steepen. Despite our best efforts, we can't get our bodies to feel better, our minds to think better, our spirits to lift.

As the days pass and the streets become more familiar, we want to find more meaning than we have, but we can't. We want to feel some semblance of progress, something more than the mere march of time, but we're left disappointed. We want to stop the endless parade of people we're meeting (*all the faces you see, all the voices you hear in your sleep*), but there aren't enough boundaries to keep them away. In the end, I suspect, we'll want closure, only to be denied. Meaning, progress, boundaries, closure: these seem to be privileges we enjoy only when suffering is past, or when we choose to stand apart from it. When we're in the midst of it, the privilege is survival, without the loss of our humanity.

DAY 38

FRIDAY, MARCH 26

ARMS

Three days. Three *terrible* days of waiting.

In White Castle Jan pulls Bobby into a long, tight hug, then pushes him away and bawls him out.

HOSTILITIES

6:45 AM. The right side of Jake's jaw is swollen, and an ugly purple bruise is raised on his cheek. Otherwise he's unhurt. He and Sarge tell me they were attacked at their camp around 3 AM. I remember. I was jolted from an uncommonly sound sleep by a flurry of sharp cracks and dull pops. James was already awake, and nervous, convinced that at least some of the sounds, coming from Jake and Sarge's, were gunshots. I wasn't sure. After much listening, we decided that no, somebody was throwing things, mightily hard, against the walls of the shack, all the while screaming a blue streak. We recognized the voice.

Jake and Sarge say they were fast asleep when Rooster burst in, armed with a big stick. He slammed it against their stove, their chairs, their walls. Then he lit into Jake, first with the stick, then with his fists. "We were *sleeping*, for godsake," Jake says in a painful mumble. "I was *in bed*—penned in. Couldn't defend myself. He was crazy, screaming. Said I was telling people he's smoking crack. Hell, Missus Ingalls, the only people I really talk to is you and James.

He shakes his head. "It ain't safe for me to be out here anymore. Maybe I'll call Harold and Ada, see if they can help me leave. I told them the other day it's getting crazy down here, I need to get off the riverbank."

"Can you *believe*," Sarge says, his eyes wide, "Rooster *apologized*, to *me*, before he left? 'Got no quarrel with *you*, Sarge,' he says. 'Sorry to wake you up!' *Hell!* You know, I think he's trying to drive us off because he wants our shack. Well, he ain't going to get it! I'll burn it down first!"

SMOLDERINGS

James greets me outside our shelter with a birthday present. I'm now thirty-seven years old. With all the hostilities, I'd forgotten.

"Stand here. Close your eyes."

I hear him strike a match. Sweet smoke wafts up, tickling my nostrils. Breathing it in, I begin to smile. By some miracle, he's conjured up some dried sage. He passes the smoldering herb around my head, my torso, my legs, smudging my bundled body.

"Take off your gloves. Hold out your arms."

His voice is quiet but firm. I obey like a child. Soon the air is full of the heady fragrance. I feel clean, new as rain.

When he finishes the smudge, the woods are still but for birdsong. I listen. Then, opening my eyes, I bow deeply to him, palms together as if in prayer, and take the smudge stick from his hand. The bundle of dried white sage leaves is as big around as a fist. Wherever had he found it?

"Close your eyes," I tell him.

Not a breeze stirs. The sage smoke hangs in the air, wispy as floss silk. For a few minutes, I don't think of the feud between Rooster and Jake. I don't think of the bombing in Yugoslavia, the atrocities in Kosovo. I don't think of homeless people, of refugees, of victims. For these few minutes, the world has righted itself. Fanning the sage lightly with my free hand, I weave the smoke around James.

He says that he found the smudge stick at the bottom of a dumpster, still packaged in crinkly plastic. Indigenous cultures around the world commonly use white sage for rituals of purification and blessing. For me, today, it also serves as evocation, summoning up memories of home, of writing at my desk, wrapped in the fragrant smoke of braided incense from Nepal.

I stub out the still-smoldering stick. The rest we must save. For the end.

MANEUVERS

Jake stops by camp in late morning, carrying two duffel bags and a sleeping bag. He says he intends to set up a new camp, somewhere along the river where Rooster won't find him. "I won't be telling you guys where I've moved to. Rooster might lean on you to say."

Wherever Jake ends up, may he be warm. May he be dry. May he be safe.

EXPOSED

Over in the Bottoms James hides behind a stack of railroad ties to change photo paper. He works quickly, feeling exposed. At least the area isn't busy at the moment; just some kids playing on the other side of the street.

Up to his elbows in the sleeves of the lightproof bag, he has finished changing his first camera and started in on the second when suddenly a white man and a black woman appear around the piling. Their eyes look like pinwheels. They're high, and jonesing for more.

"*Shit!*" they say. "Somebody's here, too!"

"Hey, I'm leaving in a sec," James says, his blind fingers fumbling in the bag.

They have no idea what he's doing. Evidently they couldn't care less. "Naw," they say, "you don't have to leave. You straight. You was here first." They light up some crack in a pipe, only a few feet away.

ARMS (2)

Behind Holy Family Church, a shrine to the Virgin Mary. Her outstretched arms are welcoming. James clears away dead pine needles from the walkway and sits down cross-legged amidst bird droppings. Being here is a comfort, like being hugged by a woman.

Though raised Roman Catholic, only once before has he felt a powerful connection to Mary—several years ago, in a chapel in Medjugorje, a small village in Bosnia-Herzegovina where almost daily since 1981 people have reported seeing apparitions of her. That day, a special worship service for children and young people had been led by a visionary named Ivan, one of several villagers to whom Mary regularly appeared. When after the service Ivan led the worshipers out of the chapel, James lingered, not yet ready to leave. He went to the front of the shrine to stand near the Queen of Peace. The energy of the place was intense, healing.

Suddenly, a touch on his shoulder—Ivan. The two men's eyes locked for an intense, otherworldly minute. Finally Ivan smiled. "It's time to go." Afterwards James couldn't stop crying, and didn't know why.

That day in Medjugorje, Mary had been for him a heavenly, angelic figure. "Don't be afraid," she seemed to say. "Open your heart."

Today, in this place, Mary is mother, arms ready to gather him in. "Rest," she says simply. "Rest."

Mary, Queen of Peace

HOME FRONT

We visit Sarge in his shack. He's camped with Jake a long time and (being "a bit slow," as he puts it) very much depends on him, tagging along like a little tyke after a brother he adores.

"You going to stay on?" we ask him.

Sarge shrugs. He says he thinks his wife might have lifted the restraining order against him. If she'll let him, he might just go home. "I wasn't allowed to be around there for a while. I didn't like the neighbors. Made some threats and stuff. Stupid. I really miss my kids."

NEGOTIATIONS

I run into Rooster along the tracks. He looks bloated, jaundiced. His appearance has deteriorated profoundly these past weeks.

"Sorry if all the ruckus kept you guys up last night," he says with a grin. "It's all on Jake's head. He come over to my place yesterday when I wasn't there and cussed out my old lady. Just ain't right. Nobody got a right to talk to her like that." He wags a finger in my face. "Now you tell me, wasn't I right to stick up for her?"

I say nothing.

"Well, *wasn't* I?"

"I'm not your judge." I'm watching him carefully, afraid he might come unhinged. "But to be honest, Rooster, when all that fighting was going on last night, James and I were afraid you'd be coming after us next."

"No *way!*" He steps back as if I'd thrown a punch. "I like the *heck* out of you guys! You're damn straight. *Damn* straight! No need to worry."

He holds out his hand, and I grasp it, somewhat relieved. But now he doesn't let go. His grip tightens.

You know what he told James. He thinks you're an ex-con. He likes you because you're tough.

I tug my hand hard, to wrench it away.

You know what he said to you, that one time in the woods—"You can trust me, I'm not trying to get into your pants."

I yank even harder, and he's still not letting go—

But here comes Sarge up the tracks. Rooster sees him, too. Abruptly he drops my hand and struts off in the opposite direction.

DAY 39

SATURDAY, MARCH 27

PUBLIC RELATIONS

Along the tracks James and I run into our reclusive neighbor Calvin, the old white man who lives in the next camp north. He surprises us by initiating a conversation, or, more accurately, a monologue. He's eager to talk when he chooses.

Calvin is a very proud man. Proud of his strict moral code. Proud of his camp, so neat and clean. Proud of his ability to keep himself going, doing the best he can.

He's deeply resentful of Take It to the Streets. This is easy to understand, given not only his pride but his fear. Whether or not he's clinically paranoid, as James and I suspect, he's very distrustful, quick to frighten, and extremely protective of his camp. How must he feel when six carloads of volunteers (and he does keep count) suddenly converge on his camp in the darkness? Recently, he says, he told the Martins that he wants to be left alone, and since then things have been somewhat better: he hides inside his tent while a single volunteer delivers his rations.

He worries that somebody from the Martins' organization will either put his picture in the newspaper or videotape him for the news. "I know they got to have publicity to get money, to do what they do. But a lot of times they don't get a person's permission. I know that for a fact. If they ever use *me* that way, I tell you, I'll *sue* them. You can understand, probably. Somebody might see you, and recognize you from the paper, and then they'd know you was homeless. It'd be *embarrassing*."

OPEN WINDOW

The other day at a Twelve-Step meeting, James heard somebody define forgiveness as the letting go of the wish that the past had been other than it was. Whenever I think of the Martins, I try to practice this letting go. Instantly my attention boomerangs to the present, and my spirit lightens, for a stretch. I'm no saint—forgiveness is often a struggle—but my sense of indignation is slowly receding. It'll just take time.

Sometimes when a wild bird is in the house, swooping room to room, you can chase it through an open window with a broom. But sometimes it's best to put the broom down, let the bird find its own way out, in its own time. Just keep the window open wide, however long it takes.

HIT

In Deaf School Park James sits quietly at a picnic table. Nearby, three gang members are hanging out. Wind brings him snatches of their rap. One of their homies is missing; they haven't seen him in days; they're afraid he's been hit by a rival gang. "Hey, I'm telling you, man," the loudest guy says, "if them badasses gets mad at you, you just disappear. Don't *nobody* ever know what happened."

Suddenly James sees a woman's face, staring up at him from the weathered gray wood of the tabletop. Drawn in black dry marker, her features are soft as charcoal, faded by the sun. He'd almost missed her.

Lying atop another table, I laze in a patch of sunshine. With the arrival of more favorable weather, I'm suddenly a person of leisure, relatively speaking. Coping takes less planning, less effort, less energy; a good thing, since I have no reserves left. I can't imagine trying to hold down a job, living this way.

The top of this picnic table is my chaise lounge. I sink, beginning to relax, my body warm, slackening.

Suddenly, just at the edge of sleep, I don't like the feel of it. Beneath the easing tension, there's no contentment—just pain—vulnerability—a distress I can't name. I yank myself out of it, sit up straight, heart racing—

Maybe I'd rather have winter.

NEUTRALITY

Around 9 PM headlights from half a dozen vehicles spray across the scruffy field above the woods. Returning from the laundromat, James and I drop into a crouch beside the railroad tracks. Concealed by darkness, we listen to the shouts and watch the wagging flashlights. Tonight we'd prefer not to deal with volunteers from Take It to the Streets. Grateful as we are for their help, it does get a little tiresome, twenty or thirty people showing up at your house two or three nights each week, sometimes unannounced, maybe even with a videocamera. You begin to feel they own you.

Spotting several flashlights down by Calvin's camp, I wonder what he's thinking, holed up in his tent. Then, suddenly, I'm wondering, too, if my wanting to write down something of his life, tell something of his feelings, to bear him witness, isn't also an intrusion.

Tired of waiting for the volunteers to leave, we stand up and walk into headlights.

At our approach, Sabrina Martin hurries up to greet us, making sure we're safe. She laments the feuding between Jake and Rooster. "This is a war zone now, At least you seem to be in neutral territory."

She's just come from Rooster's camp, where she left some rations. "Even them that's causing the trouble's got to eat."

Now a woman hails us from a mini-van. "It must take lots of strength to stay out here," she says to us, through a window half rolled down, "especially with the bad weather we've been having. I admire you two for your strength."

"You're helping us be however strong we are," we say.

Long after the volunteers drive off, the woman's words keep rising in James's mind like a mirror in the hand, reflecting the image of what, not so long ago, he desperately thought he needed to be: Strong. Unbreakable. A rock.

No more.

Now he knows: he doesn't need to be strong. He needs only to be who he is. Who, after all, can be more?

PART 4: END TIMES

DAY 40

SUNDAY, MARCH 28

TIE THAT BINDS

I'm sleepwalking up an early morning alley when my wedding ring and amulets spill with a clatter onto the pavement. I've been wearing them on a cord around my neck ever since I left home. Now, after all this time, with only a week left on the streets, the knot in the cord has come untied. It almost feels like a sign.

FIT

James: "I dreamed that Dad and I were spending forty-seven days homeless in New York City. The two of us were sitting at a table in a deli, staring at each other over cups of hot water. Suddenly Dad broke down, started screaming, 'I can't take it anymore! Give me some money! I want to buy some bacon and eggs, rye toast!'

"For some reason I had a bank card in my hand. Dad snatched it away from me and ran outside to an ATM, but instead of withdrawing money, he stopped short and squatted down on the sidewalk. Now, instead of the bank card, he was holding my tool kit (credit-card-sized, you know). The little tools were scattered all around him on the pavement. One by one he picked them up and tried to return them to their proper places in the case, but every tool was twisted and bent. He groaned. Nothing fit like it used to."

DOOMED

James and I settle with our trays at an empty table in the Fellowship Hall of Central Presbyterian Church. Before long, a barrel-chested, thick-necked Anglo sits down in the chair across from us. He sizes James up and mumbles a few words.

James smiles. "I'm sorry, I didn't hear—what did you say?"

The man glares, working his thick lower lip. His brow creases. The lip starts to tremble. Then an animal growl issues from his belly. Elbow on table, he points a stubby finger directly at James's nose. He doesn't say a word, just points. James looks like a mountain climber who's seen the start of an avalanche a thousand feet above him. Doomed.

You saw this man just yesterday. He walked past you into the library, with A History of the American People *tucked under one arm.*

James takes several deep breaths and lowers his gaze to his plate. Intense minutes pass. The man still doesn't move. James glances sidelong at me. *Keep quiet,* my eyes warn. He forks up more biscuit.

Finally the man starts wolfing down his food. James visibly relaxes. Eyebrows arched, he shoots me an incredulous look.

"You know," the man says then, suddenly friendly as a distant cousin, "all that coke they found is coming out of Haiti. Twenty-four pounds."

"*Really,*" James says, clueless.

"Yeah. That's something, huh?"

The man's no longer eating. His eyes dart all around, as if watching a swarm of insects, till he seems to remember his food. One big hand starts spooning furiously.

"We've only got eight months left, you know," he says after a bit, sounding now like a scared little boy. "Governor Taft said in the paper he's going to live in a bunker when Y2K comes. Don't know what the hell *I'm* going to do."

THE CITY

For Palm Sunday mass we walk from the riverbank way north to St. Patrick's Church on E. Naghten; an old church, built by the Dominicans in 1852.

The nave's abuzz. Unlike at St. Joe's, where you whisper, if you say anything at all, as you slide into a pew, here you can speak in normal tones and laugh without apology. No elegance to be maintained. This is a working-class church with a neighborhood feel. Fathers carry young children high on their shoulders, mothers reach up and wipe a last bit of breakfast from the corners of jabbering mouths. Elderly men snore or stare at their bulletins, waiting for mass to start; elderly women dig into purses for a mint, wave white-gloved hands at friends across the aisle. In the back, just inside the sanctuary doors, a big, bearded Dominican gives final instructions to two altar boys.

The church is packed. There's a rare empty seat beside James, right along the aisle. Several times a parishioner starts to sit down there, only to notice him, back away and awkwardly retreat to the back of the sanctuary. Standing Room Only.

The Palm Sunday procession finally begins, recalling Jesus's triumphal entry into Jerusalem shortly before he was killed. The priest sprinkles holy water, swinging the pot from side to side as he plods up the aisle. We in the congregation wave palm fronds with (feeble) shouts of Hosanna.

"As Jesus came near and saw the city, he wept over it, saying, `If you, even you, had only recognized the things that make for peace....'"

TRIAL

This old church, we discover after mass, houses a humble shrine devoted to the Blessed Margaret Castello. Margaret, a brochure tells us, was born in 1287, a child of Italian nobility, but her life was hardly one of luxury and ease. She was a "midget," a hunchback scarcely able to walk, and totally blind. Her parents, the story goes, were so ashamed of her physical impairments that when she was only six years old, they locked her up in a cell adjoining a chapel. For the next fourteen years, they allowed her out only to attend mass and receive the sacraments. Finally, as a last resort, they packed her off to a shrine in a distant city, where they prayed for a cure. When the miracle wasn't forthcoming, they abandoned her to the streets. She remained homeless till some Dominican laywomen took her in.

Margaret spent the remainder of her life ministering to the imprisoned, the sick and the dying. She died in 1320, at the age of thirty-three. In Roman Catholic belief, she continues even today to intercede for the poor, the disabled, the rejected—and the homeless.

I dip my fingers in her holy water, touch them to my forehead.

Apparently the artist who sculpted the statue of Margaret for this shrine hadn't known her story. Or maybe the artist had meant to suggest that true beauty is an attribute of the spirit. Whatever the reason, the lovely woman who gazes down at me, arms full of red roses, shows no sign of infirmity.

Scripted in red above Margaret's statue:

If you are willing to serenely bear the trial of being displeasing to yourself, then you will be for Jesus a pleasant place of shelter.

PALM

At the base of the Statue of Peace is a palm frond. Settling in for meditation, James and I stare at it with wonder. Who could have laid it there?

When our period of silence ends, James says that he'd like to come back in a few hours when the sun is softer to photograph the frond. In the meantime, he suggests we hide it from the blustery wind.

I carry the frond to a flowerbed, some distance away, and delicately push it down among blooming daffodils.

The day's good for taking pictures, sunny with occasional billows of clouds; a full spectrum of light, from bright to shade, with which to work. For more than two hours we walk the railroad tracks that cross beneath High Street, James looking for shots among the solid concrete pillars and screaming graffiti.

Spray-painted on a cement wall: "HAROLD FOR PRESIDENT." Harold Martin, maybe?

Nearby, a double mattress on springs, neatly made, covered with colorful children's comforters. *Some things,* James tells himself, *you don't take pictures of.*

ALTAR

In mid-afternoon we return to the Statehouse grounds.

"No way!" I exclaim.

"What?"

My hands probe gently among the flowers, but the palm frond isn't there. "It's *gone!*"

"Maybe the wind got it?"

"Not down in there. It *couldn't* have!"

James grabs my arm. "You're not going to believe this. *Look—*"

The palm frond is back at the Statue of Peace, exactly where we'd first seen it, now held in place by a beautiful yellow apple. Lying beside it, a yellow daffodil. Offerings on an altar.

RELICS

Lately, when I'm alone in camp, I've been working on celebratory gifts. Large gift-boxes of gratitude: for Jihong, so unwavering; for James, and his companionship on the journey. For others, smaller tokens of appreciation, like the bookmarks I'm making now, cut from dried river reeds, pressed between bricks, inscribed with lines by W. S. Merwin:

I will take with me the emptiness of my hands

Palm frond at the base of the Statue of Peace

What you do not have you find everywhere

The impulse to give gifts in exchange for favors and kindnesses rendered is probably very middle-class. Gift-giving helps not only to express gratitude but also to assuage a sense of indebtedness; generally speaking, bourgeoisie don't like feeling beholden. But though something of this middle-class civility might have prompted my desire to give gifts as I leave the streets, the gifts themselves—recycled from dumpsters, scavenged from sidewalks, scrounged from the riverbank, transformed by hand—will speak of something more than blushing courtesy.

There are also a few objects that I intend to keep for myself when I go, chief among them the golden pen with which I've been writing lately, and a tin candleholder, stashed each night with a book of matches within easy reach. The urge to keep these things feels almost primal. I read once about civilian survivors of war who keep in their homes certain relics of that terrible time, not to honor it, but to domesticate its savage memory. In this way they manage to make life in peacetime more livable. I remember reading this, and not understanding. Perhaps I still don't understand fully, but somehow the candleholder and the golden pen—these I must take home with me when I leave the streets. Not for forever. Just for long enough.

WORLD AWAY

In the nighttime darkness of a High Street phone booth, James hears Phoebe ask how he's doing. He tells her this happened, that happened.

"Yeah," she says, from a world away, "but how do you *feel?*"

He almost buckles beneath her question. He has no idea how to answer, or where to even start. "I feel *everything*," he says, beginning to cry. "Everything *at once—*"

His body convulses. He hears his own sobs as if they were somebody else's.

People say, with a dismissive air, "Why can't the homeless just get help from their families?"

God, they don't know what they're asking—

DAY 41

MONDAY, MARCH 29

TRUCE

White Castle, 6:40 AM. Jake shows up out of nowhere. Three days have passed since he moved out of the shack, trying to avoid more fighting with Rooster. He tells me that he's pitched camp in a remote part of the woods.

Things have been quiet between him and Rooster; a temporary truce, but he doesn't trust it. Word is, Rooster's easing up on him so he'll let down his guard. "Then he's going to kill me. Gut me on the tracks. That's what he's been saying."

Across the aisle a few men over sixty are debating the war. One of them, red-faced with fury, talks the others down, says, "If you're going to help another country, at least help somebody who's going to help you back, *goddammit.*"

Jake shakes his head. "I got in with Rooster for the wrong reasons. When somebody's buying you smokes and liquor and food, it's easy to be their friend. You don't realize there's going to be a price to pay in the end."

NAMES

I'm into the entertainment section of the newspaper when Jake tells me his real name, given *and* family, for the first time. At least he *says* it's his real name, and I believe him. His revelation is entirely unexpected. Out here, people use first names, nicknames, aliases—no more. They don't want to know, or be known, too much; a matter of survival, just like not asking or answering too many questions.

He tells me he's forty-three years old and has never had a real home. Born to a fourteen-year-old girl, at once he became a ward of the state. He spent his childhood in a blur of orphanages and foster homes. "No wonder I been a drifter all my life. A modern-day hobo. I work when I can and lay my head where I will."

"Speaking of work," I say, "didn't you tell me you were starting a new job today?"

He stares into his coffee cup.

"Sorry, Jake. I didn't mean to butt into your business."

"It ain't that." He rubs his forehead. "Look, Missus Ingalls, I ain't going to lie to you. There never was a new job. I just said that, trying to give myself a little hope."

He looks me in the eye. I smile a little. "It's okay, Jake. We're straight."

Jake, I call him. Not his real name, but Jake.

STAR TREK

Jake's a trekkie, though he rarely sees an episode these days. "I especially like the Voyager series."

"Why's that?"

"I don't really know."

"What's it about?"

"The starship Voyager is lost, eons and *eons* from home, and Captain Janeway—she's a woman, you know—she's trying to get them all back to where they came from." His face lights up. "It's the *theme!*" he cries. "It's the *theme* that makes that show! It's all about *going home!*"

REVELATION

From behind the metro section of his newspaper, Jake asks if I'm religious.

"I'm interested in the spiritual life."

He lowers his paper. "What's that mean?"

"I believe there's a little truth, a little wisdom, in every religion. Outside religion, too. I'm interested in whatever opens the mind and heart, regardless of where it's found."

He says that he once was a seminary student, but he had a crisis of faith and dropped out. "That's a story for another time," he says with a sigh, "but I was wondering—you ever read the Book of Revelation?"

I nod.

"PEACE" engraved on the sidewalk outside the YMCA

"Well, Revelation and the teachings of Nostradamus—if you believe what they're saying, things are coming to a head. We're coming to the *end*."

I sip my water. "You know, Jake, I'm not going to worry about that."

He deliberates a moment. "You know, I'm not either. I believe if you try to do the right thing, and you say a prayer sometimes, and you do the best you can, God'll see you. He's all the time *seeing* you."

The air between us feels suddenly charged; the moment delicate, like a bubble floating on breeze. I lean forward, elbows on the table, and look directly into his eyes. "It feels good to be seen, doesn't it, Jake?"

"Yeah," his voice almost a whisper, a tear in his reddened eyes, "it does."

FENCES

Camp, 8 A.M. James and I lounge outside the shelter, soaking up sunshine, our fuel for the day. I'm screwing open a can of sliced government peaches, the perfect accompaniment to stale dumpster bagels, when a City of Columbus truck brakes to a stop across the chainlink fence separating our little strip of woods from the water treatment plant.

This has never happened before.

Despite our feeble attempts at camouflage, our camp has always been in clear view of the plant. The tall fence around the city's property is a mere thirty feet away, and the gravel drive to the plant maybe another ten feet beyond that. For weeks now we've watched city trucks come and go. Early on, whenever a truck showed up, we'd hide, afraid of being reported; a futile exercise, since our shelter was plainly visible, but we were acting on instinct, not reason. As time went by and no police materialized to roust us, we began to feel more secure. Bold, even. Sometimes when a truck appeared, we'd wave at its occupants. Nobody ever responded in kind. These days, when a truck arrives, we scarcely pay attention.

But this truck has stopped. The city worker on the passenger side rolls down his window. "Hey, you guys want a cup of coffee?"

James and I exchange a look, dumbfounded. The moment is downright historic. Whether or not we actually want coffee, there's no way we're turning it down. "Sure, that'd be great. Thanks!"

"You drink it black?" the man yells as the truck lurches forward. "Cream and sugar?"

The city workers are shortly back from White Castle. The man on the passenger side jumps out of the cab, quickly hands two bags over the fence to James, and climbs back in. The truck drives off.

In the bags are two large coffees, a handful of creamers, and two sausage-egg sandwiches. Manna in the wilderness.

Beneath our feet is a carpet of woods flowers, purple and pink. They just poked up overnight.

FOOL

I'm sitting on my favorite tree stump, munching on dumpster popcorn, when a white van lurches into the field. A rangy sandy-haired Anglo jumps out from behind the wheel and struts off toward Sarge's shack in obvious annoyance. Soon I hear him hollering, first for Jake, then for Sarge. There's no reply. Before long, the guy is back at his van, hands on hips, glaring at the woods.

Here in the thicket, tree branches only beginning to bud, my bright green coat can't be missed. When the guy catches sight of me, he comes striding down the path toward camp.

I don't trust him. Not at all.

"Where's Jake?" the guy barks.

"Don't know," I say stupidly, chomping away on my popcorn. *Let him think you're a fool.*

"Seen Sarge today?"

"Nope."

"Were they around yesterday?"

"Couldn't tell you."

He cusses under his breath. I glance up at the van. A young black man is standing there now, watching us, holding an empty trash-bag. I recognize him. He's been staying at Rooster's. Word is, they're both dealing crack. Word is, maybe Jake's dealing, too.

"When will you be seeing Jake again?"

"No idea."

More obscenities. The guy glares. "When you do see him, tell him I was here looking for him."

"And you are—?"

"*He'll* know."

TRAINS AND RAILS

Near the city junkyard north of camp stands a lonely railroad car. James crawls under and nestles his cheek against a cold rail, carefully positioning his pinhole camera to photograph one of the wheels on the steel track. A strange shot, maybe, but it's his way of paying homage to the railroad. The trains, out here, have been an inspiration to us both. There's something reassuring about how they follow the tracks beyond where you can see, with a strong surety; something beautiful in the fit between their wheels and the rails. Rail gives, wheel receives: a powerful, steady exchange, made possible by the emptiness of the groove.

He peels back the shutter-tape over the pinhole, exposing the photo paper inside the camera. Waiting for the shot to take, he recalls an early morning in Bexley when he'd sneaked off to a park instead of loitering with the guys at the bus stop. He was breaking the rules—homeless men were strictly forbidden to enter that park—but he didn't care. He needed to be alone.

A cop car had turned into the park on routine patrol. He dodged its head-lights, scrambling for cover. Once the squad drove off again, he explored a little, eventually climbing up onto a frostbitten railroad bed to wait for sunup. His hands and feet were already numb, the temperature in the teens.

Maybe an hour later, a train far down the tracks had blasted its horn,

Train wheel on railroad track

approaching from the south as a bright sun mounted the eastern horizon. Motionless, he watched it come. The train finally passed only a few feet from where he stood, the orange rust on its cars blazoned by dawn. His lonely shadow had run with the cars, going nowhere.

The memory brings tears.

He closes the shutter.

GOURMET

Suppertime. James is in the mood to cook. With misgivings I watch him improvise a recipe from our meager store of food. He dumps a can of fatty government shredded pork into our cookpot. He combines it with a can of government spinach and tosses in some sliced jalapeño peppers from Grubb Street. After heating the concoction over a small fire, he rolls up some of the runny green mess in a couple stale tortillas dug from a dumpster. Keeping one tortilla for himself, he offers the other to me.

I take it half-heartedly. "Grateful, grateful," I say, praying the simple prayer that has become our custom. He smirks, suspecting sarcasm.

Warily we each take a bite.

Make a face.

Laugh out loud.

Eat the whole nasty potful.

CHARGED

Eudora Welty, quoted in *American Photo*: "Insight doesn't happen often in the click of a moment, like a lucky snapshot, but comes in its own time and more slowly and from nowhere but within. The sharpest recognition is surely that which is charged with sympathy as well as shock—it is a form of human vision."

DAY 42

TUESDAY, MARCH 30

RAPID-FIRE

James and I are conversing on a bench near the Ohio Statehouse when a woman in high heels scurries by on rapid-fire tip-toes. Her pace is so brisk that we both stop talking to watch her all the way up the sidewalk, then all the way up the steep capitol steps.

"You know," I say, when she hits the top, "I couldn't walk that fast now even if I tried. Besides, I don't think I *want* to walk that fast, ever again."

James nods. He knows.

In our other life, time squirts like thin ketchup from a bottle, and somebody or something always seems to be squeezing, pressuring us to speed up the pace, to crowd the day's schedule, to accelerate the plan. But time on the streets is thick. It oozes. Out here, we walk slow as the day. We joke that we only have one gear left, the rest stripped.

SPACE

I sit in the dimly lit quiet of St. Joe's, writing on the back of spacewalking astronauts; they float above an earth muddied by photocopy grays. Around me, the church is trimmed in yellows, golds and virginal white, as if for a lavish wedding. Up in the loft, an organist begins practicing a fugue for Easter. A disciplined piece of music, resoundingly triumphant. I close my eyes. The pew vibrates with sound.

"Hey, you got some money you can give me?"

I look up. The voice belongs to a wild-eyed Anglo. His clothes are clean, his beard a day old. I shake my head.

The man sidles back out the pew, then strides up the aisle toward the only other person in the nave, a woman kneeling at a shrine up front. She's been kneeling there, her head bent over clasped hands, ever since I arrived. Under my breath I plead with the guy to let her be, but he's too bold, or too desperate, for such delicacy. He interrupts her prayers with a brassy voice that echoes all the way back to my ears: "I want some money!"

"This is too much," I mutter.

The woman's purse is resting on the floor beside the kneeler. The man pleads and pleads. She tries to ignore him but finally snaps and scolds. In that instant I fear for her safety, but the man turns on his heel and strides back down the aisle. After he slams through the door, the woman crosses herself, rises slowly and leaves.

My anger remains, without an object.

James soon joins me, weary after an afternoon of shooting photographs. He lies down on a pew not far away and adjusts his body to its hard wooden curve. Before long he's drifting in thought and prayer.

Suddenly his feet are shoved violently off the pew. His sore ankle strikes the kneeler. He groans.

"No sleeping!" our old friend Sam says sharply, glaring down at him. "Sit up!"

"I wasn't sleeping," James says with a grimace. "Sometimes I just pray better lying down—"

"Not in *this* church!"

Sam turns on his heel and marches down the side aisle. Before he exits the sanctuary, he kneels and genuflects before a statue of the crucified Christ.

FACE

The reclusive Calvin pays us a visit in camp. We're delighted. Though often invited, this is the first time he has come. Sitting with us by a slow-burning fire, he's jumpy but eager to talk.

"Heck of a basketball game last night," he says, referring to UConn's national championship win over Duke. "Yes, sir, I listened to it on my transistor." He gives us an amazing play-by-play, practically a re-broadcast, of the last few minutes of the hard-fought contest. "Would have liked to hear the whole game, but had to save my batteries. Batteries cost plenty. Nobody'll bring me none either.

"Last fall them Take It to the Streets people wanted to put my picture in the paper. No way I was going to do that. Now, *some* people—and I ain't going to say who—they agreed to have their pictures taken, and they get a lot more stuff now. *A lot* more than *I* do." His eyes, when they land on you, are piercing. "Sometimes I've asked them people for stuff, like batteries, or a kerosene heater, or some laundry detergent, some aspirin. They always tell me they'll bring it, and they never do. They just lie to you. *Lie* to you, just because you won't agree to being in the paper.

"Don't get me wrong," he says. "I can get along just fine *without* them. They bring me gobs of stuff I don't need. I mean, who can use a whole bottle of vitamins every single week? What you supposed to do with a dozen tooth-brushes? They tell you, `Just pass them on if you don't need them.' Well, I don't have nobody to pass them on to."

Some volunteers, in my presence, have referred to Calvin as the "mean guy" and the "crazy old man." "He's not crazy," I've tried to tell them. "He just gets scared. He likes to keep to himself."

The other day, Calvin says, he was over at Sarge's, and he spotted a wooden cross the volunteers had given him in celebration of Holy Week. "Nobody brought *me* no cross. I would have liked one of those."

James and I trade glances. Ever practical, we'd used our crosses for kindling. They burned like glory.

"You know," Calvin says, after a moment, "them people's lining their own pockets. It's the same with the shelters—they don't really help homeless people. Nothing changes for *nobody* in this places, not *really*. They're just keeping their own people employed, that's all."

He stands up as if to go. "How long you two been out?"

"A little over six weeks," James says.

"Why, that's not long at all. Not *a*-tall. Bobby told me he'd seen you out here a couple years ago."

"Wasn't us."

He sits down again. "You know, I'm worried about Sarge. Since Jake's moved out he's started to fall in with Rooster. Rooster's buying him liquor, feeding him steak, just like he did Jake, at first."

For a recluse, he seems remarkably well-informed about his neighbors on the riverbank. Now that he's trusting James and me a little, he gives us a full report. Listening to him prattle on, I begin to suspect that gossip, for him, is more than just a way of connecting with us; it's also a way of facing, sidelong, some of his greatest fears. If this is true, maybe his worst fear of all is dying a death you're driven to, and dying that death alone. So I gather when he tells us, at the very last, about the homeless man who had sat down on the railroad tracks in front of an oncoming train, and the woman who had jumped not long ago from the south bridge. He doesn't know who those people were, only that they died—alone.

His stories are frightened slivers of lives. They cut. His face is crisscrossed with lines.

CUSTOM

In my other life, the question "What do you do?" often breaks the ice between strangers. That, and "Where do you live?" and "Are you married—any kids?" First exchanges so commonly revolve around job, house, and family that two people, upon being introduced, can almost predict the course of their conversation.

On the streets, such questions are rare. "Don't ask, don't tell" is the unspoken rule. Take our neighbors, for instance. Even after a month, James and I know little, if anything, about where they came from, or why they're homeless, or how long they've been on the riverbank. Withholding information, like manufacturing lies, is wisdom on the streets, a strategy for survival. As it turns out, James and I, in deliberately disclosing little about ourselves, are only following custom.

What we try to offer in place of particulars is presence. We've stripped ourselves to the essentials: Here we are, and this little light, this little fire we have, we'll share with you till there's no more wood. When it dies out, we'll shiver with you in the dark.

DAY 43

WEDNESDAY, MARCH 31

BAG OF BAGELS

A few days ago, returning to camp in late afternoon, James and I had swung past Einstein Bros. and rescued another full trash-bag of day-old bagels from the dumpster. After saving back a week's supply for ourselves, we abandoned the bag by the railroad tracks, out in plain view, hoping they wouldn't go to waste. We were simply too beat to make deliveries to our neighbors.

By the next morning, the bag of bagels had been gone. We took not a little satisfaction from that.

Now, though, we run into Calvin along the tracks. "You know," he says, "the other day I found a whole bag of bagels, dozens of them, right near here. I took them over and dumped them in the weeds. Somebody might have seen them and come snooping around, looking for whoever might have put them there."

GOODBYE

Eating lunch alone at Holy Family Soup Kitchen, I catch a glimpse of Jake across the crowded cafeteria and give him a wave. Already finished with his meal, he soon comes by my table. His face is sallow, his eye sockets sunken and dark.

"I'm going into a treatment program this afternoon," he says, his voice dead. "Got to get myself cleaned up."

Please be telling me the truth, I say to him silently, as I rise to give him a hug.

I wish him well, warning him, whatever he does, to steer clear of Rooster. "I saw Calvin early this morning. Rooster charged into his camp late last night, looking for you. Calvin told him to go away. Told him you weren't staying with him. Told him he ought to leave you be."

Jake stares at me without speaking. Another hug goodbye, weaker this time, and now he's walking away.

You'll never see him again.

FRIENDS ARE FAR

James stuffs his hat into a pocket and unzips his sweatshirt. The temperature must be around sixty. On his way to meet Aaron at a Parsons Avenue soup kitchen, he's enjoying the warmth, and the walk. This part of town is new to him.

After a half hour's hike through mostly poor, tumbledown neighborhoods, he sees a man two blocks up, staggering on the sidewalk. A sick gnawing in the pit of his stomach tells him it's Aaron, but the man disappears before he can be sure.

Just before he reaches Parsons Avenue, he turns his head to look down an alley. There's Aaron, staring straight at him. He goes to join him.

Aaron reaches out to shake hands, keeping a tight grip on his bottle. "Morning, James," he slurs loudly. "You're my friend."

He's far gone. Inwardly grieving, James tries to keep his voice light. "Hey Aaron, how's it going? Ready to eat?"

"Naw." He holds up his bottle. "This is my second of these. I ain't a bit hungry yet."

Together they shuffle up the alley. "Aaron," James says, "I could use some food."

"Well, Parsons ain't open yet," he says roughly, "and I need to sit down!" He flips an abandoned shopping cart onto its side for a seat and motions for James to join him. "Come on! You're my friend! Sit with me!"

James sits down to appease him. This isn't the Aaron he knows.

Aaron takes a few swigs of his Strawberry Cisco. "Liquid crack," he says, "that's what this is."

Nearby is a dirty yellow metal shack, maybe ten feet square. "The Golden Goat," reads a rusty sign across the top. A very short Anglo is feeding one of its machines soda cans for dimes.

"That's Carl," Aaron says.

The man looks at James with sunken eyes, his face haunted, like a man who's been terrorized.

"Carl showed me a way to get a dime with four cans instead of ten." Telling this, Aaron brightens, as if it were remarkably fortunate.

"Where'd you sleep last night?" James asks.

"Down around here. I got kicked out of the shelter because of my drinking."

"You know this part of town?"

"Yeah, my sister used to have a place near here. Last year I slept under her old pool when I didn't have nowhere else to go. The house is abandoned now, but I climbed the fence last night, and sure enough, the pool's still there." Suddenly he grows quiet. "James, this liquid shit has got me. If only.... Friends are far, James."

"No, they're not, Aaron. I'm your friend, right?"

"If—yeah—but friends are—friends are—*far*...."

He drifts. He sits with James in silence. Then, like a hellfire preacher, he roars, "Let's pray! *Pray* with me, James!"

James closes his eyes. Aaron rambles on, talking to Jesus about wanting to do right and get himself saved. When he finishes, Carl's still feeding cans to the Goat.

"I still got that book you gave me," Aaron says, in a voice loud enough to be heard a block away.

"I'm glad, Aaron. Check it out sometime, okay?"

He nods, staring at the ground. "I will, James. You my friend, James."

Now a rangy black man shows up. He flaunts his height over the five-foot Carl, trying to provoke him. Carl doesn't take the bait, but Aaron, not very tall himself, rises to his feet, sticks out his skinny chest and screams, "What the hell you doing?"

"*You* talking to *me*?" the black man says menacingly, squaring up to Aaron.

Oh God, James thinks, as the two men yell at each other, bumping chests. Aaron raises his bottle as if to strike—

Suddenly, laughter. The black man throws an affectionate arm around Aaron's neck, and the two guys start jiving. Their hostility had all been an act.

"This here's Frank," Aaron says to James.

Relieved, and exasperated, James gets up to go. "Aaron, I got to eat. I'll see you at the soup kitchen."

"Yeah, man," Frank says. "We'll be there after this bottle."

"Don't go, James," Aaron begs, as loudly as before. "James! *James—*"

FRIENDS LIKE THESE

Under a bleached-blue sky and a glorious sun, every bench on the capitol grounds is full of people on lunch break. To James's surprise, sitting a short distance from the Statue of Peace are his friends Tyler and Marela, both from out of town. The sight of them brings tears. Tyler has traveled all the way from Maine, just to be here for noon meditation.

Aaron, James says to himself, *if only you had friends like these....*

HOPE

Jake had agreed to meet Sarge here in White Castle at 4 PM. "He's an hour late," Sarge says to me. "It's not like him, not to show up. Maybe it's true— maybe Rooster *did* beat him up. That's what Rooster's been saying. Said he hurt Jake *bad.*"

"When?"

"Last night."

I smile. "Sarge, I saw Jake today at Grubb Street, and he was okay, far as I could tell. He said he was going into a treatment program this afternoon."

His face lightens. "That makes sense. I went by Jake's new place earlier, and all his stuff was gone.

"You know, I was drinking with Rooster last night. Don't remember much. Passed out. I shouldn't drink with that guy. He's too dangerous. You wake up, and there he is, ready to beat your face in."

His eyes lock on mine like I'm his last hope, "So you *really* think Jake's okay?"

DAY 44

THURSDAY, APRIL 1

A PLACE AT THE TABLE

During the night, a Holy Thursday dream:

In the middle of a wild forest, you happen upon a farm, generations old. There's a three-story brick house, a huge red barn, and a cluster of outbuildings, all carefully maintained and abundantly full. The mow is stacked high with hay, the stalls and pens are fat with animals, the smokehouse is crowded with hams and sides of beef, the root cellar's crates and burlap bags are bulging with apples and pears and potatoes and onions…. Surely more bounty is here than could ever be raised on a farm in the heart of a forest, but you accept what you see without question, as you're apt to do in dreams.

You step up onto the front porch of the house and open the door. Walking inside, you find the rooms unremarkable, except for the fact that each is a garden plot. Corn stalks, vining cucumbers, melons and squash, stands of lavender, bushes of basil, rows of beans and peas and pepper plants are growing out of the floor. A man whose age you can't guess is tending the plots, pruning here, harvesting there.

Finally you enter what must be called, despite its rich vegetation, a dining room, since it's filled with tables covered with starched white linens. The sight of the tables stuns you. Suddenly you're aware that there's a multitude who must be fed, an invisible throng of fellow travelers.

Now a woman appears, elderly but by no means frail. She hands you a tall stack of bread plates. Everyday dishes, showing signs of wear. Without needing to be asked, you begin setting them around the tables, which all at once are overflowing with platters of fried chicken and roast beef, tureens of different kinds of soup, bowls of mashed potatoes and creamed spinach and corn, brimming gravy boats, pans of fruit cobbler, filled pies—so much food, more than any holiday meal you've ever seen. As you try to squeeze in the bread plates among the serving dishes, you ask over your shoulder, "Will there be enough room for everybody?"

"Of course," the old woman says, as if she's been asked this question every day for the last hundred years. "Not everyone will be fed here—there are thousands and thousands of rooms—but *everybody* has a place at the table."

HARD TIME

Another Holy Thursday dream, this one from James: After serving a prison sentence, hard time, you're riding on a bus full of new parolees, about to be released in the city. When the bus finally pulls over to the curb, you all get off, stand there looking at each other, bewildered. Where do you go from here?

STAYING (4)

April Fool's Day.

The first day of Passover, when the Hebrews were delivered from slavery in Egypt.

Holy Thursday, when Jesus, the Jew, took the unleavened bread of Passover in his hands, and blessed it, and broke it, in the presence of somebody he loved—somebody he knew was about to betray him.

It's wisdom to know that loving is never easy; folly, many believe, to love anyway.

In this morning's *Dispatch*, a photograph: a teenage girl from Kosovo wiping away the tears of her young sister, the two of them finally safe but all alone in a Macedonian refugee camp. I look closely at the teenager, and know nothing: not her name, or whose eyes she has, or the lullabies she heard as a baby, her favorite color, the childhood toy she'd kept hidden away while pretending to be all grown up, what she wants to be someday, or whether she'll always be a mother, now, to this crying little girl....

Grief is heavy in these last days. The many people James and I have come to know a little and to care for, here on the riverbank, at Grubb Street, other places—when will *they* make their way home, and how? As if by agreement, we don't speak of this. In the same way, we don't speak anymore of going home early, even though there seems no real reason to stay for just a few more days—

No reason but Easter itself—

We stay on the streets for those who feel trapped here. We stay for those who can't leave.

MANTRA

James and I trudge through cool gray mist to Holy Family Soup Kitchen, arriving before the line opens. This being Thursday, the little dictator's on duty. In a brief interval of silence as he begins his prayer, we hear a radio playing out in the hall. Some lyrics reach our ears, faint but clear:

> *If you feel like lovin' me*
> *when you get the notion*
> *I second that emotion*

"Sounds like a mantra for the streets," James whispers.

Almost every day the same woman is stationed at the bread and dessert table. We don't know her name. She's in her sixties, at least, and can barely speak or understand English. If you ask for a cookie, she might shingle six of them across your plate, despite your protests. If you ask for a slice of brown bread, she might toss on a muffin and a slice of white as well. Language difficulties alone can't account for her behavior. It's more, we suspect, the gift of generosity, well concealed beneath a dour veneer that sometimes puts you off and makes you feel you're a bother.

Last week we tried to talk to this volunteer a little, and she made us understand, finally, that she'd immigrated to this country years ago from Hungary. We asked her how to say "Good day!" in Hungarian. She taught us syllable by syllable, drilling us to her satisfaction.

Today, as we're leaving, we pass by her table. "Jona-pot-kiva-nok," we stammer, pronouncing the words as best we can remember.

"Oh, jó napot kívánok!" she cries, laughing, pressing one veiny hand to her ample bosom. Beside her, two girls in prep school uniforms, also volunteers, shoot her a quizzical look.

"It is *Hungarian!*" the old woman brags, absolutely beaming.

THIRST

Sarge drops by as the sun's going down. Never before has he ventured into our camp without Jake.

"You guys mind if I sit with you for a spell?" He's gripping a liter bottle of water.

Back when Jake was around, Sarge never had much to say. Tonight, though, he practically tells us his life story. Says his father was an alcoholic, and he's been an "alky," too, since he was thirteen years old. As a youth he'd run off and joined the Marines, become a machine gunner. At the end of his stint, he wanted to re-up, but since he was a "non-reader," the brass wouldn't let him.

"Never learned to read. I didn't like school much. I was the only white kid in my class. Didn't fit in. Finally I just dropped out."

After the service, Sarge got married, worked construction, had four kids. "Then there was the drinking, and the thing with the neighbors, and the restraining order. Don't know how to go home now. Don't know how I can face my kids. Really miss them though. You know, some people's got kids and don't have no feeling for them at all. Rooster, that's the way he is. That ain't natural. I ain't like that.

"I'm thinking about going into rehab. If Jake's really going to do it, I could do it with him. He probably checked into Maryhaven. But you got to use the phone to get into them kind of places. I'm not too much on using the phone."

He probably can't read a phone book. "Sarge," I say, "if you want me to, I could go up top, call Harold and Ada, tell them you need some help getting into a program. They do that sort of thing."

He mulls it over. "Maybe tomorrow. I got to do *something*. I need to get off the riverbank. I'm spending too much time with Rooster. Keeps giving me liquor, you know. But not the crack—I *don't* smoke crack. Jake, he'd get crazy on the stuff.

"You know, one time some cops was hassling me in United Dairy Farmers. But one of the guys working the counter stuck up for me. He said to the cops, 'Look, Sarge is a nice guy, he don't bother nobody' —and I *don't*, you know. I don't mean nothing.

"Guys, I *really* need a drink. Would you mind if I went and got a forty, brought it back here and drank it?"

CONQUERORS

Long into evening, a hot-rod pickup pulls into the field above camp. James and I go to greet the volunteers. Sarge stays on his log by the fire, clutching his brownbagged forty. He doesn't want them to see him drinking.

Two Anglo couples climb out of the truck, all wearing black leather jackets. A guy with a mustache crawls into the back, which is crowded with coolers and picnic baskets and water jugs. He starts filling large styrofoam containers with food. James and I try to say that while we're very grateful, we aren't at all hungry, having already eaten our supper, and their food, which is no doubt excellent, won't keep in this warmer weather—but nobody's listening. We watch the man spoon up huge mounds of mashed potatoes and top them with thick brown gravy. A woman hands me two gallons of water and loads James's arms with loose soda cans.

The quartet follows us back to camp, each carrying two big bags of food-stuff, which they deposit at Sarge's feet. After an awkward pause, the mustached man starts in preaching. Says he's a biker who had nearly gotten killed in a bad accident. "God knocked me off my bike, and that's how I found Jesus. We all come to him in our own way, don't we?"

He wants us to know that Jesus will save us, too, if we let Him. He recites, in dramatic fashion, his favorite passage of scripture, the last few verses of Romans 8:

> Who shall separate us from the love of Christ? Shall tribulation, or distress, or persecution, or famine, or nakedness, or peril, or sword? As it is written, `For thy sake we are being killed all the day long; we are regarded as sheep to be slaughtered'—

Sarge slumps lower on his log. The fire's dying. I give it a poke.

> —No, in all these things we are more than conquerors through him who loved us....

PLUSH

One of the biker women, hanging back as the others leave, presents me with a gift bag containing several sets of stationery, a book of stamps, three expensive pens, an address book, and last but not least, a variety of Clinique cosmetics and beauty aids. Then she hands me a cosmetics storage box, in which I discover two plush hand towels and washcloths, and a polished brass hand mirror sheathed in burgundy velveteen.

I sigh.

The woman leans in, murmurs in my ear, "I just don't know how you do it. I know *I* couldn't. Guess I wouldn't make a very good pioneer."

NOBODY THERE

By the time the bikers drive off, our tiny camp is cluttered with eleven bags of food, more than a dozen soda cans, and several gallons of water. Wearily James and I sort out a stash to send home with Sarge, who is wasted; the remainder, we'll worry about tomorrow. If nothing else, we'll lug the supplies up to Grubb Street, the Salvation Army, or Volunteers of America. We've done it often enough.

We sit with Sarge by the fire till there's nothing left but coals. Again and again, he thanks us for letting him drink in our camp. Again and again, he thinks he sees people sneaking around in the night woods, up to no good. "Who *was* that?" he says, panicked, pointing into the darkness. "Did you see them? *Tell me*—didn't you *see* them?"

Nobody's ever there.

DAY 45

FRIDAY, APRIL 2

BARE HANDS

A Good Friday dream: You're planting trees in the downtown in memory of all the homeless people who have died, and are dying now—so many people, so many trees, there's not enough room for them all. So, big as a giant, you begin knocking down skyscrapers, angrily tearing them apart with your bare hands, making room for the planting....

LIFE FOR LIFE

In early morning, James and I walk the tracks toward White Castle. Between us and the path up top, a train is stalled. It might not move for an hour.

"My bowels can't wait," James says. He drops on all fours, starts to crawl under a coupling.

Suddenly the train lunges. Terrified, he scoots through to the other side, just as the train groans and begins to roll forward.

Now he feels the pain. A bloody slice across his palm, cut by a broken forty.

Today is Good Friday. A day of crowing cocks and gut-wrenching betrayals; of false accusations, illegal interrogations and rigged trials; of riotous crowds and unbearable silence; of portentous dreams, ignored because they were dreamed by a woman; of handwashings, and the trading of life for life; of floggings, mockery and spit; of nakedness and thorny branches twisted into a crown; of crude wooden crosses, too heavy to bear, borne to the Place of a Skull—

A day of darkness, descending on the land in the middle of the afternoon —the agonizing cries of a dying man—

Earth shaking—rocks splitting—wails rending air—

How much time had to pass before somebody began to call this day *good*?

REFUGEES

On the front page of the *Dispatch*: Thousands of refugees walking the railroad tracks through winter mountains, approaching the Macedonian border. A long, long human line. After these weeks of walking the railroad toward Grubb Street, I can better imagine how the tracks might feel beneath their slow feet. At the very front of the line, a man assists an elderly woman (*is she your mother?*), hand gripping her elbow, his body ready to bear her up. These two carry nothing. Behind them, other refugees are bent beneath bundles of possessions.

What would you choose to take with you if you had to leave behind the life you'd always lived, and all you could take with you is what you could carry?

Perhaps what is truly yours, to keep and to give, can't be carried at all.

NAMES (2)

Shortly after James leaves White Castle for camp, Sarge sits down at my table. "Thanks again," he says, "for letting me come over last night and drink in your camp. I really needed to talk to somebody."

A homeless black man is begging quarters from the customers. I wave him over, give him 30¢.

"Rooster was picking on me this morning," Sarge says, his voice grim. "I'm scared, man. Never got hold of my wife. I'm going to try to get in touch with my sister. Maybe she'll let me come over. I got to get out of here."

Now, for the first time, he tells me his name. A name of many names, each delivered with emphasis. He laughs at the expression on my face. "Oh, it's a good Irish Catholic name."

I'm touched by his trust, and amazed that he should make this personal revelation only days after Jake had done the same.

Bobby's sister Jan is sipping coffee at the table across the aisle. Once Sarge exits the restaurant, she leans my way. "He's lost without Jake," she says softly. "He's absolutely *lost* without Jake."

KIND OF CRAZY

I nearly collide with Rooster on my way out the door. He's hopping mad at Sarge, threatening to beat him up. "I'll *get* him, goddammit! Put him in the hospital, just like I did Jake!"

A flicker of dismay must have shown on my face, because suddenly he calms down. He gives me a thoughtful look. "Hope you guys ain't going to leave. I know things are kind of crazy around here right now, but—"

"We'll be going soon."

His face reddens. He rubs at his eyes. *What'll become of you, Rooster?*

"Hey," I say, remembering the wheelbarrow episode, "any word on Joseph?"

"Oh, Joseph. He's back sleeping in his dumpster, up behind the Starlight pub."

SPIKES

Up and down the railroad bed, old spikes lie scattered in the gravel. Once upon a time they held the crossties in place; rusty now, some of them bent and twisted, you don't think of them as all that substantial, till you pick one up and feel its solid weight in your hand.

James and I begin collecting them, tossing them into piles along the tracks. It's a task we've saved till today; appropriate, somehow, for Good Friday, when Jesus the Nazarene was nailed to a Roman cross. We want to take the spikes home with us—relics again. One by one, we want to give them away as reminders of how every human being, homeless or otherwise, must inevitably suffer; and how no human being, homeless or otherwise, can endure that suffering without love, without compassion. Love and compassion: These two —our wish for another's happiness, and our wish for their anguish to end— are the strength of us. Like old railroad spikes, they might not be perfect, but they can endure.

Sun's just broken through the clouds. Blue sky opens. As James walks along a set of tracks, a short, skinny Anglo, apparently drunk, waggles toward him pushing a rickety bike, fishing pole in hand. "What you doing, man?" he slurs.

"Gathering spikes," James says, as if it were the most natural thing in the world to do.

"Oh. Need some help?"

James grins. "Sure."

The fellow lays his bike on the ground. He stumbles up the tracks, his head bent low. After finding a few spikes, he loses his enthusiasm and totters back to his bike.

"Have a good day, man," James calls. "Good luck with the fishing."

"Yeah, you too." The man leans into his handlebars and wobbles on up the tracks.[6]

WALKING AWAY

Behind a warehouse on Church Street, two black men stand smoking and drinking. Between them, lounging on the loading dock, is Aaron, entertaining them with stupor humor. Catching sight of James and me, Aaron waves us over. "Hey, where you going?" he shouts, as if we were a world away.

"Grubb Street," we say.

Aaron tries to stand up, teeters, falls off the dock. His buddies and James manage to catch him before he hits the ground. "Naw," he whines, "you guys don't want to go there. Let's go get some hot dogs and ice cream."

"We don't have any money, Aaron."

"I'll treat you," he says, as if flush with cash. "What the hell time is it anyway? One o'clock?"

"Around ten," James says, looking at me helplessly. Seeing Aaron this way is painful, but there's nothing we can do. We back away. "Aaron," James says, "we'll see you over at Grubb—"

"James—no, come on! Sit down with me here—let's bullshit—*come on,* man!"

We turn around and start walking. We force ourselves not to look back, even when we hear Aaron fall down as he tries to follow us and prevent our leaving. He shouts after James all the way down the street. "Hey, James! —*James!*—come on back, man! You my *friend!*"

We keep walking. A block away, our eyes full of tears, we can still hear him yelling.

RAIN

Morris, the graybeard who once propositioned me, is ahead of us in the serving line at Holy Family. I greet him with a cool nod, wishing to discourage further overtures.

"How's it going?" James asks him.

"Oh, okay, James," he says wistfully, remembering James's name for the first time. "But you know, don't you, it's going to rain today. Around two or three o'clock."

"Why's that?" James is baffled, remembering the brilliant blue of the sky after the morning murk had burned off.

"Why, it's Good Friday," Morris says. "It always storms at the hour Jesus died."

BLACK BOX

We seat ourselves at the very front of the cafeteria. Nonchalantly James removes a camera from his duffel and places it between two food trays, aiming the pinhole at the serving line and the painting of da Vinci's *Last Supper*, hanging above. The light in the room is poor; the exposure will take at least an hour—a true shot in the dark, but he wants to try. He peels back the shutter-tape, hoping for the best.

Before long, a weatherbeaten Anglo sits down at the head of the table, right in the camera's eye. With so long an exposure, his presence probably won't register on the photo paper.

The guy points at the camera. "What's that, your lunch box?" he says, with his mouth full.

"Yeah," James says.

The man inspects it with his gaze, a battered box covered with black tape. Then he shrugs. "I don't eat here much." He glances around nervously as he slurps and chews. "You can't trust anybody. There's some people in here that shouldn't be, even though this place has got security cameras. They watch everybody who comes, especially when they're having a summit. Couple of weeks ago, all the world leaders were here. They kept real close watch. I don't like being watched. Not at all."[7]

WINE TO BLOOD

We're walking east along Broad, headed for the Statue of Peace, when James grabs my arm. "Is that *Maddy?*"

I follow his line of sight. On the other side of the busy four-lane street, a woman lies on the sidewalk, her shoulders propped against a building. I stare, trying to convince myself it's not Maddy, but now she waves a bony arm at us, removing all doubt.

She's drunk. We can tell from here.

The last time we talked to Jeff, a week or so ago, he hadn't known where she was. She'd disappeared on a binge. "I don't know how to help her," he said. "Maybe I *can't.*

"She misses her kids, you know," he'd told us. "Especially when school starts, and holidays. With Easter coming, she just lost it."

Now, across four lanes of Broad Street traffic, we wave back at her. "What can we do?" I say, heartbroken.

"Nothing. Not really."

First Aaron, now Maddy. Crucifixion. Bodies, spirits, broken.

"Takes on a whole other meaning, doesn't it," James says, "'wine turning to blood?'"

PEDESTRIAN

I'm standing on the corner near St. Joe's, waiting for the streetlight to change. A Good Friday mass has just let out. Worshipers spill out the cathedral doors, turn pedestrian. An older man and what appears to be his grandson, six or seven years old, walk up next to me, hand in hand, dressed in their Sunday suits. I glance down at the boy and drop a smile. He presses closer to his grandfather.

Compliments of the Hungarian lady at Grubb Street, I'm toting a grocery bag filled with all kinds of cookies, clearly seen through the plastic. The man, whose features look Mediterranean, points at my bag and laughs merrily. "She has many cookies, no?" he says to the boy, his accent delightfully rich.

"Do you want one?" I ask the little guy, lifting my bag high to show off its bulge, and his grandfather laughs again, from down in his belly.

"I'm going to have a *donut!*" the boy says with great seriousness, staring straight ahead.

"That's where we are going," his grandfather explains to me. "To get a donut."

I glance across the street. Don't Walk, in red neon.

"Now," the man says to the boy, "why don't you ask the nice woman if maybe *she* would like a donut?"

The boy stares up at me with a forlorn expression, chewing on his lip. For all the world he doesn't want to ask me, but he doesn't want to disobey either. I smile at him again. "Thanks anyway, but I'd better eat my cookies."

"Okay," the boy says, relieved.

"Happy Easter!" I say to them both.

"Same to you!" the man exclaims. "Yes, happy, *happy* Easter!"

RECEIVING

At the *Columbus Dispatch* loading dock, a sign reads "RECEIVING MONDAY — FRIDAY, 7 AM — 4 PM." James smiles, taking a photograph of it, one of the last pictures he'll probably shoot on the streets. When he and I first came out, we had difficulty accepting the kindness of others. We wanted to put limits on their help, and on our own requests for help. But now—well, let's just say we're trying to be receptive, every hour of every day.

Receiving hours at the Columbus Dispatch

LAST THINGS

It isn't till we're preparing for bed that we realize we've visited Holy Family Soup Kitchen for the last time. These last things are hard to register at the moment they're happening. A sense of finality requires a feel for the future, and we don't seem to have much of that anymore. Time has shrunk, the world with it, and so, it feels, has my flagging spirit. Every day I feel smaller, more shriveled, more self-absorbed. What will be left when I go home?

When I was a child, being tucked into bed on the eve of a much anticipated day (my birthday, maybe, or the last day of school), my mother would always tell me, "The faster you go to sleep, the faster tomorrow will come."

Only two more days.

I snuff the candle, pull the blankets in tight.

DAY 46

SATURDAY, APRIL 3

STRANGERS

White Castle, 7 AM. Though warm, my night was rough due to extreme leg pain. I just have to make it through one more.[8]

The high temperature today is supposed to be near eighty. T-shirt weather. I can't wait to strip down.

How typical of central Ohio to pretty much skip spring and head from winter directly into summer. The grass, greening fast, is looking almost Irish. Down in our neck of the woods, a squabbling parliament of birds has returned from midwinter recess. Chipmunks dart. Squirrels chatter and scold, contending for grazing rights at the bags of dumpster cereal we've hung in a sapling. The flat, bare ground between the field and the railroad bed has become a thoroughfare for cottontails. Soft anthills are swelling. Sometimes weeds and wildflowers rustle when there isn't a breeze, and you say hello, out loud, to the tiny critter that would rather be heard than seen.

There's more human activity in the neighborhood, too. Strangers (men mostly) are walking the tracks and poking around in the woods, maybe scouting sites for fair-weather camps. Their presence adds to the already mounting tensions on the riverbank. James and I have confessed to each other: "It's good, for us, that we're leaving tomorrow."

The fellow who wears the army coat and argues with himself about grave matters of consequence ((I call him the Philosopher) is back in White Castle this morning after a long absence. He's shaved off his beard. Another indicator of spring.

No sign of Sarge. Did he call his sister? Did she take him in? *Will you see him again before you go?*

So much will end tomorrow. So much will begin.

PASSING ON

This morning I feel much in common with certain elderly folks I know who, coming to the end of their lives, say they now understand a little better what's truly been theirs. Not their money or property, not their personalities or talents or successes, not even their loved ones—all these have a place, but in the end they're transitory. They don't survive.

What's mattered most, these people say, and what will endure, are the endowments of the heart, which across a lifetime they've had endless opportunities to develop:

Their capacity for love, and for giving themselves to another person—

For feeling another's suffering, and doing something about it—

For embracing change, even if it means a sacrifice—

For rejoicing—

For exercising faith—

For making peace—

For having visions that are beautiful and just and true, and finding the courage to speak of them, and to somehow try to give them flesh—

Capacities such as these will survive because they belong to us all. They're powers we human beings possess in common, a shared plot of fertile land that mustn't lie fallow for long.

EMPTY POCKETS

James and I return to the Agora. Here, shell-shocked on our second day out, we'd taken refuge for an afternoon. While James slept on his cot, I'd wandered the building, finally ending up here, in the Five Loaves café. At one of these tables I'd been told stories and offered food by people who bothered to care.

Now, for our last lunch on the streets, we order a turkey club sandwich, a bowl of chicken noodle soup, and a chocolate pastry, all to split between us. Then we deposit our remaining money on the counter—several crinkled dollar bills, a sweaty five, and a pocketful of street change. "Put it all in the till," we say to the server.

She looks us up and down. "But that's way too much. Are you sure you don't need it?"

Smiling, we walk our tray of food over to a table. Any profit the café makes goes to support the Agora's socially concerned ministries in the Bottoms. Empty pockets never felt so good.

POSTLUDE

If you cock your ear, you can hear Guitar Man under the bridge north of camp, singing a ballad in falsetto. His lyrics make no sense, but his plaintive strumming, and his voice—they cling. I've never known Guitar Man to be down in these parts.

I've never met Guitar Man, and till now I've never heard him play, but I've been aware of him from my first day on the streets. That afternoon I saw him on the third floor of Main Library, leafing through an art book, the neck of his guitar resting against the edge of his table. The thought never occurred to me then that he might be homeless. I guess he didn't fit "the profile." His guitar, though, made him a marked man, and after that day I was always seeing him, if only from a distance. Across the street, across the soup kitchen, across the park, across a crowded McDonald's. Always, it seemed, he was alone, except for an invisible, talkative muse.

His playing is beautiful as home.

REMEMBRANCES

After supper it begins to rain. James and I scramble into our shelter, where we exchange humble gifts in gratitude, and remembrance. My favorite of the gifts he gives me is an 8"x10" photograph from a downtown dumpster: a black and white close-up of two white girls, five or six years old, standing along a neighborhood street. A photo taken in the seventies, maybe. Whoever did the developing had applied a hint of blush to the cheeks.

The girl on the right glowers into the lens. Something has rankled her. Or maybe it's sadness, rather than temper, that tugs her eyebrows down. Her eyes are sober and testy, her hair unkempt, her mouth a frown.

The girl on the left is laughing hard at the camera, her nose wrinkled in glee, her short hair in angelic wisps around her face. She holds her cheeks between her pudgy little hands as if otherwise her face might bust.

Two realities, in the same frame.

"'Pain and Wonder,' remember?" James says.

FIRE

The rain has stopped, at least for now, and the sun's going down. With wet wood we struggle to start a smoldering fire in the firepit. Our last fire, here.

Back on February 17, as we were about to leave home, we felt the need for ritual—the imposition of ashes. Now, as we prepare to leave the streets, we feel it once again. Beginnings and endings seem to demand some semblance

"Pain and Wonder": a gift from James (photographer unknown)

of ceremony—some sort of container bigger than we are, capable of holding the strong emotions that might otherwise overwhelm us.

We place our cookpot between us. We fill it with white sand, dirty and damp, scraped up from the ground in front of our shelter. Then we remove twenty-four birthday candles from their little box (these, a token from Jihong, discreetly given on my birthday, along with a package of cupcakes I'd not had the heart to refuse). We'd saved the candles for a more practical use. Now we stick them, one by one, into the sand.

Each of us lights a slender eighteen-inch taper (found in German Village trash). James touches his taper to the wick of a birthday candle. "I light this candle for Jake."

"I light this candle for Sarge," I say, following his lead.

"For Aaron."

"For Maddy."
"Jeff."
"Joseph."
"Rooster."
"Enid."
"The Professor."
"Calvin."
"Blue."
"Elena."
"Morris."
"Sweetness."
"Manuel."
"Grace...."

On and on the names, as by turns we light candles for every homeless person we've known or met on the streets. As the names keep coming, fire begins to leap between wicks—there's a flap of air as each wick ignites—and we watch the flame spread, till all the candles are melting down into one fiery pool of wax.

Still the names come, and tears too, now, as the wax suddenly blazes up with a quiet roar, then slackens and burns itself out.

Rain begins to sprinkle again. A breeze kicks up.

We huddle closer over our cookpot. We press our lit tapers into the sand. We cup our hands around their two flames, still naming names, using descriptions when names are unknown, till finally no more can be said.

Our voices now silent, the tapers continue to burn, drops of wax sliding down their sides like tears. The candlewicks sizzle and spit, rain dripping on them through the trees. We can't protect them enough.

In the distance, the bells of St. Mary's.

Blessings come now, and thanksgivings too, for everybody who has helped us during these forty-seven days—for all the people who have taught us by their kindness, or their ignorance, or their hardness of heart; for all the places we've found rest, and smiles, and warmth, and food, the humblest of amenities....

At last, we're spent. Silence again. A few minutes more, and we can bear to look each other in the eye.

A GOOD THING

Sabrina Martin shows up in late evening with three carloads of volunteers on Saturday night rounds. We draw her aside for a private word. "We'll be leaving soon," James tells her quietly, avoiding specifics. "I've got some work. So don't be worried if you come out next week and find us gone."

Tears spill down her cheeks. "You *leaving* me?" She throws her arms around us both and pulls us close. "I don't want you to go!"

Her reaction startles us. "Sabrina," we say, "this is a *good* thing. We've got work, a place to stay—"

"Where you going?"

"Up north," we hedge. "Don't worry about us. We'll be fine. We're *happy* to be going. This is a *good* thing."

She sniffs, wipes her eyes, rubs the tears off her face. "Will you guys promise me something? If you ever need a place to stay, you'll call me? You can even stay with me awhile, if you need to. You got my number, *right?*"

DAY 47

SUNDAY, APRIL 4

PROVISIONS

To bed last night at 11:30, but not to sleep—there was no sleep for either of us, all night long. Too much pent-up anxiety. *How to end things, here. How to start again, once you're home.* Too much, too much.

I remember a Columbus cop who, back in January, as a favor to a mutual friend, tried to dissuade me from the streets. "What'll you do," he said, making one last appeal, "if you like it so much out there, you don't want to come home?"

Yeah, right.

The time now is 6:10 AM. In less than an hour, Jihong and Ron (the old friend who hadn't recognized me at the federal courthouse) will be meeting us with a truck behind a dilapidated office building, a quarter-mile north of camp. How ironic that, having left home with little more than the clothes on our backs, James and I should now need a pickup to pack out all the stuff we've accumulated.

James fumbles in the dark, packing up his pinhole cameras and other gear. I begin to stuff our bedding and clothing into McDonald's trash-bags (one last courtesy of Iris). I save out two blankets, the best we can offer, and the piece of foam rubber James has been using as a pillow; these we'll leave behind on our makeshift mattress. Now that the weather's warm, the rest of the bedding would just be in the way of whoever might move into camp. Besides, the bedding's not smelling so good. We'll take it home, wash it up, and donate it to Take It to the Streets.

James wants his wool pants to go to Jake, somehow. "Woolies," Jake always called them, with envy in his eye. Once they're clean, maybe the Martins can pass them on.

We stow a variety of nonperishable supplies in two boxes just inside the shelter door. The camp will be relatively well-stocked for its next occupant (the Professor, we suspect, but can't be sure): some government canned goods, a full bottle of vitamin C (*Calvin: "Who can use a whole bottle every week?"*), matches and lighter, candles and candle holders (*"a different kind of light"*), Sarge's watch face (*"no Rolex"*), Repel bug spray (*volunteers brought it last night, just in time*), sodas, two gallon jugs of water (*"Don't ever drink from the river"*), a few toiletries, several rolls of toilet paper, flashlight (*dead*), small metal bowl (*our cookpot*), plastic forks and spoons, plastic containers for food storage (*Grubb Street carry-out*), several sticks of Big Red gum, masking tape, scissors, pens and scratch paper (*what might you want to say? to whom?*), a few photography magazines, plastic grocery bags for all sorts of uses, clean white socks, a sturdy pair of men's shoes (*if you're a small-footed woman, wear thick socks and stuff the toes*), winter coat (*just in case the weather turns*), safety pins, rope and wire (*for shelter repairs*), and our last lucky penny (*for you to find when you're not looking*).

We bag up the little perishable food we have left, to take home. We'll either return it to the Martins or donate it to a city shelter. We'll do the same with various other supplies that either were given to us in exorbitant quantities or were simply too impractical for camp life.

We pile extra kindling next to our meager stack of firewood and cover all of it with plastic. We rinse out the bucket that served as our toilet, turn it upside-down. We dump the ashes from the grill and replace the lid.

Jihong and Ron arrive with the truck, right on schedule. No time for sentiment. We have to hurry. The sun's up, bright and warm; the heavy morning mist is lifting. An early-bird neighbor might see us. James and I scuttle back and forth between truck and camp, loaded down with boxes and bags.

Over the next month or so, we hope to visit the Martins, Sam at St. Joe's, and other people who have helped us on the streets. We want to tell them who we are, what brought us here, and what their assistance meant to us.

More than anybody, though, we'd like to reveal ourselves to the people we've known here on the riverbank, especially our near neighbors. Sadly, that can never happen. Jake has disappeared into treatment. Sarge is gone, too, apparently. Rooster we can't trust; he's too volatile. As for the reclusive Calvin, our confession would do him no good. He's paranoid enough as it is.

No, it's over now. There's no way to say goodbye.

We hurry.[9]

SAGE

The truck drives off, completely full. James and I return to camp. There's little time. We have to leave soon for center city. Our morning is booked solid: breakfast as usual at Central Presbyterian; Easter mass at St. Joe's, joined by Jihong and Phoebe, who's driven down from Connecticut; a final noon at the Statehouse, where we'll each lay a crooked spike at the Statue of Peace—

Then, at last, the going home.

James picks up the smudge stick saved from my birthday. He flicks the lighter and kindles the bottom of the herbs, blowing gently to encourage the burn. Then he crawls inside the shelter to ceremonially cleanse and bless it. One last ritual. As the scent of sage wafts faintly out the door, a feeling I can't name rises in my throat.

How inseparable are Lent and Easter, one requiring the other, like winter needing spring. In winter the old world gives itself up and lays down to die; in spring a whole new world strides forth from the grave, starts dancing to a penny-whistler's jig. This is the nature, the rhythm, of things. This is the way. Sometimes our lives are nothing but ash, other times they're butterflies and lilies. Often, as now, they're *everything at once*—

SILENCE

He backs out of the shelter on his knees, as you've seen him do a hundred times, shoulders hunched so he won't hit his head on the ceiling. He reaches back, hands you the smudge.

You circle the shelter slowly, trailing smoke. The air is still as death, or grace. No birds. No noisy hum from the treatment plant. No sirens. No planes. Only light freeway traffic, dimly heard, and the snap of a twig underfoot, the brush of a dewy branch against your shoulder.

Little remains now. You stub out the smudge stick and scatter the charred leaves over the damp ground.

One last time, he lowers the plastic flaps over the shelter door and anchors them with full water jugs. By tomorrow night, if not sooner, somebody else will be living here. The tomb's not empty. Not yet.[10]

No words now—they'd just slip between worlds, and vanish. Only a glance between the two of you, then together you walk up the path and out of the woods, through the field. Hands empty, you cut one last time across the railroad tracks, high-stepping the rails.

Somewhere, not so far away, a lone bird is singing. Whistling, right through you.

Railroad switch north of camp

Yashir koach

Before setting out, early on February 17, 1999 (photo credit: Jihong Cole-Dai)

Upon their return, April 4 (photo credit: Jihong Cole-Dai)

NOTES

INTRODUCTION

1. National Coalition for the Homeless, "Why Are People Homeless?", Fact Sheet #1, June, 1999.
2. Barbara Poppe in Alice Thomas, "Study on Homeless Families Goes Beyond Obvious," *The Columbus Dispatch*, March 11, 1999.
3. Ibid.
4. A finding of the National Law Center on Homelessness and Poverty, 1999, cited in National Coalition for the Homeless, "How Many People Experience Homelessness?", Fact Sheet #2, February, 1999.
5. Philadelphia, 1,478,002; Boston, 558,394 (1996 figures).
6. 27% of homeless people are children (U.S. Conference of Mayors statistic).
7. Thomas, "Study on Homeless Families...."
8. The chronically homeless are described as spending more than 160 days over a two-year period without a home. They tend to be older than other homeless persons, and are approximately 86% male (*Comprehensive Community Needs Assessment*, Columbus Community Shelter Board, January, 1998).
9. The following information on the criminalization of homelessness is based primarily on a study by the National Law Center on Homelessness and Poverty, dated March 17, 1997.

THE EMPTINESS OF OUR HANDS

1. Pronounced YAH-sheer KO-ock, this Hebrew phrase means "Grow in strength." Some weeks before hitting the streets, James and I had received in the mail the well wishes of a Jewish friend, who concluded his note with this blessing. On the streets it became our traditional way to end each day.

2. Some weeks after leaving the streets, I revisited the café, told the employees who I was and paid this young man back. He was dumbfounded. When I apologized for having deceived him, he said, "The greater deception would have been if you'd never come back. Besides, you know what the Bible says—show hospitality to strangers, for you might be entertaining angels unaware." It turns out the man had once been homeless himself.

3. Families comprise around 40% of the nation's homeless population. An estimated 1,300 homeless children, elementary-school age or younger, live in the Columbus metropolitan area. No information was found on older children and youths.

4. I later learned that the Spanish phrase I used best translates to "Very beans!"

5. After we came off the streets, James and I were both diagnosed with post-traumatic stress disorder and received counseling to alleviate panic attacks. Now, fortunately, most of those difficulties have passed, though I remain claustrophobic.

6. Little more than a month after James and I came off the streets, a shanty fire along the railroad tracks claimed the life of an unidentified homeless man. Given the location, we were almost certain the victim was our neighbor Blue until a well-placed friend called a contact in the coroner's office. From him we learned the approximate height, weight, and race of the victim's body, which had been badly burned. The description didn't resemble Blue at all. However, it did match one person we'd met on the riverbank: the short, skinny Anglo with the fishing pole. Since James and I never knew that fellow by name, we couldn't confirm our suspicions once the body was positively identified.

The fire's cause was never determined. The death was ruled accidental.

In a December, 1999, issue of *Columbus Alive*, the associate director of a homeless shelter claimed that in recent years railroad police have been regularly burning encampments alongside the tracks. A spokesperson for the railroad company said in response that while he wasn't certain the charge was true, taking such action wouldn't be "unreasonable."

7. Perhaps fittingly, this photograph didn't turn out.

8. My knee and my back would both require surgery.

9. When James and I revealed ourselves to the Martins a few weeks after leaving the streets, we learned that Jake had in fact entered a rehabilitation

program. Sarge had taken up residence in his sister's backyard, somewhere in Columbus. Rooster had been arrested on an unknown charge. Calvin was still in his tent camp, doing fine, for him.

Astonished at our self-disclosure, a speechless Harold and Ada greeted us with laughter, tears and hugs. During a two-hour reunion, James and I were able to explain to them what had led us to the streets, express our immense gratitude for their help, and also discuss matters about which we felt ambivalent. The Martins' goodwill was remarkable. Parting was sweet.

Ada Martin died of kidney failure on July 29, 2000. She was fifty-one. Though she's missed, her spirit endures. Take It to the Streets still ministers to homeless people in Columbus.

10. The Martins told us that the Professor moved in almost immediately after our departure.

ABOUT THE AUTHORS

Phyllis Cole-Dai seeks in her writing to cross deep divides to promote understanding and respect. She has edited or authored works in multiple genres, including historical fiction, spiritual nonfiction, and poetry. She makes her home in Brookings, South Dakota, where she resides with her husband, teenage son and two cats in a cozy 120-year-old house. Learn more about her work at www.phylliscoledai.com. There you can join her mailing list and receive a free sampler of her work.

James Murray is an artist, writer and clinician—who holds multiple graduate degrees. His primary work for over a decade has been with his firm, Breakthrough Interventions, which offers therapeutic interventions to individuals and families in crisis. He lives a creative life of service and strives to be present. Currently he resides in Wyoming and has a wonderful partner, Hana.

FREE BOOKS FOR YOU

The Book of the World: A Contemporary Scripture

Phyllis edited this contemporary scripture on behalf of an unknown author. It speaks on behalf of no religion but offers alongside other holy books its own poignant witness to compassion, love for the neighbor, love for the enemy, care for the earth, and more. Read and test its truths in everyday life. Perfect for daily meditation or group study.

Get your free e-book at http://www.phylliscoledai.com/nonfiction.

Practicing Presence: Insights from the Streets

This is a companion reader to *The Emptiness of Our Hands,* which Phyllis co-authored with James Murray (3rd edition, 2018). She wrote this series of forty-seven blog posts in 2009 on the ten-year anniversary of living voluntarily for 47 days on the streets of Columbus, Ohio. The book includes photographs that until now have never appeared in print. Deepen your understanding of the practice of being present while learning more about Phyllis's time on the streets.

Get your free e-book on Amazon.

DON'T FORGET YOUR FREE PHYLLIS COLE-DAI SAMPLER!

Get a taste of her music, poetry, fiction and nonfiction by joining her mailing list.

Visit www.phylliscoledai.com today!

ALSO BY PHYLLIS COLE-DAI

(RECENT WORKS)

NONFICTION

Practicing Presence: Insights from the Streets. Deepen your understanding of the practice of being present while learning more about Phyllis's time on the streets. She wrote this series of forty-seven blog posts in 2009 on the tenth anniversary of her streets experience. A companion reader to *The Emptiness of Our Hands,* each of its brief chapters is based on an excerpt from that book. Also included are photographs that until now have never appeared in print. Available as an e-book.

The Book of the World: A Contemporary Scripture (edited on behalf of an unknown author). Enter the mystery of this contemporary scripture, whose origins and author are unknown. Speaking on behalf of no religion, it offers alongside other holy books its own poignant witness to compassion, love for the neighbor, love for the enemy, care for the earth, and more. A book of truths to be read and tested in everyday life. Perfect for daily meditation or group study. Available as a paperback and free e-book at www. phylliscoledai.com.

FICTION

Beneath the Same Stars. Based on the life of Sarah Wakefield, this historical novel presents the story of a white woman, big as a man, who gets embroiled in the Dakota Uprising of 1862, forbidden love and the largest mass execution in U.S. history. Available in e-book and paperback formats.

POETRY

Poetry of Presence: An Anthology of Mindfulness Poems (co-edited with Ruby R. Wilson). Find "good medicine" in this collection of more than 150 mindfulness poems, mostly by contemporary or recent poets. Mindfulness poems invite us to bring our whole self to whatever moment we're in, and truly live it. They encourage us to be more present, more attentive and compassionate, in the living of our days. They grant us a taste of being good enough, just as we are, in this world, just as it is. Anthologized poets include Margaret Atwood, Wendell Berry, Billy Collins, Thich Nhat Hanh, Joy Harjo, Seamus Heaney, Galway Kinnell, Ted Kooser, Mary Oliver, Rainer Maria Rilke, Rumi, William Stafford, Alice Walker and many more. Available in paperback from all major retailers. Learn more at www.poetryofpresencebook.com.